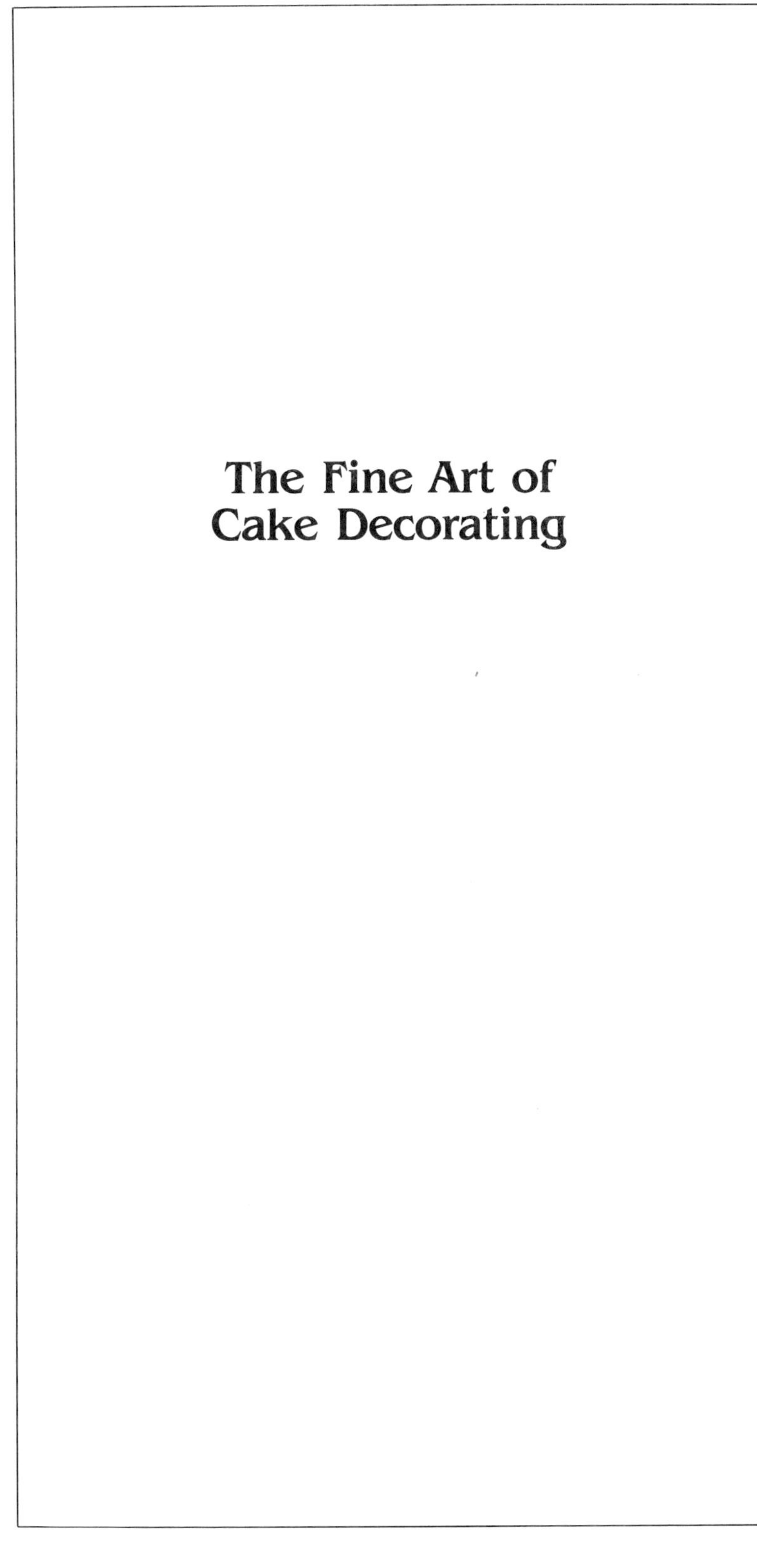

The Fine Art of Cake Decorating

The Fine Art of Cake Decorating

Cile Bellefleur Burbidge

A CBI BOOK
Published by Van Nostrand Reinhold Company
New York

A CBI Book
(CBI is an imprint of Van Nostrand Reinhold Company Inc.)

Library of Congress Catalog Card Number 84-5059

ISBN 0-442-21861-3

Printed in the United States of America
Designed by Ernie Haim
Photographs by Richard Burbidge, except for Bride's Magazine Cake, reprinted from *Bride's* magazine Copyright © 1983 by the Conde Nast Publications Inc.

Published by Van Nostrand Reinhold Company Inc.
115 Fifth Avenue
New York, New York 10003

Van Nostrand Reinhold Company Limited
Molly Millars Lane
Wokingham, Berkshire RG11 2PY, England

Van Nostrand Reinhold
480 La Trobe Street
Melbourne, Victoria 3000, Australia

Macmillan of Canada
Division of Canada Publishing Corporation
164 Commander Boulevard
Agincourt, Ontario M1S 3C7, Canada

16 15 14 13 12 11 10 9 8 7 6 5 4 3

Library of Congress Cataloging in Publication Data

Burbidge, Cile Bellefleur.
The fine art of cake decorating.

"A CBI book."
Includes index.
1. Cake decorating. I. Title.
TX771.B954 1984 641.8′653 84-5059
ISBN 0-442-21861-3

DEDICATION

I would like to dedicate this book to the following people who contributed so much of their own special talents.

Frank Raneo	*My personal "Leonardo da Vinci" whose wonderful drawings have always said more than words.*
Lillian Diehl	*My "Girl Friday" who is always ready to come in my desperate moments and whose constant encouragement I dearly cherish.*
John Burbidge	*Husband, photographer, and artistic adviser. Whenever I call his helping hand is always there.*

Contents

Preface

For as long as I can remember, sewing and cooking have been a part of my life. Needlework of all kinds has been my relaxation and I always have projects planned and projects to finish, including a lovely twelve × twelve-foot hooked rug purchased in Montreal on my honeymoon thirty-two years ago. The canvases, by now a collector's item, are still in the original box, but there is always a rainy day.

My love affair with the stove started in my mother's kitchen, spurred partly by a fascination with cooking and partly (or mostly) by a love of eating.

When not bending over a hot stove, I was busy at the sewing machine making my own clothes. My youthful adventures as a dressmaker convinced me that the world needed another fashion designer; after high school I entered the New England School of Art in Boston, Massachusetts.

After graduating I stayed on to teach fashion design at the school. Although I never scaled the ramparts of Seventh Avenue, or took Paris by storm, I did the next best thing—I married a fashion designer. My husband was a student at the school and after we graduated he went on to become a fashion designer. He has been designing wedding gowns for Priscilla of Boston for the past thirty-six years.

I, like other married women in those days, stayed home to care for my house and children. We had five. After my son Richard (number three child) was born, I went through a time of depression (nothing to do with Richard). My doctor advised me to get out and do something; so a friend and I, decorating bags in hand, joined a cake decorating class at the local YMCA. Twenty-six years later here I am in print!

Needless to say a lot of frosting has oozed since then. For many years, I taught cake decorating in the North Shore area of Massachusetts. I loved those teaching years and all the wonderful people I had in my classes (by last count about 3000).

So many of my students urged me to put it all on paper that in 1978 I published my first book, *Cake Decorating for Any Occasion*, made up of the lessons that I had prepared for my classes.

Cake decorating is one of the few arts where total destruction is the artist's greatest tribute (probably accounting for the lack of international cake museums). The only logical place of preservation for this fragile and nonenduring art seems to be that of the written page.

This new volume, *The Fine Art of Cake Decorating*, starts at the very beginning with the first lesson I teach my new students—the American Flag Cake. From this humble but patriotic beginning, the book will carry you through an assortment of flowers, basket weaving, and wicker work to the constructional details of building elaborate wedding cakes. At the end of the book are instructions for some of my more spectacular efforts; though I hope that you will use them primarily as pathways to your own personal style.

In closing I must say that my involvement in frosting has provided me with a wealth of adventures and friendships.

One of my cakes (a small one) was made for the wedding of a Massachusetts girl in the mountains of Colombia and carried by her mother through the jungles. My husband and I journeyed to the charming Swiss village of Brienz to view first hand a chalet I had reproduced from a photograph for the owner's birthday. One wonderful evening in Rotterdam with a Dutch baker, I discovered that cake decorating can break the language barrier.

Perhaps my most unforgettable cake adventure was our odyssey to the African country of Nigeria where we were the guests of honor at a ceremony of the Bestowal of the Titles of Chieftaincy on a Nigerian chief and his wife. We had met the chief's daughter the previous year in Paris at the Cordon Bleu. After seeing photographs of some of my cakes, she came to the United States to study with me and proved to be an amazingly gifted pupil.

Upon her return to Nigeria, she invited us to the ceremony that was to honor her father and mother. In the days preceding the ceremony, she and I worked on a large cake for the festivities.

Never in those far away YMCA days did I dream that my husband and I would one day be standing under the African sun, dressed in cream and silver ceremonial robes, participating in a scene straight out of the pages of the *National Geographic*.

My greatest satisfaction, though, was in being invited to design five cakes for the windows of Tiffany's on Fifth Avenue in New York. The simple and elegant presentation of my work by Mr. Gene Moore and

Mr. Ron Smith of Tiffany's will always be one of my most treasured memories.

With practice and patience this art can be your piece of cake. Wonderful ideas are out there waiting for you; with knowledge and skill you can translate each one into reality.

So, good luck, and remember this (a quote from my first book), "A good cake decorator never shows her mistakes—she eats them!"

Acknowledgments

No book of this subject and scope could have been written alone. I was fortunate in the encouragement and support of my family and friends.

I would like to give special thanks to Ruth Johnston and Betty Levin for providing me with "author's refuge," a home away from home where so much of this book was written.

My special thanks also go to that valiant group of proofreaders who burned the midnight oil on my behalf: Lillian Diehl, Anne Gargan, Carolyn Michel, Phyllis Morin, Rena Opolski, and Loretta Tenaglia.

After many years of cake making, I have accumulated an enormous gallery of photographs. From this mass I selected about a hundred of my favorites and conducted a survey.

I am most grateful to the following people who graciously helped me settle upon the chosen few: Anne Burbidge, Mary Boyne, Carl Cassman, Christine Crowley, Rebecca Denis, Carmie Dennis, Lillian Diehl, Patricia J. Holmes, Claire McLaughlin, Gene Moore, Phyllis Morin, Paul Noel, Rena Opolski, Linda Sams, Ron Smith, and Kathleen Wheelright.

My sincere thanks to my oldest daughter, Christine Crowley, who typed this manuscript, and to my youngest daughter, Jenifer, who so willingly entertained my grandson, Sean, so his mommy could keep her typewriter going.

PART I
Beginners

In 1978 I published my first book, entitled *Cake Decorating for Any Occasion*, which is now out of print. This book was based on the lessons that I have taught over the past twenty years. It was as much a book for beginners as it was for those who, having had experience in the subject, wanted to learn different methods.

When I asked to do a second book featuring the very elaborate style of cake decorating that is my specialty, I decided to incorporate the first publication, thus making a complete volume.

There is a definite relationship between this basic section and the intricate work of the second. All buildings must have a foundation from the most simple to the ornate, and any cake decorator is, if nothing else, a builder.

These first sections are presented in a very simple step-by-step manner with complete listings of supplies, tips, and materials needed to do the various cakes. I have included many hints and suggestions that I have learned from my years of experience. However, if practice makes perfect, then perfection has eluded me for I still eat a lot of mistakes!

The first cake is the American Flag Cake, which I have found to be an excellent beginning project. This cake introduces the novice to the use and handling of a decorating bag, the control of frosting, the planning and marking out of designs, and the mixing of colors. In this exercise, that old complaint "I can't draw a straight line" may be voiced when doing the stripes on the flag, but I have yet to have a student whose first effort was not satisfactory. The beginner will get a wonderful lift when his cake is greeted with "oohs" and "aahs." And, as my husband once said, "Who would dare criticize the flag!"

If you study the cakes shown throughout this book, you will note the development of these basic techniques. My entire style evolved from these early pages, and as a decorator you will find that there is always a new experience or a different twist of the frosting that can create a fresh look.

A cake decorator is both a creative artist and a craftsman involved in a continuing learning process. The results are what make the long hours seem so short.

CHAPTER I

Basic Methods and Supplies

This book is divided into four sections and is written for the beginner as well as the professional decorator. I recommend that both read it from the beginning as the information in each chapter is built upon the preceding chapters. As in all crafts, there are certain fundamentals to be mastered; the rest is practice. Once you have learned to make a rose, constant repetition will make it perfect.

The first section is a text for the novice. The American Flag Cake will teach many of the basics of decorating, such as the mixing of colors and how to fill, hold, and control a bag. The arrangement of the thirteen stripes and the field of stars provides a very good lesson in dividing a cake surface. The end result is very gratifying. When you have mastered the basics of this first section, you may proceed to something a little more complicated.

Pots and Pans

Plan the cake you would like to do; then choose a pan. It is not necessary to buy every pan on the market. A look in your own cabinet, where you should find a saucepan, roasting pan, frying pan, and mixing bowls, will yield an array of sizes and shapes. Any container that will withstand the heat of the oven can be used to bake cakes. You cannot use a baking pan for roasting, but you can use a roasting pan for baking. Baking pans are often made with seams, while a roasting pan is pressed so that there will be no leakage.

If you buy a cooking pan, select a pan of a good heavy quality and it will last a lifetime. The investment will pay off in the better quality of the final product. The heavy-duty aluminum loaf pans I use were received by my mother-in-law as a bride over fifty years ago; they are still in excellent condition. The only exceptions to the rule of quality are the disposable heavy-aluminum roasting pans, which are fantastic for baking odd-shaped cakes.

The first oval cake I made was baked in a large rectangular roasting pan. I then cut the cake into an oval using a paper pattern. This worked very well. I have since found oval pans of the disposable heavy-aluminum type in all sizes and have been able to make oval wedding cakes in graduated sizes. These pans can be used again. You should be aware when removing a cake in a disposable pan from the oven that it needs to be supported from the bottom so that the cake does not bend and crack.

Cake Batters

Once you have decided upon a pan for your cake, the next question that comes up is, "How much batter do I need?" A very simple method for determining volume is to take the pan that you would usually use for your favorite recipe and fill it with water to the level that your cake would reach when it is baked. Now empty it into the large pan that you want to use. Repeat as many times as it takes to fill the container to where it should be when the cake is baked. Let us say it takes eight containers of water to fill the large pan; that means you need eight recipes of cake.

Remember when choosing a recipe for a large cake that some recipes cannot be doubled. A basic one- or two-egg cake or a pound cake can be doubled and quadrupled with no problem at all. I have not had very good luck in doubling chocolate cake recipes; they either fall or end up dry.

If you have a very large commercial mixer, you can mix all your ingredients at once, but, if you have a regular home mixer with a three- or four-quart capacity bowl, your mixing instructions will be a little different. A four-quart bowl is sufficient to mix a cake using four cups flour without spilling. If you are planning a cake that requires eight recipes of batter and each recipe needs two cups flour, you will need eight bowls in order to mix it properly. In four bowls, you put sugar and shortening ready to be mixed. Into the other four bowls, you measure the sifted flour, baking powder, and salt and set these aside. Next you cream the shortening and sugar and add the eggs. Do this with each bowl, then set it aside. When all four bowls have been thoroughly mixed, add the flour mixture alternately with the milk into each bowl, with flour going in first and last. The flavoring may go in before the flour mixture or at the end when everything is thoroughly mixed. If the vanilla is put in direct contact with the flour, it sometimes forms lumps that remain in the batter and will mar the texture. With all the ingredients premeasured, the mixing process will go very quickly, and the first batter will not set so long that it becomes heavy.

This method of measuring and mixing batter can also be applied to cake mixes. Use the pan indicated by the mix directions as a measure to determine how many boxes of mix you need. Again, have all your equipment and ingredients ready so that the mixing can be done quickly.

Baking

Before the batter can go into the pan, the pan must be greased using waxed paper with vegetable shortening, then lined with waxed paper and greased again. Square cake pans are no problem to line. Just pull out the waxed paper until you get the proper length, then tear on serrated edge. The excess paper on the sides may be cut off or extend up the sides of the pan. The waxed paper is then greased again.

If you are working with a round pan, place waxed paper on the bottom of the pan. Using the sharp edge of a knife, rub against the side of the pan until the paper tears away. Another method that takes a little longer but that I find more satisfactory is to place the round pan over waxed paper, trace around the base of the pan with a pencil and then cut out the paper circle. Grease the pan, line the bottom with cut-out paper, and then grease again. If the pan is larger than the width of the paper, use two sheets of waxed paper, one over the other.

If you are baking in a bowl, grease it and sprinkle about a teaspoon or tablespoon (depending on the size of the bowl) of flour in the container. Tilt the bowl from side to side so that the flour covers all the shortening in the bowl. Turn the bowl over and tap it lightly on the counter to remove excess flour. If too much flour remains, it will not harm your cake, but it will leave an unattractive white surface.

An average-size cake is baked in a moderate oven, temperature about 350°F, unless it is a fruitcake. A fruitcake is baked in a slow oven for a long period of time in a pan lined with waxed or brown paper to keep the outer edge from overcooking. When baking a large cake, 12 to 14 inches in diameter (round or square) and 3½ inches high, lower the temperature 35 to 40 degrees. A problem with baking large cakes is that the edge of the cake is overdone by the time the center is completely baked. One aid in controlling this overcooking is to wrap the pan in a damp towel. Cut an old cotton terry towel lengthwise down the middle, sew the two short ends together so that you have a long narrow strip. Wet the towel and wring it out just enough so that it does not drip when you are handling it. Fold the towel lengthwise until it equals the depth of your pan. Wrap it around the outer edge of the pan and fasten with a large safety pin. The towel will discolor but will not burn. I wash the towel after every use and can use it about three or four times before it literally falls apart.

Another method I have found very helpful in baking large cakes is to line the sides of the pan, as well as the bottom, with waxed paper. Grease the pan, line the bottom with waxed paper and grease again as you would for a smaller cake. Then cut or tear strips of waxed paper about five inches wide and place one long strip against the side of the pan. The paper should be about 1½ inches higher than the pan. Grease the first strip; then overlap it about half by a second strip. Grease this paper and overlap it by another strip until the circle is completed. The sides of the pan should have a double thickness of waxed paper, which will prevent a very thick crust on the outer edge. When the cake is baked and slightly cooled, place a cooling rack over the pan and invert. It will slide right out of the pan when turned over.

Now you are ready to bake the cake. Never fill the container more than two-thirds to three-quarters full; or the cake may overflow and fall. As your leavening agent (baking powder or baking soda) is performing its duty, a gas is forming lightening the batter and making the cake rise. When the batter overflows, the gas escapes and the center of the cake sinks. If the batter is spilling over the pan, tear a piece of heavy brown paper bag a little smaller than your hand and quickly put it against the pan and batter. The uncooked batter holds the paper, the paper holds the batter, and the cake is saved. If the batter has not yet gotten to the overflow stage, you can slip the brown paper between batter and pan. This must be done very quickly without moving the cake.

No matter what size cake you are baking, if the top is browning but the cake is not baked thoroughly, a piece of brown paper placed over the cake will prevent it from getting any darker while it finishes cooking.

It is very difficult to predict exactly how long a cake should be baked. Your pan may not be the correct size or there may be a difference in altitude, or your oven could be too hot or not hot enough. The first method of checking the cake for doneness is to tap the pan lightly with your fingernail to see if the batter is set. When the pan is tapped, the batter should not jiggle like gelatin. With a small pan, the batter leaving the edge of the pan would mean the cake is done, but, with a larger cake, testing with a cake tester, a toothpick, or a thin roasting fork will be necessary. Years ago, a cake maker would test with a piece of straw from a broom, but in this synthetic age I would not try it. Do not be too anxious to use your cake tester; you could put a hole in the center of the cake causing it to fall. A cake may be a very delicate brown color, but this does not mean it is cooked. Doneness can also be tested by touching the top lightly with your finger; if the cake springs back it is done. Most cakes, when baked, will pull away from the pan.

When the cake is finally taken from the oven, you should let it stand about five minutes unless directions specify otherwise. Then carefully go around the edge with a table knife or a metal spatula and invert the cake onto a cooling rack.

The use of a cooling rack is important to cool the cake evenly. If a hot cake is inverted onto a plate or board, steam will not be able to escape, and the cake will be soggy and of inferior quality.

Preparations for Decorating

For most of the projects in this book, the cake is inverted to guarantee a flat surface with right-angle edges for decorating. Just about every cake that comes out of the oven can be made suitable for decorating. If your cake comes out lopsided, you simply level it by cutting off the mound and inverting your cake.

The board or plate that the cake is placed on should be at least two inches larger than the cake on each side. Your cake-decorating supply store carries corrugated cardboard circles, rectangles, or squares that are used with matching glassine (grease resistant) doilies. You may make your own cardboard disks from corrugated cardboard boxes, but make sure the cardboard is strong enough to support the cake. If the cardboard bends or gives, it will crack the cake. I have gotten a stronger base by arranging two pieces of corrugated cardboard in opposite grains. Whenever using a cardboard disk or wooden board under your cake, wrap it with heavy-duty aluminum foil being careful not to tear the foil at the corners. There was a time when a glassine doily could be wiped with a damp cloth when the cake was completed. However, the quality has changed and this can no longer be done. Now when I use doilies, I completely decorate the cake with the exception of the lower border. Take the baking pan that was used for the lower cake, place it over the doily, half on, half off, allowing 3 to 5 inches at the widest part depending on the size of the cake. Trace around the pan with a pencil, cut it out, and try it on the cake. If it is too large, place the pan over it and trace it again until it looks pleasing to the eye. Use 10-, 12- or 14-inch doilies and make a scalloped edge, using as many doilies as necessary.

For a special effect, a piece of Plexiglas at least ½ inch thick for a tiered cake is an excellent choice. The cake looks as if it were set directly on the table. The Plexiglas is expensive but it does save time.

A pink and white cake complemented by a pink tablecloth showing through the clear Plexiglas is very attractive. Greens of any type around the edge of the cake complete the setting.

A silver tray can also enhance your "sugar sculpture." When using a tray of this value, cut corrugated cardboard to the exact size of the cake and wrap it in foil. Place a small amount of icing on the tray and place the foil-wrapped cardboard over it leaving the smooth section up for the cake. The cardboard keeps the tray from being scratched when the cake is cut.

If the tray has a lip that makes your cake look sunken, wrap two or three cardboard layers together and place these under the cake. This will give it better proportion. You will be forced to work at a disadvantage if decorating a cake in a container or tray with a "fence" around it as you will not be able to get the decorating tip inside at the proper angle.

Whether the cake is frozen or freshly baked and cooled, you can keep the cake from sliding by placing a small amount of decorating frosting on the board or tray and then inverting the cake onto it. If you are using a doily, put a little frosting under and then on top of the doily to keep the entire assemblage stable. The recipe for frosting that follows is one I have successfully used for years.

BASIC FROSTING

6 cups confectioner's sugar
1 cup white vegetable shortening
⅓ cup cold water
½ teaspoon salt
½ to 1 teaspoon white flavoring

Yield: 5 cups

Sift the sugar before measuring 4 cups. Place the sugar in a mixing bowl with the remaining ingredients. Beat at low speed, using a rubber spatula to scrape the bowl while mixing. When creamy, add remaining 2 cups sifted sugar; continue to mix at low speed until smooth, about 5 minutes.

You may substitute butter or margarine for up to ½ cup of the shortening, but keep in mind your frosting will no longer be white. Any white flavoring, such as vanilla, almond, or lemon, may be used. Pure vanilla extract will discolor the frosting. If mixed at high speed, this frosting will have air bubbles that will create problems when frosting the cake or making flowers. This frosting does not have to be refrigerated; if placed in an airtight container, it will keep for a few months at room temperature.

Crumbing and Glazing

Now for the crumbing of the cake. This process is called crumbing because it sets the crumbs of the cake; it also seals the cake, keeping it moist. You begin by placing some of the frosting you have just mixed in a small bowl. Let cold water run into the bowl; then invert the bowl, holding the frosting in with a spatula. The few drops of water that adhere to the frosting will be enough to thin it down when it is mixed. This technique may be used for any too stiff frosting; simply use whatever liquid is called for in your recipe. With the frosting thinned down, it is easier to get a thin layer of frosting all over the cake. When doing a small cake, I find it easier to do the sides first, but there is no set rule. Do whatever is easiest for you at the time; just be sure that none of the cake is visible when you have finished. If your cake is not perfectly flat on the board, fill the space with frosting.

Once this frosting is dry, you may glaze the cake. Go through the same process: Place a small amount of frosting in a bowl and add a few drops of cold water to thin it down. Then frost again, this time adding a little more frosting to cover the cake completely. Using a small six-inch spatula at a ninety-degree angle from your board, make long, straight strokes. When the cake is completely frosted, heat the blade of the spatula in a glass of hot water, wipe the blade quickly to avoid getting icing too wet, and go over the cake. The hot blade will melt the frosting giving it a shiny and smooth surface. Your cake is now ready to decorate.

Crumbing and glazing is done on just about every cake. Crumbing is not done on cakes from molded pans, such as Disney characters. The only time you do not have to glaze is when the decorations completely cover the cake, for example, the top surface of the Flag Cake or the basket full of flowers.

Bags, Tips, and Coupling

Before starting your first cake, you should become familiar with decorating equipment. You can find all of the following items in a cake-decorating supply shop, but some department stores, craft stores, card and gift shops, and kitchen specialty shops are also good sources for supplies.

Cake decorating bags range from six to twenty-four inches long. All are plastic coated for easy washing. The very large bags are used by professional bakers decorating many cakes in a mass production process. For projects in this book, an eight-inch bag is sufficient.

In order to change the tip of a bag without removing the frosting, you need a coupling. Some bags come fully assembled with coupling and nut (screw-top ring); if yours does not, you must cut about a ¾-inch opening in the bag (illustrated in Chapter 2). Remove the nut, insert the coupling into the decorating bag, and push until you can see the threads of the coupling. If these threads do not show, remove the coupling, cut another ⅛ inch from the bag, and try again. Cut just a small amount at one time as the bags stretch to make a larger opening. Full details on cutting bags are in Chapter 2.

When you have finished with the bag, remove the tip and coupling and wash the bag in soapy lukewarm water. Rinse well and let stand to dry thoroughly.

Parchment paper is often used to make decorating bags. The parchment can be bought precut in triangles or on a roll and cut into a triangle to make a cone. Some people prefer parchment paper to decorating bags because it is disposable. The bags are not strong enough to use with a coupling, but you can cut ½ inch off the pointed end and insert the tip into the bag before putting in the frosting. Chapter 4 provides details for folding these papers into conical bags. The bag is then filled and folded like any decorating bag. The paper bags are also used without a tip for certain details as explained in Chapter 4.

For decorating tips, I find Ateco Domestic Standard Decorating Tips made of nickel silver to be of superior quality. For excellent results, one should use quality merchandise.

There are hundreds of decorating tips to choose from, but each person seems to favor certain ones. As you master the art of decorating, you will find your own favorites. For this reason, buy only the numbers you need for a specific cake and try them out. You should become familiar with the numbers and what each tip produces before investing in a large quantity. The numbers are about the same for all brands of tips; although individual tips will vary slightly, depending on the manufacturer.

Following is a list of decorating tips and what they may be used for.

Numbers *1 through 12* have plain hole openings. Number 1 has a very fine thread opening; the numbers increase as the openings get larger up to number 12 with a 5⁄16-inch opening. Many of these tips may be used for the same things, such as lines, stems, writing, centers of flowers, lattice, figure piping, beading, dots, Australian lace, and decorating petit fours or even sugar cubes. If you want to decorate with fine details, use small tips (numbers 1S, 23S, 65S, and 101S). For heavy figure piping, use a larger tip. A fine line requires a fine tip, a thick line requires a larger tip. Experiment until you find the right size for the job.

Numbers *13 through 22* are open-star tips and numbers *23 through 35* are closed-star tips. The lowest number in a grouping is usually the smallest tip. All these tips can be used for stars, borders, scrolls, garlands, shells, and side-of-cake decorations. Holding the bag at different angles creates new designs. Cakes may be decorated using only the star tips.

Numbers *41, 42, and 43*, small, medium, large, are double-line tips and are excellent if you want just two lines as decoration. For best results, the frosting should be a little soft and free of air bubbles. For lattice work, I prefer the single-line tube (number 3 or 4). The lattice may take longer, but the results are superior.

Numbers *44 and 45* are ribbon tips. The ribbon frequently frames a design on the top of the cake or on the side. To make a wide flat ribbon, use tip number 45 and make two ribbons side by side. Then dip a narrow metal spatula in hot water to heat the blade, quickly wipe the blade dry, and go over the joining to make it look as if it were all one. (In a pinch, tips numbers 101 through 104 series can be substituted.)

Numbers 46 *through* 48 are similar to 44 and 45 except that one side is smooth and the other is serrated. These make an excellent basket weave. When these tips are marked with a degree symbol next to the number, it means that both sides of the tips are serrated.

Numbers 49 *through* 54 are the cross tips, also known as aster. They may be used to accent a border, to make scrolls, or to write.

Numbers 55 *through* 58 are oval tips creating a half-round effect. They may be used for lattice, but the tube must be held at the same angle to keep the oval effect.

Numbers 59 *through* 61 are tips shaped to resemble a comma (available in right and left). These tips make rosebuds, pinecones, and all kinds of daisies. 59°, the smallest of the group, is particularly useful for making the ruffle on the flute of the daffodil and very tiny flat flowers scattered over a cake.

Numbers 62 *through* 64 are tips used to make accents on a border design.

Numbers 65 *through* 70 are the leaf tips. They also make excellent garlands and leaf-type borders.

Numbers 71 *through* 78 are combination leaf and star tips. If you look closely, you will see the groove of the leaf. Both sides make an interesting border.

Numbers 79 *through* 81 are excellent for chrysanthemum and fantasy flowers. In this group, number 79 is the largest tube. This tip is shaped like a horseshoe and can be used as well for concave or convex designs.

Numbers 82 *through* 84 are square tips with concave sides. Number 82 is the largest. All may be used to trim a border.

Number 85 is a triangular tip and used in the same way as number 82 series.

Numbers 86 *through* 88 are double tips, combining number 104 and number 16 in one tip. Many interesting designs, such as ruffly garlands, can be created with this tip. The ruffle can go either on the upper or lower edge depending upon which way the tip is turned. If you want the ruffle on the lower edge, you must work the cake from left to right. This is one time when it is an advantage to be left-handed.

Number 89 is a triple hole, making three lines at one time.

Numbers 94 *and* 95 are French leaf tips, giving a fernlike effect. A beaded trim added with a plain or star tip down the center makes an interesting design.

Number 96 is a mock drop flower tip. Hold the bag at an upright position and squeeze with a little pressure to form frosting petals. Release pressure, push in on the tip slightly to break the frosting, and pull away. The flowers may be done directly on the cake or on waxed paper and added later. This tip also makes a good border when used like any of the star tips.

Number 97 is a rose tip for a full-bloom rose. It creates a very open flower.

Number 98 is the shell tip; it has a curved opening with serrated ridges on the top edge. When using this tip, you must apply a great deal of pressure; the resulting shell will be 1 to 1½ inches long. The shells make an attractive border around the top edge of a cake or at the base.

Numbers *99 and 100* can be used for a border on a small cake or to enhance another border. The tip can be used on either side, with a left-to-right wave motion, or straight out, letting it ripple as it comes out of the tip.

Numbers *101 through 104* are the rose series, the most popular tips in the set. The tip is also used for a large number of flowers, rose petals, and ruffles. The rose tips are also available in a very large series, 124 through 128. The extra-large number 180 has a 1½-inch opening.

Number *105* reminds me of a chocolate kiss if used straight up. It has rounded ridges and may be used for a border.

Number *106* looks very much like the number 30 closed-star tip except that every other prong is shorter. It also makes an excellent border.

There are many drop flower tips. All of these tubes have a center pin that leaves a small space in the center of a flower. The space is then filled with a dot of yellow icing.

All drop flower tips are used holding the bag straight up. The frosting coming out of the tip must be moist; if the bag has been sitting for a while, the frosting will have dried and will not adhere to the cake or waxed paper.

Here are a few of the drop flower tips that I have found useful:

136 daisy tip—Holding the bag very close to the cake, apply pressure until the frosting forms the size flower you wish. Practice a few times before starting on the cake. Fill in the center with a contrasting color using a number 4 or 5 tip.

190 violet tip—This large tip can be used in the pastry bag without a coupling or in a parchment paper bag. With the bag held straight up and the tip touching the frosting, apply pressure, twist and make a quarter turn. This should make a five-petal flower resembling a violet if you have violet-colored frosting. Add a small amount of yellow icing to the center with a number 2 or 3 tip.

193 fantasy flower—I use this tip for my candleholders. Hold the bag straight up, squeeze and twist to the right or to the left or both. You can place a candle in the hole or add a yellow center. The candleholders can be placed on the cake or around the cake on the tray.

Numbers *224 and 225* make small five-petal flowers. These tips are great when making a spray of flowers. I use them for lilacs and add yellow centers with a number 1 tip.

Number *220* forms a stylized buttercup with five balls joined together. Hold the bag straight up and squeeze out a little frosting; don't make them too large. Stop squeezing, push down a little to break the frosting, and then pull away. This sounds more complicated than it really is.

Number *221* forms a three-ball petal flower. The flower is done in the same manner as the flower with tip number 220.

The following are large border tips:

Number *199* is the same as the number 12 plain-hole tip with the addition of very fine prongs.

Numbers *132 and 195* are large tips and cannot be used with a coupling. They are excellent for decorating large cakes and piping whipped cream. For whipped cream use a 14- or 16-inch bag and, by all means, use a stabilizer in the cream. The stabilizer prevents your cream from watering and keeps the cream stiff. If you have no stabilizer, mix ½ teaspoon plain gelatin thoroughly into the sugar before beating it into the pint of whipped cream.

Number *230* is the bismarck tip. It looks very different because it has an extension of 1¾ inches, but it is a standard tip that fits onto the delrin coupling. With an opening of 3/16 of an inch, this tube is ideal for filling bismarcks, jelly donuts, and cream puffs because the puff does not have to be cut open to be filled; the tube is just inserted into the pastry.

Flavoring and Paste Colors

White vanilla is preferred for decorating frosting because pure vanilla extract will add color. White vanilla is an imitation flavoring available wherever cake decorating supplies are sold. Any white flavoring, such as peppermint, almond, or lemon, can be used too.

Paste colors made with vegetable dyes come in a variety of shades. Color your frosting by taking a small amount of color on a clean toothpick and mixing it in. You can mix two or more colors for a special shade. Make certain you mix enough frosting to complete your project as it is very difficult to match a color the second time. Paste color will not change the consistency of your icing unless you are trying to get a deep red; then you must add more confectioner's sugar to thicken the frosting. Paste color will never spoil—if it gets a little dry, add about 1 teaspoon of glycerin to the jar (glycerin is available at a drugstore).

Before you begin, I would like to offer this charming little poem I found in *McCall's* magazine of August, 1899. I feel that all good cooks will appreciate its message.

Her First Cake

She measured out the butter with a very solemn air;
The milk and sugar also; and she took the greatest care
To count the eggs correctly and to add a little bit
Of baking powder, which you know, beginners oft omit.
Then she stirred it all together, and she baked it full an hour;
But she never quite forgave herself for leaving out the flour.

CHAPTER 2
Flag Cake

I have always found the Flag Cake to be ideal for the novice who needs a creative lift as it is virtually a foolproof exercise in decorating.

One learns how to control the decorating bag and how to color frosting. If the stripes are not quite even, you can pass it off as a Flag-in-the-Breeze Cake!

SUPPLIES

12- × 9-inch one-layer cake
2 recipes Basic Frosting (see Index)
Small metal spatula
3 mixing bowls or pint-size containers with airtight lids
Paste colors dark red and royal blue
Toothpicks
3 decorating bags with couplings
Scissors
Tips nos. 16 and 30
Glass
Thread
Dishcloth
Cleaning brush

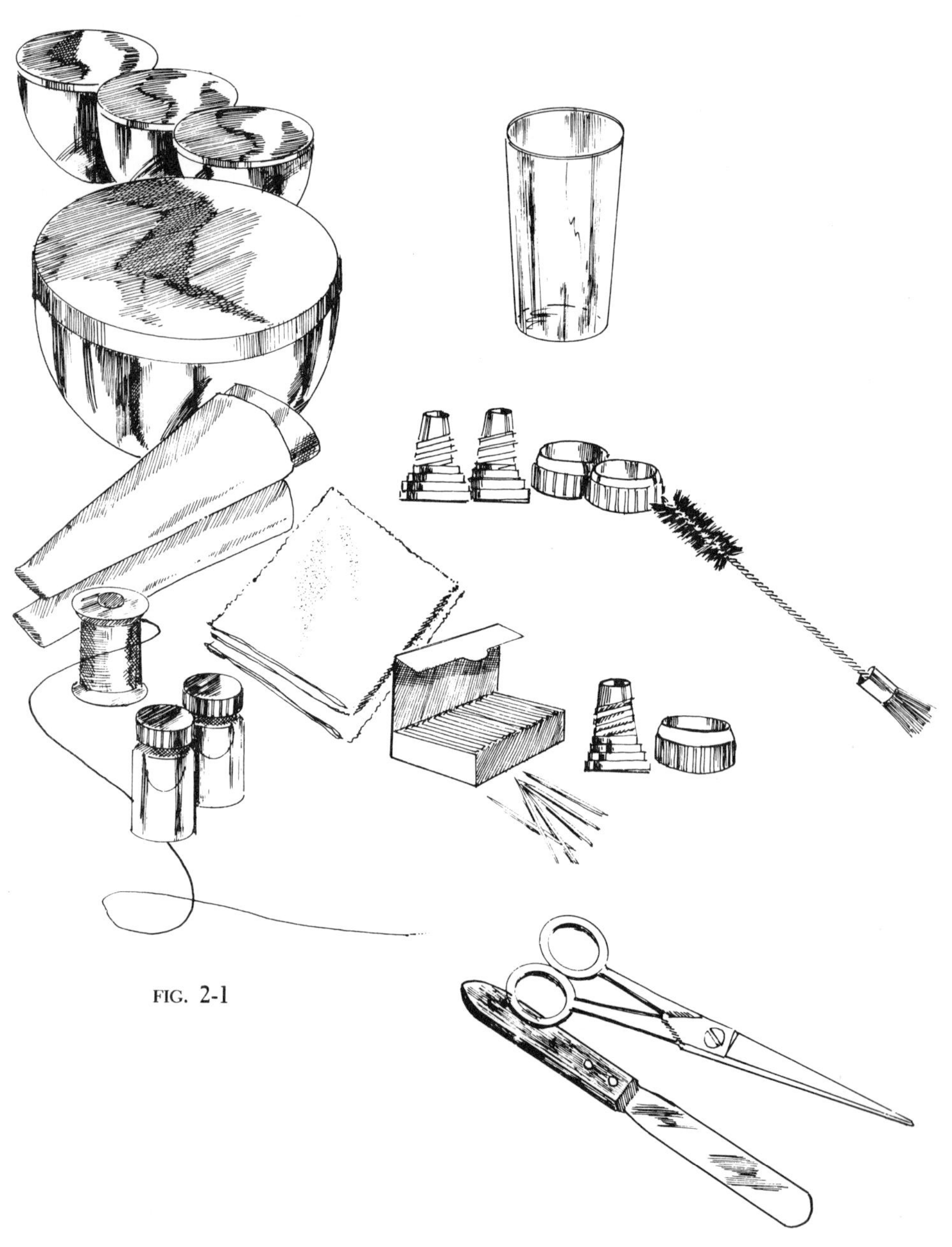

FIG. 2-1

Leveling the Surface

Almost all cakes are inverted before decorating giving a flat surface on which to apply the decorations. But a cake that is higher in the middle will crack if it is turned upside down. Cut off half the mound so your cake will have a flat surface to rest on. Cakes often bake unevenly, creating unwanted spaces. After trimming, the excess cake can be used to fill in spaces.

Your cake should be baked in a rectangular pan; a 12- × 9-inch pan is perfect. If you only have a square pan, you may use this procedure: Cut approximately 1½ inches off one side of the square and transfer it to the adjacent side, thus forming a rectangle.

Your cake should be put on a board that is at least 2 inches larger than the cake on every side. The larger the cake, the more space you should allow on the edges.

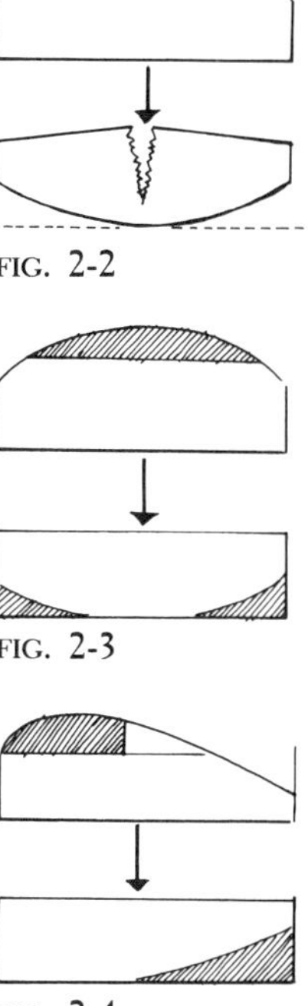

FIG. 2-2

FIG. 2-3

FIG. 2-4

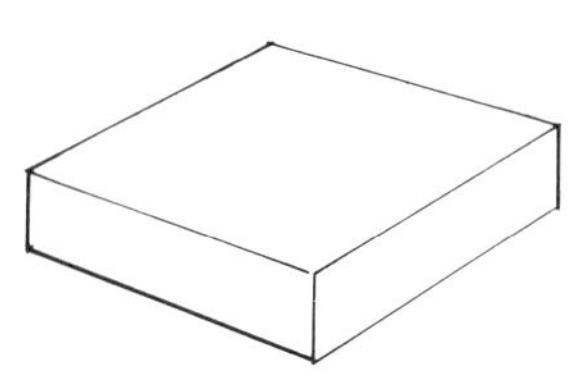

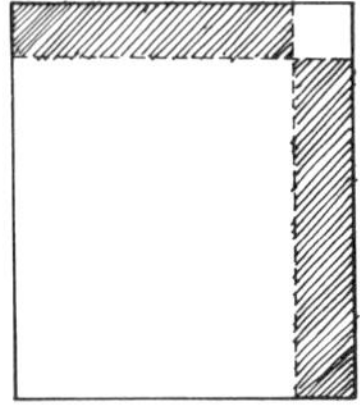

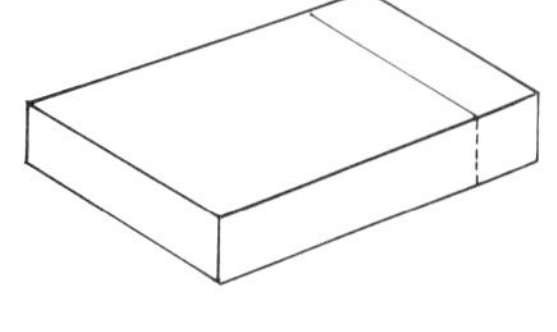

FIG. 2-5

Crumbing

Put a small amount of Basic Frosting in one of your mixing bowls. Add a few drops of cold water and mix thoroughly.

Using the small metal spatula, frost the cake keeping the spatula at a right angle to the cake (see fig. 2-6).

If the frosting is turning up crumbs, your icing is too dry. Add a few more drops of water. Adding a few drops of the liquid used in a frosting (in this case, water) will make it easier to apply.

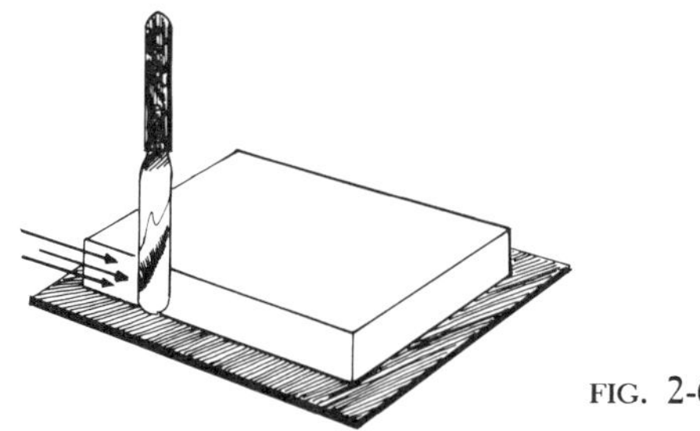

FIG. 2-6

Couplings and Tips

1. Cut off ¾ inch from the base of an 8-inch bag.
2. Remove nut from coupling. Insert coupling into bag and push through the small hole until 2 threads are showing. The grains of bags vary making one stretch more than the other. If coupling will not force through opening, trim another ⅛ inch from the bag.
3. With the coupling in place, put tip over end of coupling. Screw on the nut.
4. Prepare remaining bags in same manner. For the Flag Cake you have a bag for each of the three colors.
5. If you do not have enough tips to place on every bag after your bags have been filled with icing, place a piece of wax paper over the coupling and screw on the nut. This will prevent the frosting on the open end of coupling from drying.

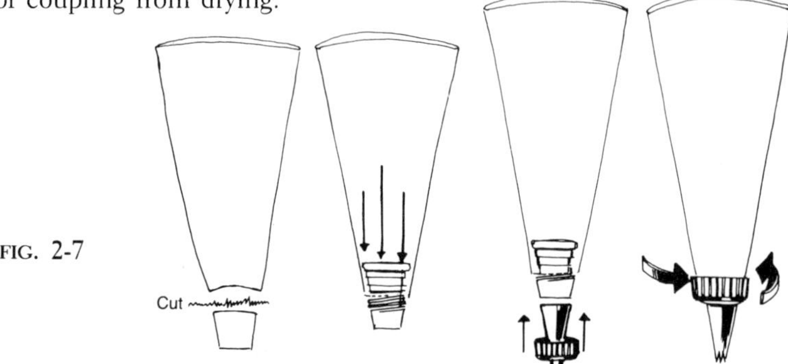

FIG. 2-7

Coloring the Frosting

On the Flag Cake, the red and blue should be bright. For the red frosting for a 12- × 9-inch cake, put about 1 cup frosting in a mixing bowl. Paste colors are very strong, so use sparingly; however, the flag cake is an exception. You may use up to a teaspoon of paste color to get a bright red. Always use a clean utensil when removing paste color from the jar and take a small amount at a time; a toothpick makes a very good applicator.

Put a small amount of frosting to the side of the bowl. Add coloring to the small portion and mix it thoroughly before mixing it into the rest. Some paste color is thick or a little dry; if you mix it through all the frosting immediately, it takes twice as long to mix thoroughly. Also mix slowly so that you do not get air bubbles in the frosting. Keep adding and mixing the red coloring until you have the desired shade. The dark colors will darken as they dry and the light colors will fade when exposed to daylight.

For the blue field, take approximately ½ cup frosting and mix in the same manner.

Filling the Bag

Using a metal spatula, take up a scoop of frosting on the blade and insert into the bag, as shown. Wipe the spatula free of frosting in the center of the bag by using your index finger (see fig. 2-8). Keep top of bag clean of frosting.

Squeeze frosting down and add more until you have filled about three-fourths of the bag (fig. 2-9). The top 2 inches of the bag should be left for folding. Follow the procedure for folding illustrated in fig. 2-10.

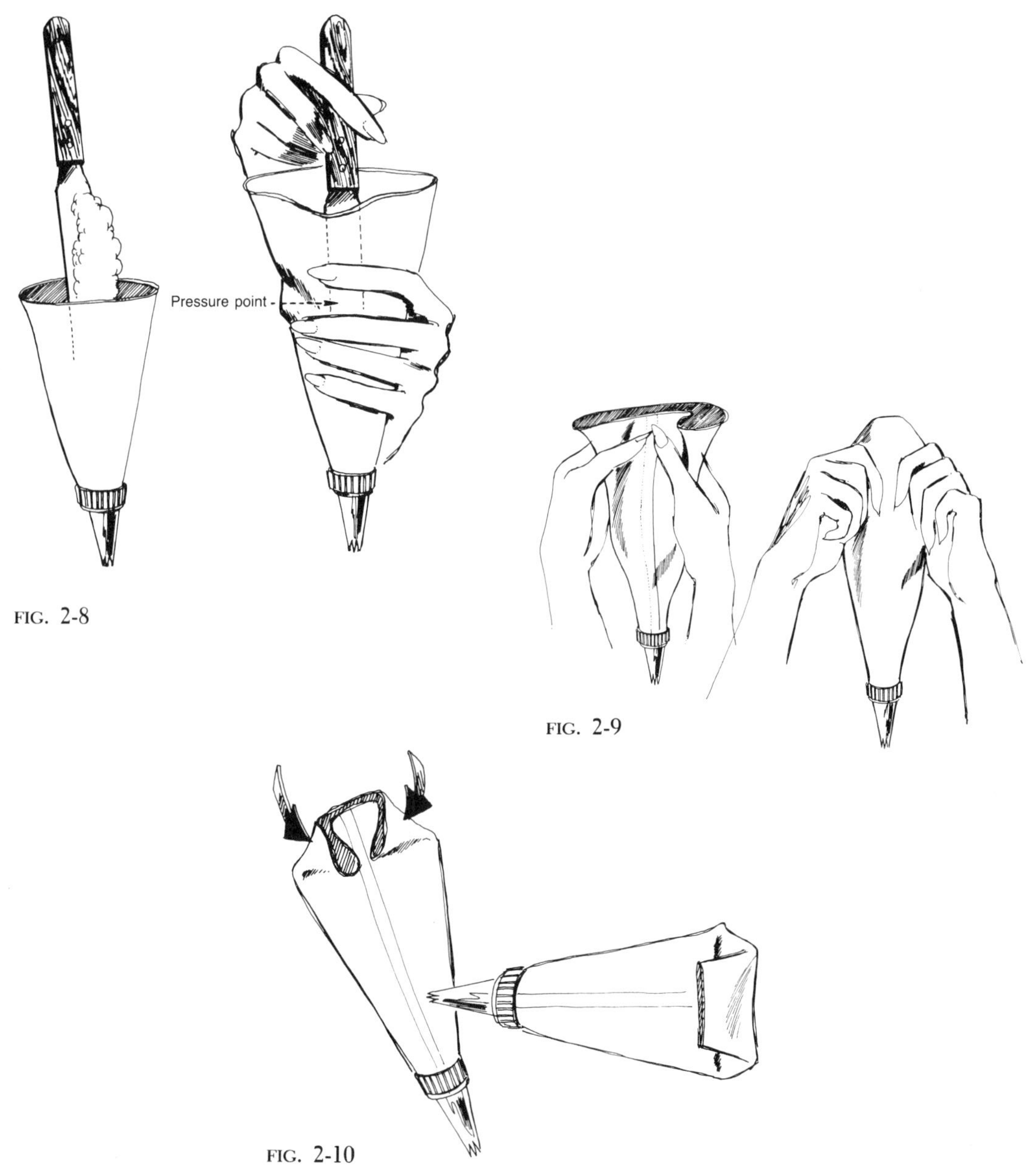

FIG. 2-8

FIG. 2-9

FIG. 2-10

Measuring the Surface

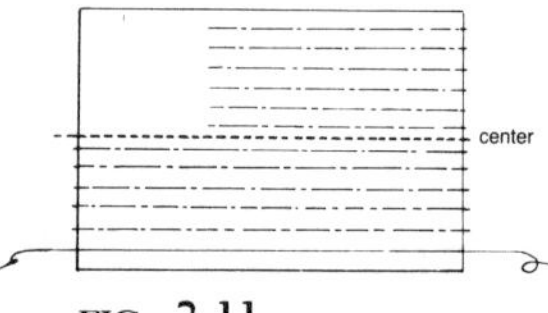

FIG. 2-11

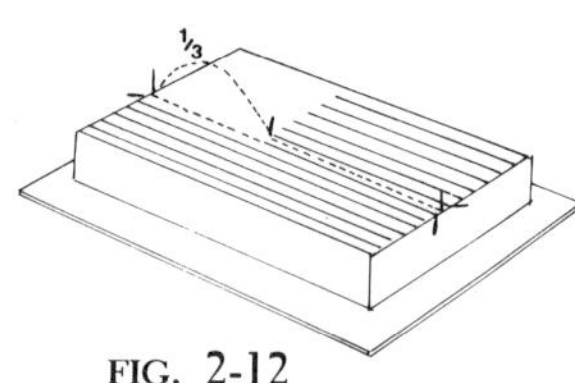

FIG. 2-12

1. Using a ruler, divide cake lengthwise in half and mark with toothpicks placed straight up.
2. Place toothpicks a generous 1/4 inch on each side of each upright toothpick. This marks your center stripe, approximately 5/8 inch wide.
3. Divide the lower section lengthwise in half, using toothpicks placed at 45-degree angles on top of the cake.
4. Divide each of these sections lengthwise into thirds, using 2 toothpicks for each division. It is not the toothpicks that indicate stripes, but the space between the toothpicks (fig. 2-11).
5. To indicate the blue field on the top left side of your cake, divide the upper area into thirds (fig. 2-12).
6. The center stripe is a short one making 6 long stripes below the blue field and 7 short stripes to the right of the blue field.
7. Mark out the short stripes in the same manner as you did the long ones. First, divide the area in half and mark with toothpicks. Then divide each section into thirds and mark with toothpicks.
8. With a piece of thread about 10 inches longer than your cake and holding tightly, rub the thread lightly against the front of your toothpicks on the frosting to make straight lines.
9. Now you have guidelines for applying your stripes. Remove the lines from the blue field with a spatula.

Hold the bag with red frosting and a no. 30 tip in your right hand, as shown (fig. 2-13). Control the bag with your left hand with a light touch (fig. 2-14).

FIG. 2-13

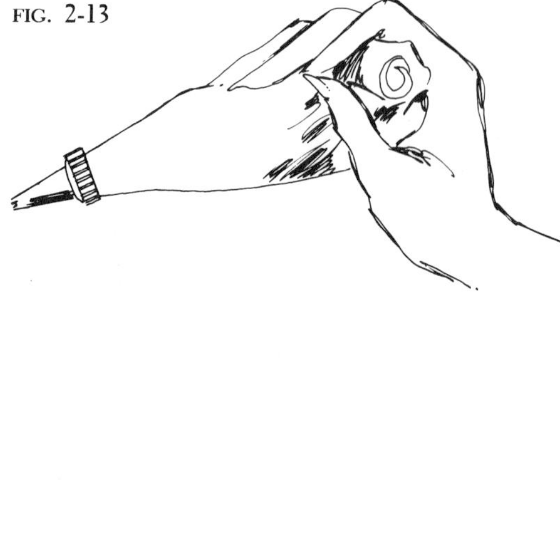

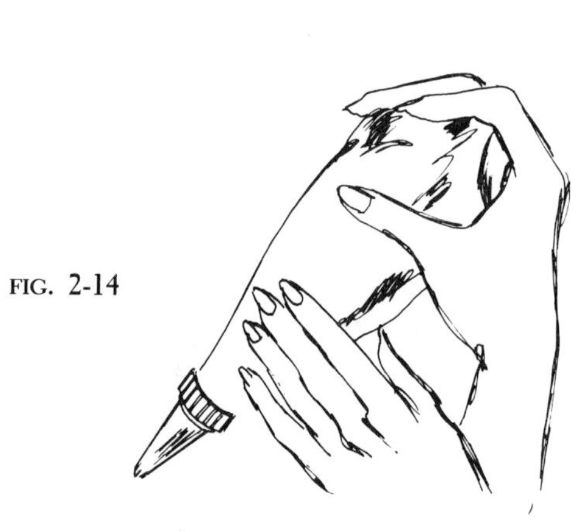

FIG. 2-14

Grand Salute

Starting at the left side of the center stripe and using the red icing, apply pressure and move the tip in an S motion, making close loops (fig. 2-15). Repeat the same process in every other space. You should now have 3 long and 4 short red stripes (fig. 2-16).

Wash the tip thoroughly using the cleaning brush and change to the white bag.

FIG. 2-15

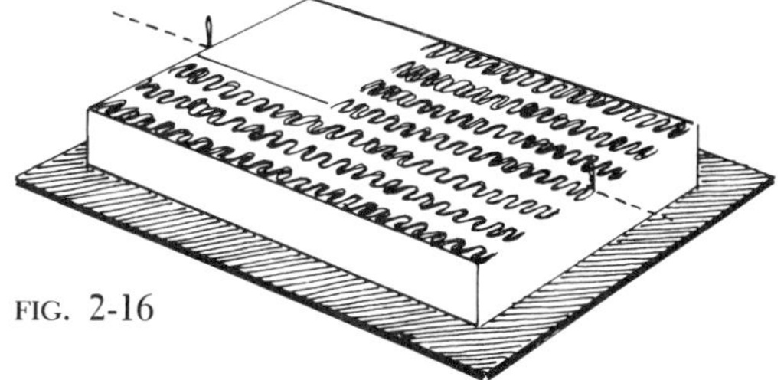

FIG. 2-16

Hold the white bag in the same manner as you did the red one. Start again at the left side of the cake, but this time apply a little more pressure so that the white frosting will meet the red. Do not allow the tip to touch the red stripe as you move from side to side.

The blue field is done with a no. 16 tip. Turn your cake so that you can start at the inner corner (fig. 2-17) and work from left to right if you are right-handed. Use the same motion as you did for the stripes but smaller.

If you are left-handed, just reverse the procedure. Start from the right side and work toward the left.

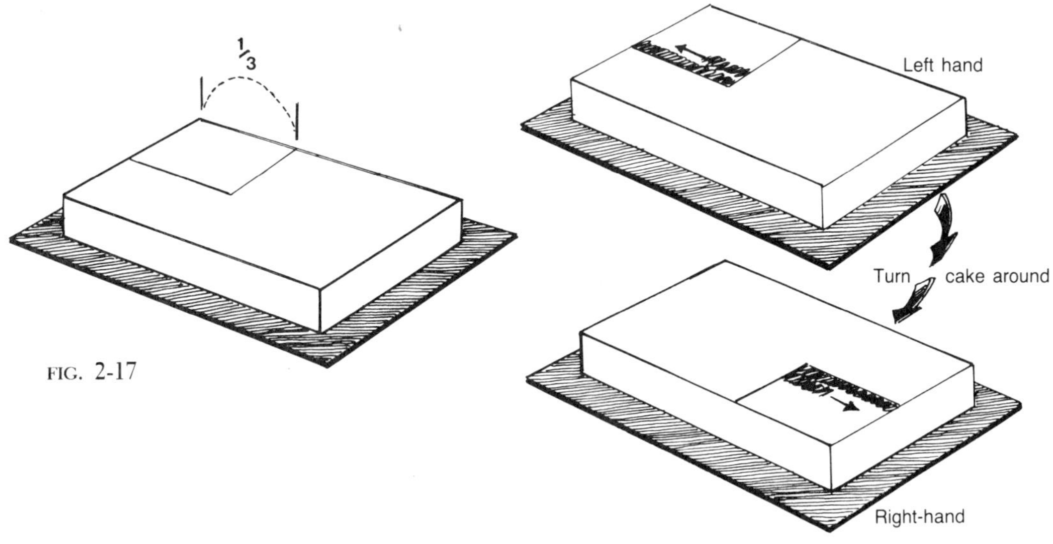

FIG. 2-17

Stars

For a small cake, use 13 stars. Make sure the blue icing is dry before applying white stars or the colors will run. Position stars approximately ½ inch inside blue section.

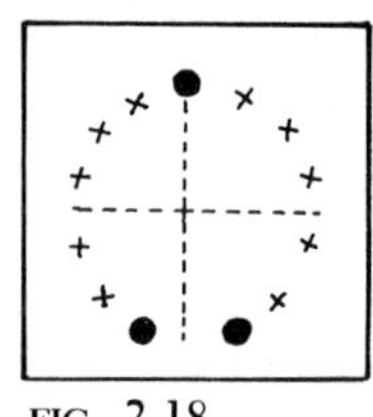

FIG. 2-18

For 13 stars, keep a clockface in mind and place a toothpick at 12 o'clock. Place the next toothpick at about 27 past the hour and the next about 33 past the hour. Position 5 toothpicks proportionally around each side of the clockface (fig. 2-18).

For a larger cake with all stars, place 6 toothpicks along the top edge and 5 along the side edge, leaving a scant ½-inch border all around. Check fig. 2-19 and place a toothpick where each circle is shown.

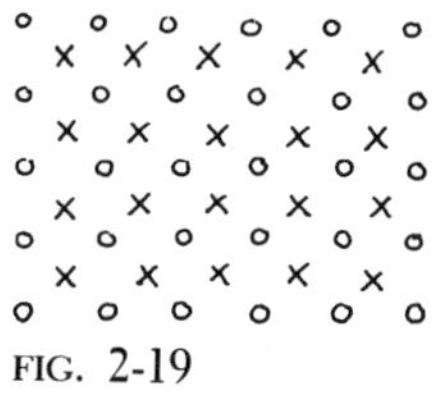

FIG. 2-19

Try making a sample star on the back of your hand or on waxed paper before applying to the cake.

With a no. 16 tip and white frosting, hold the bag at a right angle and apply a little pressure until the star is the size desired. Stop pressure and pull the bag away. Clean the excess frosting from the tip by wiping it on a towel.

Remove a toothpick and make a star; remove another toothpick and make the next star. Do this until all the toothpicks are gone.

To complete the 50 stars, add stars between stars as indicated by x marks in fig. 2-19.

Finishing Touches

The bottom edge of the cake is done with a no. 30 tip with white icing. Holding the bag at a 45-degree angle, apply pressure to make a pleasing mound. Release pressure and pull bag away. About ½ inch away, make another mound, applying pressure until it is the same size as the first. Continue around the cake.

Changing to a no. 16 tip and holding the bag at a 45-degree angle, pipe a solid line around the upper edge of the cake. This will give a nice finish to the design.

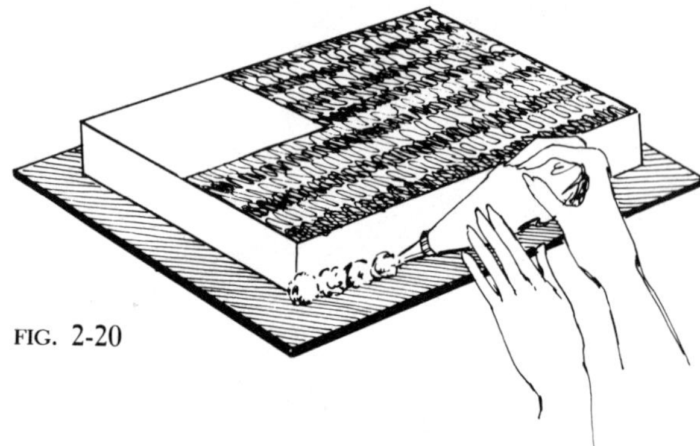

FIG. 2-20

CHAPTER 3
The Cupcake and the Rose

The rose seems to be every cake decorator's favorite. Having achieved a steady hand with the flag exercise, you should be able to take on the queen of flowers.

In order to devote your time to learning the rose techniques, I recommend using them on cupcakes, thus eliminating the need to glaze a cake. This project also provides an opportunity to do stems and leaves and to mix colors in the decorating bag. Rose-laden cupcakes served on a lovely glass dish add a delightful touch to a special luncheon. The greatest compliment will be when the guests take them home instead of eating them.

SUPPLIES

7 cupcakes baked in liners
1 recipe Basic Frosting, (see Index)
2 small bowls
Toothpicks
Paste colors pink and leaf green
Short metal spatula
3 decorating bags with couplings
Tips nos. 3, 16, 65, 67, 104
Waxed paper
Scissors
No. 7 decorating nail
Wooden dowel or skewer, ¼ inch in diameter
Dishcloth
Cleaning brush

Frosting Preparations

Put approximately 1 cup Basic Frosting in a small bowl. Place a small portion of this frosting to one side of the bowl and on the top edge. Dip your toothpick lightly in pink coloring and mix it into the small amount of frosting. By mixing the coloring in small amounts, it is easier to break down, thus avoiding streaks in the frosting. Also, by mixing in this manner, you can better regulate your coloring. If the color is too dark, add only part into remaining amount in the bowl. Mix very little for a variegated rose.

For better highlights on your roses, use two shades of frosting. Fill the bag alternately with small amounts of pink and white frostings. It is important that both icings be of the same consistency or one will come out faster than the other. Put tip no. 104 on coupling.

Mix green frosting in the same manner as the pink; mix thoroughly and put only one color in bag. If a softer green is desired, mix in a touch of red coloring. This will give you a grey green. Do not add too much or you will have brown frosting. Fill bag and use no. 3 tip on coupling.

Preparing the Cupcakes

When filling cupcake liners with batter, never fill them more than halfway. Lining paper should be a scant ⅛ inch above the cake after baking. Thin down Basic Frosting slightly with cold water, and frost the cupcakes with a short metal spatula. Sometimes during baking the paper pulls away from the cupcake; to correct this, smooth the frosting to the edge of the

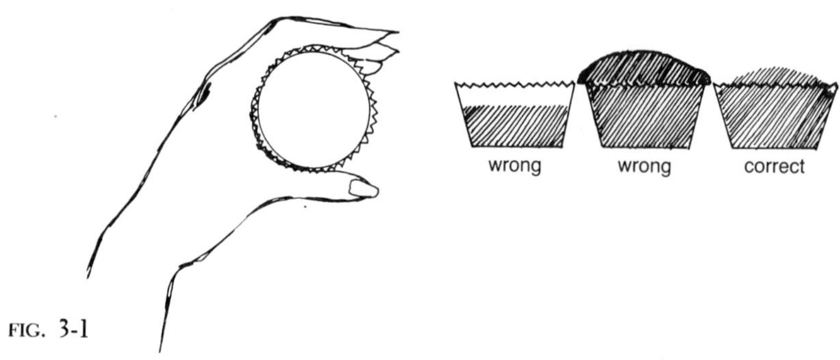

FIG. 3-1

cupcake, touching the paper. The frosting will stick to the paper, thus sealing the cupcake on all sides. Apply enough frosting to cover cake. (Crumbing and glazing is not necessary on cupcakes.)

Fold and Trim

Many flowers are made on squares of waxed paper and allowed to set before applying them to a cake.

Tear off strips of waxed paper 2 inches wide. Fold in half and cut; then fold in thirds and cut as shown. These squares fit on your no. 7 decorating nail. Do not cut papers too large—approximately 2 × 2 inches will be fine. Make as many squares of waxed paper as you think you will need to complete your project. I cut a large number of these at one time and keep them in a box for immediate and future use.

With the no. 7 nail in one hand and the bag with pink frosting, held with the thick end of the tip down, in the other, put a small amount of icing on the nail; place a piece of waxed paper over it with the natural curve of the paper down.

FIG. 3-2

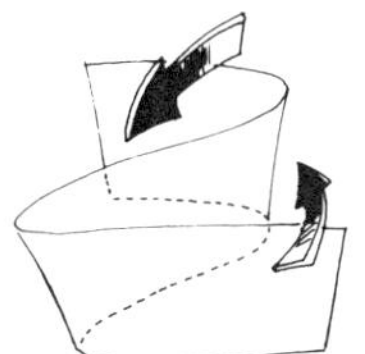

FIG. 3-3

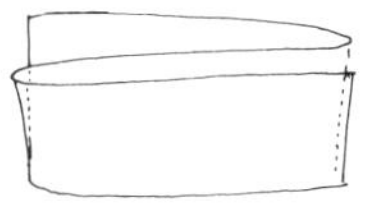

FIG. 3-4

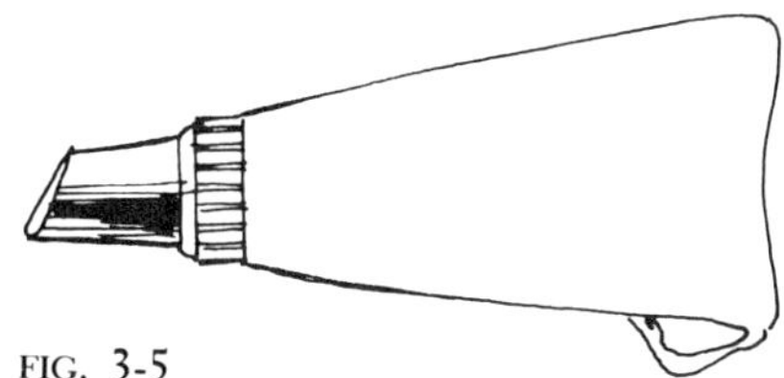

FIG. 3-5

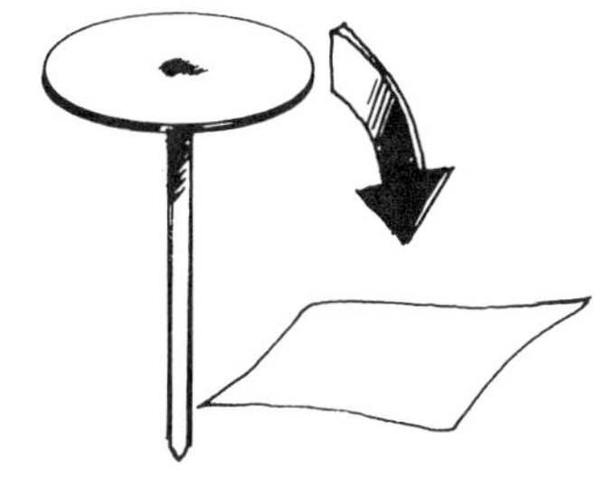

FIG. 3-6

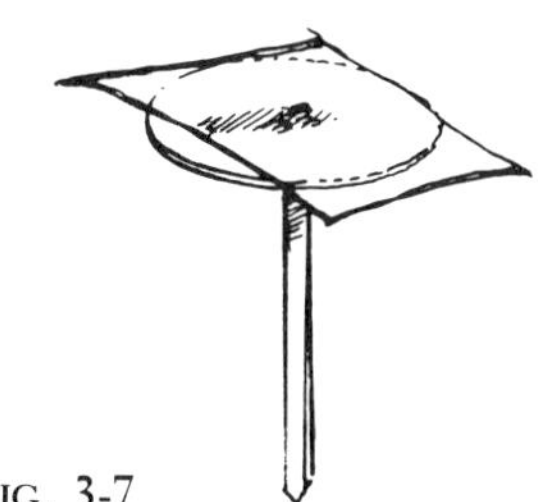

FIG. 3-7

A Sample Rose

Apply pressure on the bag with the right hand and turn nail counterclockwise with the left hand. Rest the tip lightly against and slightly off the center of the nail. Tilt the tip towards yourself. As you apply pressure, form a cone. Go around twice to make a stronger base. As you complete your second turn, stop squeezing but keep moving the bag in the same way until the frosting stops flowing and breaks off (fig. 3-8).

Hold the bag so that half of the tip is above the cone (fig. 3-9). Apply pressure, making a slight upward motion, then a downward motion (fig. 3-10). Always work the petals coming towards you, turning the nail counterclockwise (fig. 3-11). Three of these petals around the cone will form a bud (fig. 3-12). Wipe the tip clean on a wet dishcloth before making each petal and make sure that each petal overlaps (fig. 3-13).

To make a larger rose, make the petals a little larger, overlapping each one with the motion of a fan. As the rose gets larger, the thin part of the tip will be more outward. Remove waxed paper with flower from nail and let it set (fig. 3-14).

If left-handed, these instructions can be used by just reversing hands. Make all petals coming towards yourself.

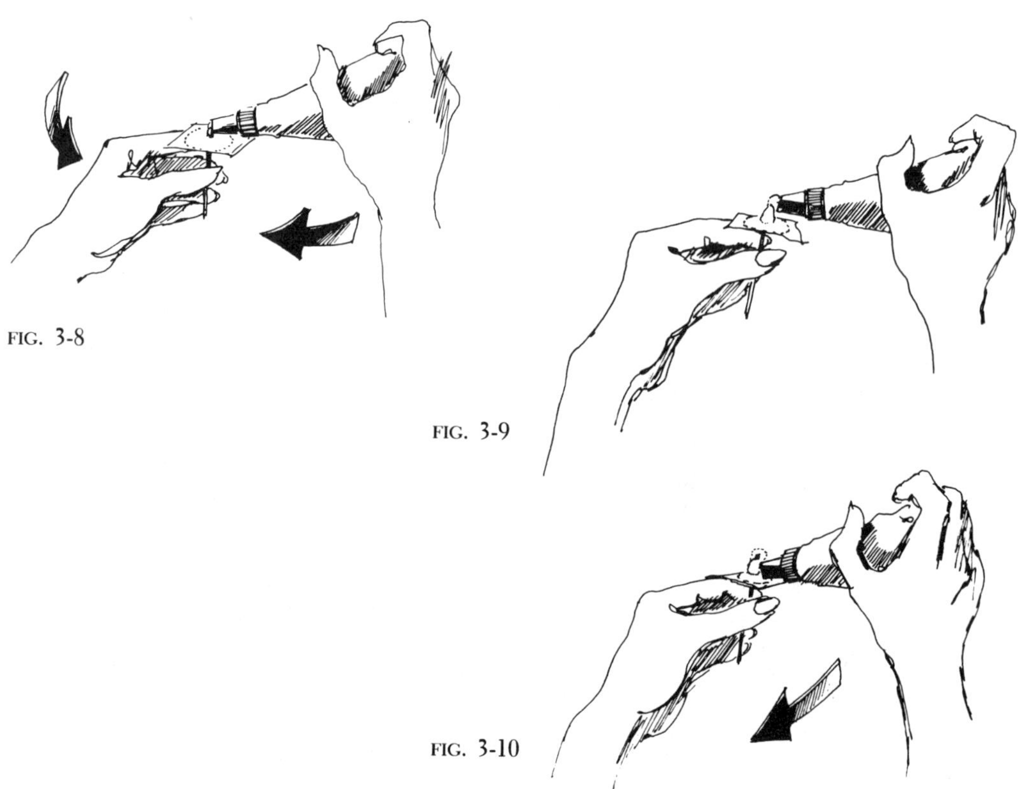

FIG. 3-8

FIG. 3-9

FIG. 3-10

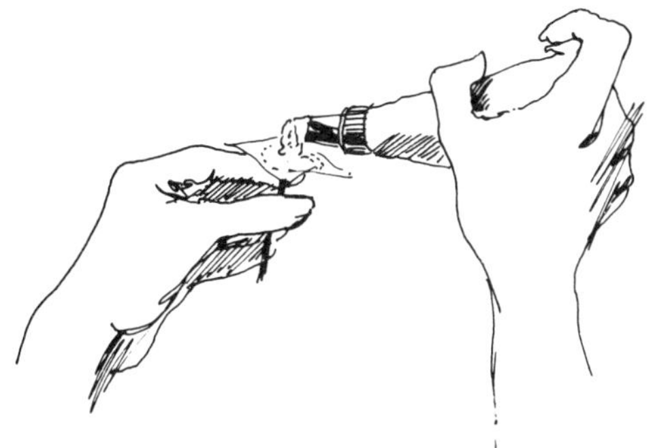

FIG. 3-11

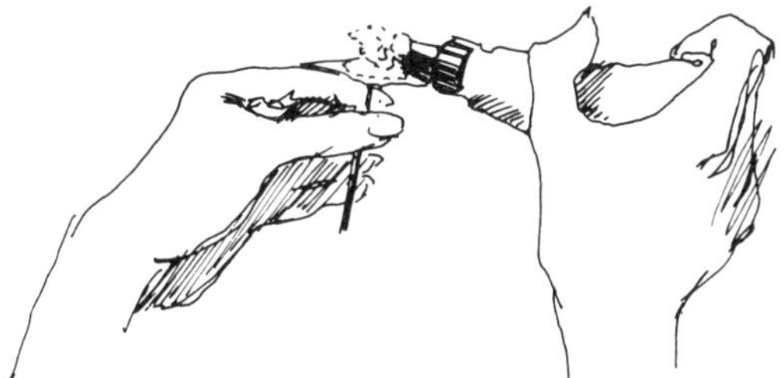

FIG. 3-12

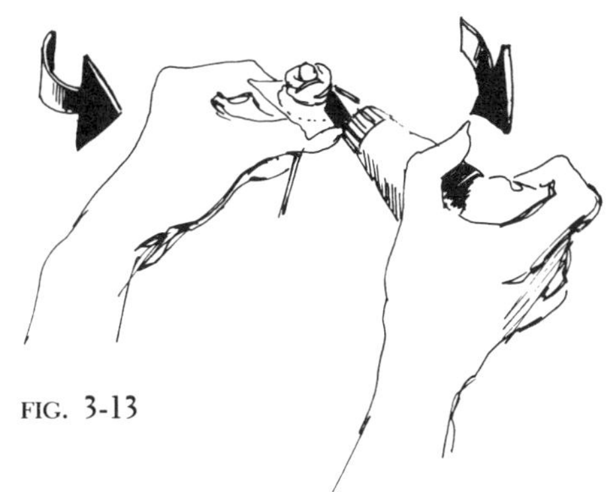

FIG. 3-13

FIG. 3-14

A Sharpened Dowel

Once you have mastered the nail, try working on a dowel. Slightly sharpen a ¼-inch dowel about 6 inches long in a pencil sharpener; then sand it smooth. For the dowel, use the same waxed-paper squares as for the no. 7 nail (2 × 2 inches.) Then pierce the paper on the bottom of the nail to make the hole. If you put the papers directly on a wooden dowel, you will ruin the point very quickly. Put about a dozen papers on the wooden dowel and separate them between your thumb and index finger to make them easier to remove after each flower (fig. 3-15).

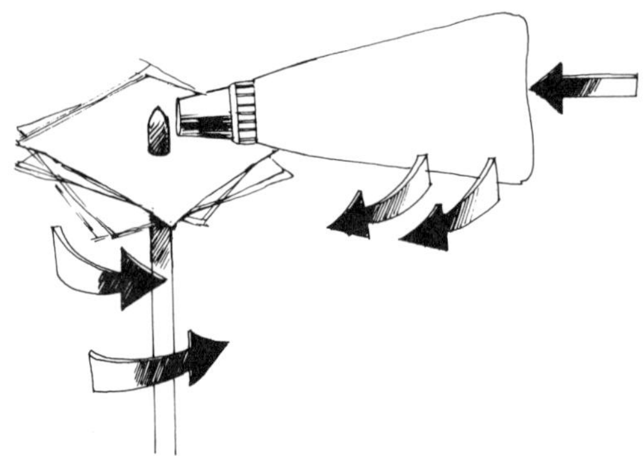

FIG. 3-15

A Rose Is a Rose

Hold the dowel in the left hand and pastry bag in your right hand. With the thick part of the no. 104 tip down (fig. 3-16), squeeze with the right hand and rotate stick counterclockwise to shape the cone, extending half above the end of the dowel. Once around is sufficient.

Clean the tip. Put tip against the cone with the thin end of tube at the level of the bud (fig. 3-17). Apply pressure and give a slight upward

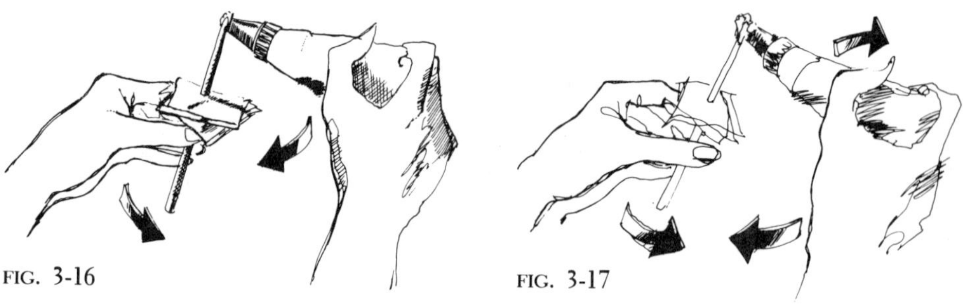

FIG. 3-16

FIG. 3-17

motion, then a downward motion. As you come down, release pressure but continue the petal. The frosting will stop flowing, and the petal will be completed. Fig. 3-18 illustrates the position of the three petals for a bud. Clean the tip. Overlapping the first petal slightly, make another petal in the same manner. After the third petal, you have a bud (fig. 3-19). If you wish to stop here, raise one piece of waxed paper from the lower part of your dowel till it touches the base of your flower. Put fingers of left hand under waxed paper (fig. 3-20) and rotate the stick to remove it. If pulled up straight, the flower can be ruined by suction. Rotation will also give the flower more depth.

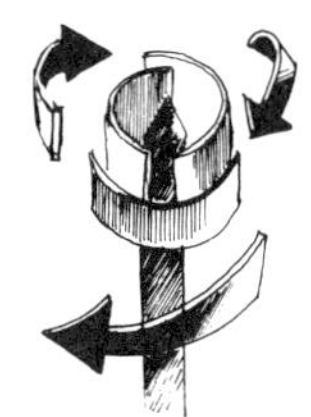

FIG. 3-18

If you want a larger rose, keep adding more petals. Make sure you overlap all petals. On the second round, make 4 petals, using the same upward motion and coming down onto the stick. On the next row, hold the tip at a more outward angle and back on the stick (fig. 3-21).

For a very large rose, use a tip no. 124 to 128. Follow the same directions, but get a larger dowel for best results (fig. 3-22).

The flowers just completed should be allowed to set for a few hours before you place them directly on a cupcake.

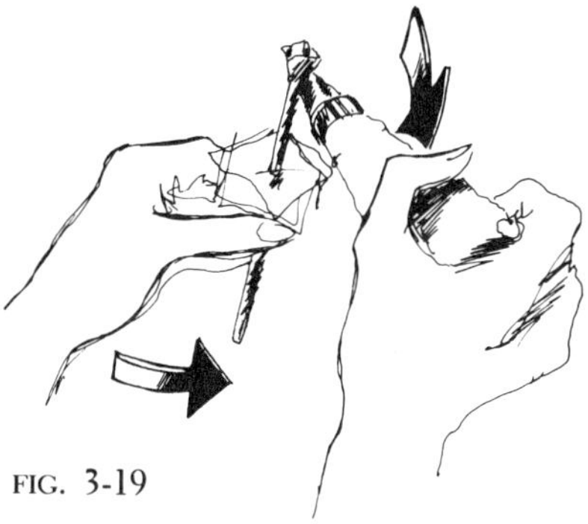

FIG. 3-19

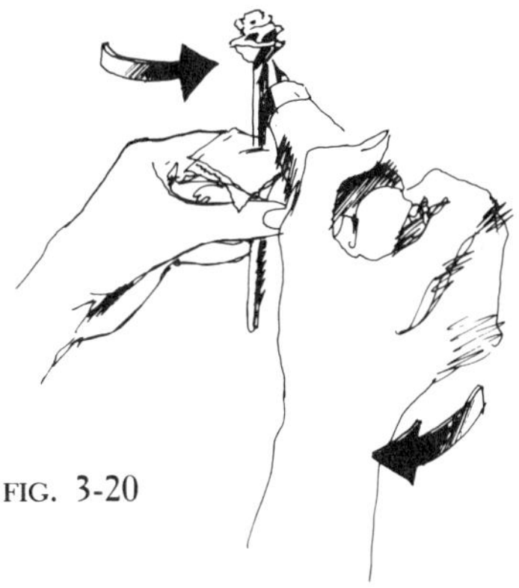

FIG. 3-20

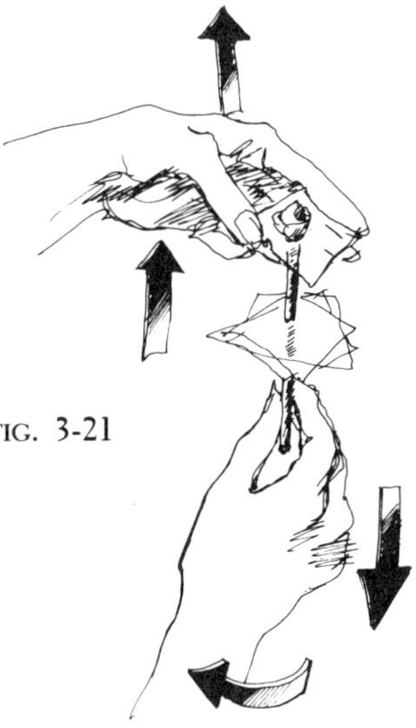

FIG. 3-21

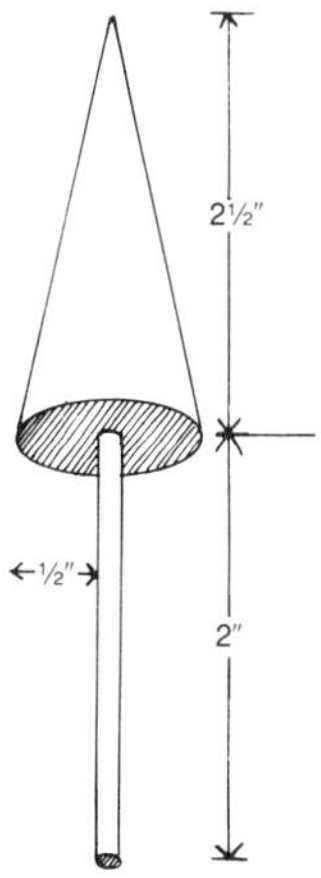

FIG. 3-22

At the Bud

The flat bud and the following flowers are made directly on your cupcakes. I suggest trying a few on waxed paper first. Hold your bag at a 90-degree angle. Again, the thickest part of the tip is down and held just above the surface of the cake. Squeeze the bag until you have a pleasing-size bud (fig. 3-23). Just this bud is very attractive on a cupcake and also very good in a flat floral arrangement.

FIG. 3-23

After you have completed a bud, take the bag of green frosting with the no. 3 tip. Hold the tip at the base of the bud, apply pressure, but do not move bag. The mound will cup itself over the base of the bud. Release pressure slightly and pull bag slowly away forming the stem.

To form the sepal on the rose, put a clean no. 3 tip in mound next to pink flower, apply a little pressure and pull out, releasing pressure very quickly. On a flower this size, I find three sepals are enough. Try to make them look as if they were a continuation of the green base, rather than pieces added on.

For a larger bud, start again, holding your bag at a 90-degree angle, and make the bud. Holding the tip with the thickest end against the left lower part of the bud and the thin section outward, apply pressure and bring tip towards you right over bud (fig. 3-24). Release pressure as you go over, but keep going towards opposite side. By stopping pressure at that point, the petal will continue a little further and break. Place the tip the same way to the *right* side of the bud and make another petal (fig. 3-25), working towards the left. Add the green base with sepals and stem in the same manner as for the smaller bud.

FIG. 3-24

To make a full flat rose, add 3 more petals to the bud. Put a petal directly over the center where the last 2 petals overlapped. To the left of the flower, put thick end down slightly in icing with thin side out. Apply pressure and make a petal coming to center, just overlapping last petal. Form a petal on the right in the same manner.

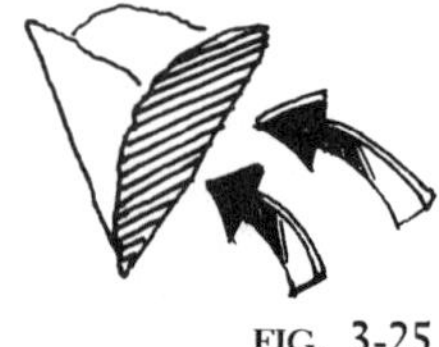

FIG. 3-25

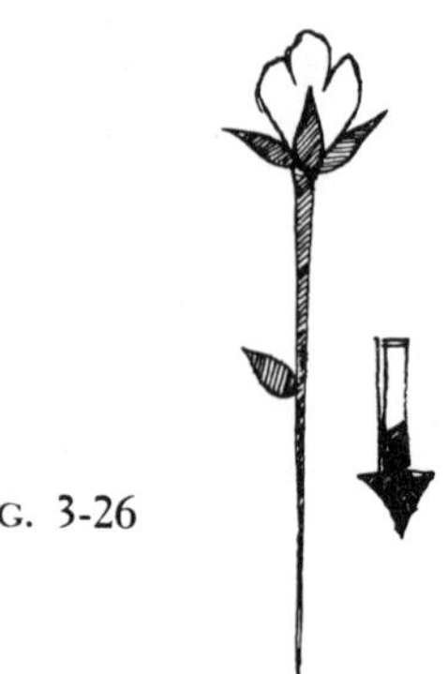

FIG. 3-26

Whenever a flower is made in a side view, the green base must be applied. When a full rose is placed on a cake, the green base is not visible; therefore, it is not added.

To add leaves to the stems, change the tip on the bag of green icing to a no. 65. Place clean tip lightly against stem and apply very little pressure for a very small leaf in proportion to your flower (fig. 3-26).

To create a small bud on the stem hold the no. 3 tip on a bag of green icing still at a 45-degree angle and apply pressure to make a rounded mound the desired size. Release pressure slightly and pull away slowly to form the stem.

Wash the no. 3 tip and attach it to the bag of pink icing. Push the tip into the center of the green mound and apply pressure until color is showing and the bud looks as if it will burst (fig. 3-27).

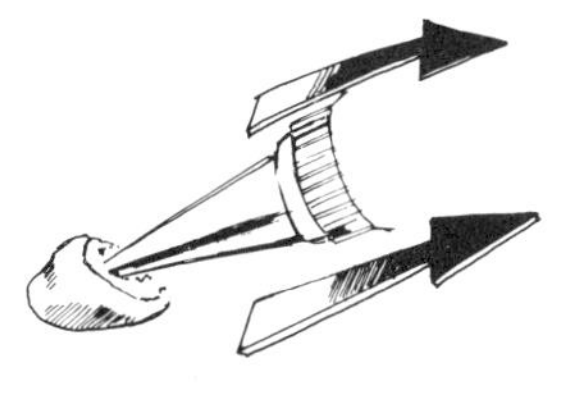

FIG. 3-27

Rose in Hand

When the roses are dry, remove waxed paper, place a small mound of green icing on the cupcake, then place the rose over it. Without this icing to secure it, the flower will fall off.

One rose with one leaf is very effective. Three roses with leaves on a cupcake makes a more elaborate design, or the entire cupcake can be covered.

When applying green leaves with a no. 67 tip, hold tip next to the attached rose and against the frosting. Apply a great deal of pressure so that the leaf will have a heavy base; then release pressure slightly and pull up. This does take quite a bit of practice. If your frosting is too dry or too soft, you will not get good results.

To finish off your cupcakes, take a bag of white icing with a no. 16 tip and pipe in a fine left-to-right motion around the edge.

FIG. 3-28

CHAPTER 4

Garden Cake

This chapter deals with the techniques of working on the sides of a cake and of dividing the surface. In addition, you will be learning the art of string or lattice work—a popular and graceful form of cake design. You will also be making and applying roses directly to a cake without the drying process.

This is also a good time to learn how to use parchment bags, which are especially useful in designs requiring small amounts of icing. The Garden Cake is charming for a spring or summer birthday and offers the decorator an opportunity to work out some of her favorite color schemes.

SUPPLIES

8- to 10-inch round high cake
2 recipes Basic Frosting (see Index), depending on size of cake
Small metal spatula
Cardboard disk or flat plate with glassine doily
2 mixing bowls with covers
Paste colors of your choice
Toothpicks
3 bags with couplings
Tips nos. 3, 16, 30, 67, 104
Parchment papers for 4 bags
Waxed paper
No. 7 decorating nail
Sharp-pointed scissors
Dishcloth

Before you begin your decorations, you need to prepare a round high cake, 8 to 10 inches in diameter. If doing a layer cake, remember to use just a small amount of frosting between the layers. Too much frosting will cause the layers to slide.

An angel cake baked in a tube pan may be used, but it is a little difficult to get a smooth finish on it. A slightly heavier icing will give better results. To cover the hole, cut a piece of lightweight cardboard or plastic ½ inch larger than the opening.

When crumbing your cake, place the cardboard over the hole and frost over it. If you plan to place any decorations over the center of the cake, the cardboard should be made a little larger.

For a single layer cake 3½ inches high, use a wedding cake pan or springform pan. This pan is greased and lined with waxed paper; the cake will take a longer time to bake because of the large amount of batter.

Before you crumb the cake, it should be placed on a cardboard disk or a flat plate with a margin of 1½ to 2 inches all around. If you are using a doily, put a small amount of icing under and over it so that the doily will stick to the disk and the cake will stick to the doily. The cake is now ready to be crumbed and glazed according to the directions in Chapter 1.

If your cake is crumbed with white icing, let it dry thoroughly before glazing with a color. You may glaze and decorate your cake in several combinations:

1. Dark glaze with light decorations of the same color
2. Soft-colored glaze used with deeper shades of the same color for decorations
3. Colored glaze with white decorations
4. White glaze with colored decorations

Frost your cake, being careful not to select too deep a color: Dark or harsh colors are not appealing to the palate or the eye. Remember to use a clean utensil or toothpick when taking paste color out of the jar.

Fill your first canvas bag with icing for the lattice and borders. Instead of putting a tip on your coupling, put a piece of waxed paper over the coupling and screw on the nut. This will prevent the icing from drying until you are ready to use it.

Fill the second canvas bag with about 1 cup of green icing. Use a no. 3 tip.

The third canvas bag will be used to make roses. The colors may be varied by adding several shades, as discussed in Chapter 3. Place tip no. 104 on coupling. If the bag for the lattice and the borders is a color, you can squeeze all the icing out when finished and add white. The first rose will be the color of the original frosting left in the coupling, but the next rose will show the new frosting.

When using a canvas bag with a coupling, you must have at least ⅓ cup of icing in the bag in order to squeeze any out.

Parchment Bags

Folding the triangular parchment papers into bags might be difficult to master at first. However, it is worth the effort because the parchment bags are so very practical for small amounts of icing. A parchment bag can be used with or without a tip but *never* with a coupling. All the icing can be used except what is left in the tip; the bag is then thrown out or refilled, if necessary. Be careful not to discard any tips.

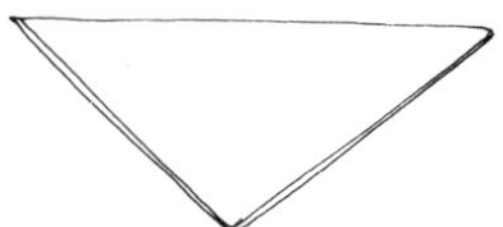

FIG. 4-1
Fold or cut the parchment sheet into a triangle measuring about 15 inches on the longest side.

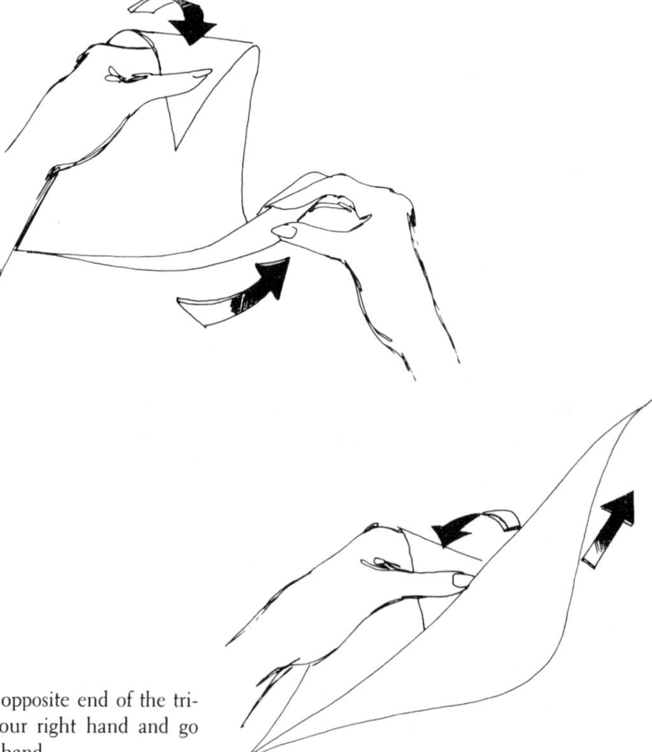

FIG. 4-2
Take the triangular paper and hold it in your left hand between thumb and index finger with the right angle of the paper toward your elbow.

FIG. 4-3
Take up the opposite end of the triangle with your right hand and go over the left hand.

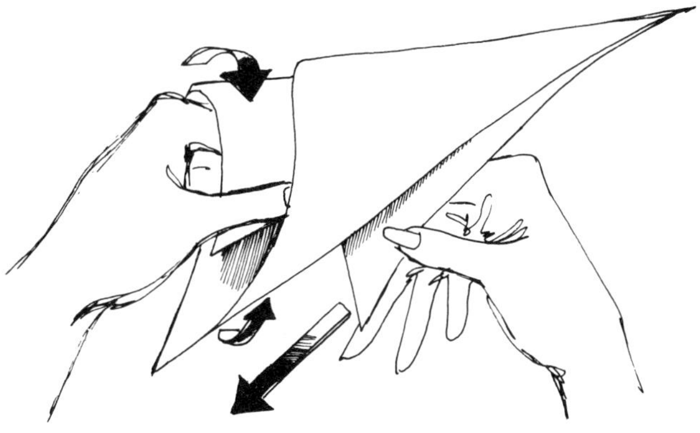

FIG. 4-4
The two points should meet at a right angle, forming a cone without a hole on the point.

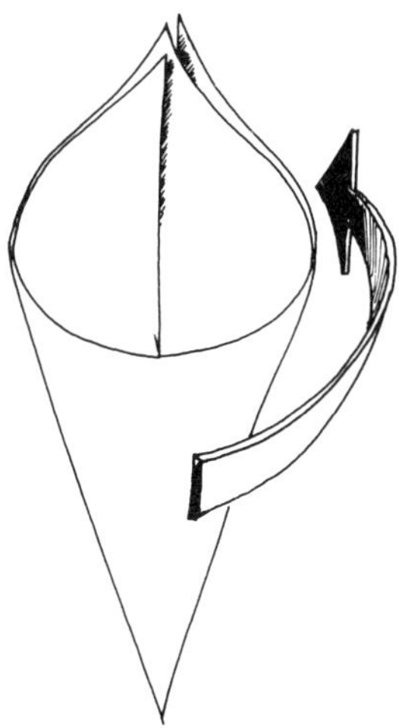

FIG. 4-5
The cone-shaped bag is now 4 thicknesses of paper with all edges meeting.

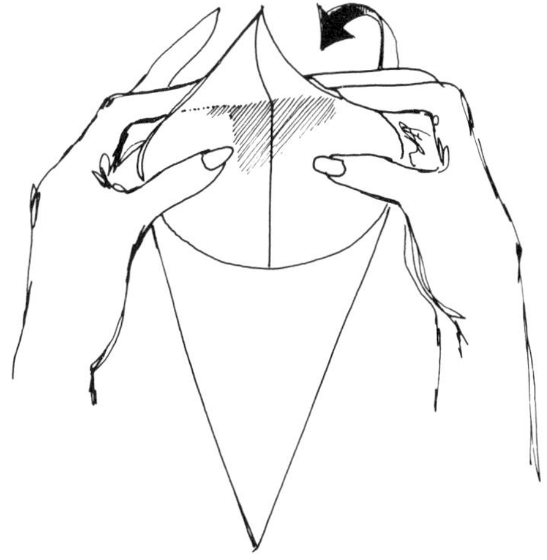

FIG. 4-6
Fold back the top point about 2 inches, then fold again ¼ inch. The bags can be used by just clipping the end or by cutting off ¼ inch and adding a tip.

For the Garden Cake, you will need 4 parchment bags. No tips are needed. In each parchment bag, you will place about 1 tablespoon of icing, each a different color, for the flower garden growing around the sides of the cake. Insert the icing; then squeeze the bag till icing is all the way down. Fold left side toward center, then right side toward center; roll flap down to reach frosting, and the bag is ready to use.

Branch Out

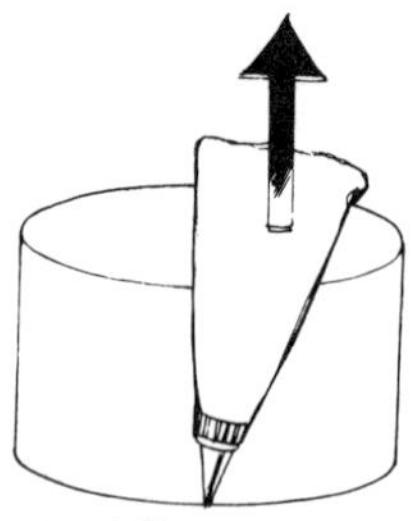
FIG. 4-7

With the bag of green icing and no. 3 tip, start making stems. Hold the bag almost straight up to the cake, as shown, so that the frosting forms a rounded stem. Three variations of stems are shown here.

When the stem motif is completed around the cake, apply flowers. The flowers can vary in color, but use only one color per stem. On treelike stems, however, all flowers should be the same color.

With a small amount of icing in a parchment bag, cut just the tip end of the bag so that the opening is about the size of a no. 3 tip. Hold the tip end of the bag to the left and then to the right of each stem, and apply a little pressure to make a small bulblike flower. Release the pressure; then pull tip away. Do this, alternating side to side, all the way up the stem to the top. Add flowers to all stems.

The larger the cake, the larger the buds may be. If they are large enough, add sepals to the base of each flower with a no. 3 tip and green icing. Put tip over the lower base of flower and apply a little pressure as you pull up slightly. Just a little touch of green should be on each bud.

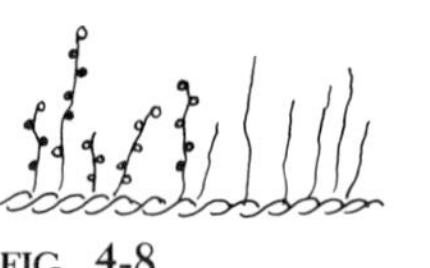
FIG. 4-8

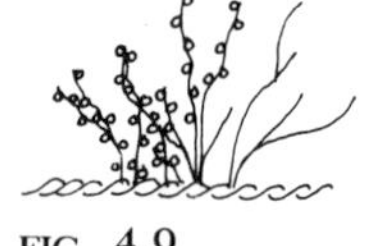
FIG. 4-9

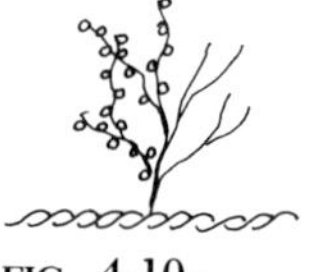
FIG. 4-10

Divide the Surface

To divide the top and mark for decorations, tear off a piece of waxed paper the width of your cake. Cut off excess to make a square (fig. 4-11). Fold this square in half, then in quarters. Cut the tips off the corners to either side of the center point (fig. 4-12). Open paper and place on dry glazed cake. Place a toothpick in the cake at each notch (fig. 4-13). The cake is now divided into 4 equal sections. This method is used to divide a cake into as many sections as needed.

FIG. 4-11
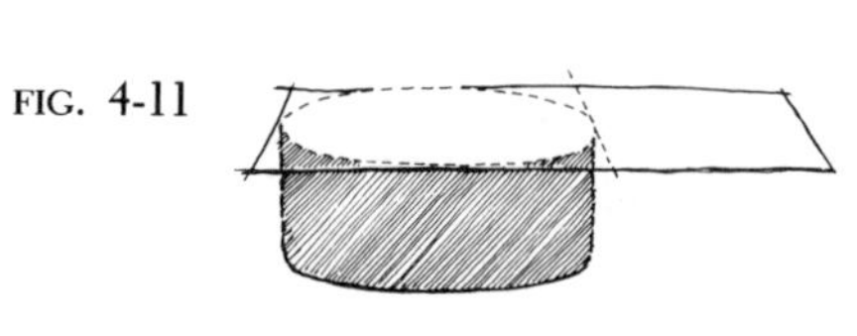

FIG. 4-12 FIG. 4-13
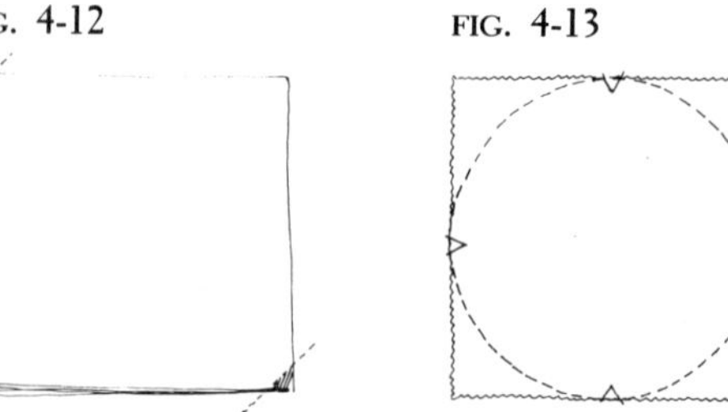

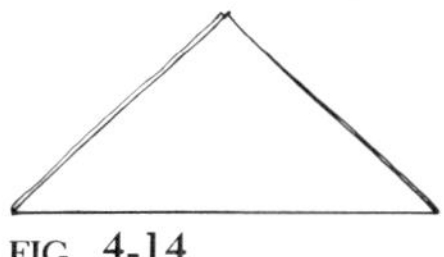

FIG. 4-14

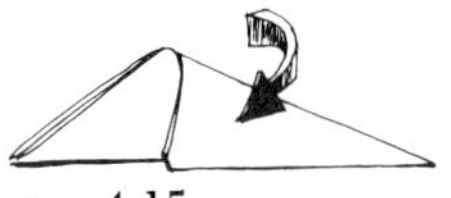

FIG. 4-15

For the Garden Cake, fold the waxed paper into quarters, then into eighths (fig. 4-14), then into sixteenths (fig. 4-15), then into thirty-seconds (fig. 4-16), keeping the pie shape. Cut off top edge at notch (fig. 4-17). If done properly, this will give you a round piece of paper. To mark the ovals for lattice work, gently place your paper on the cake as shown, keeping a scant ¼ inch away from your markings. Then mark the oval with toothpicks or a spatula.

Now wash the no. 3 tip and place on the main color bag that you previously covered at the tip with waxed paper.

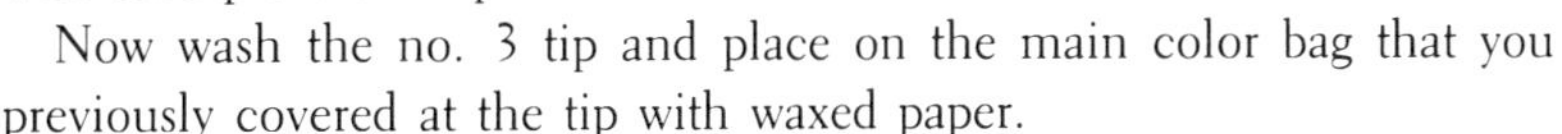

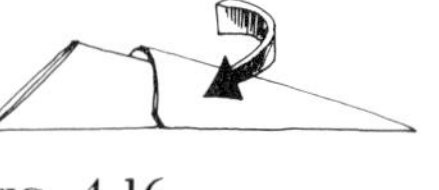

FIG. 4-16

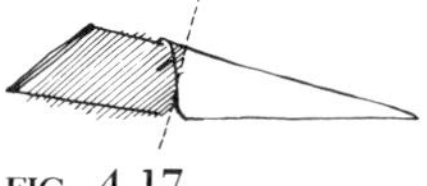

FIG. 4-17

Lattice Work

To begin the lattice, mark 1 inch on the top curve of the oval and 2 inches at the outer edge, as shown. Do this on both sides of the oval. These are guidelines for both directions of the lattice. The lines are on a slight angle. Complete all the lattice lines in one direction before doing the lines in the opposite direction. To make the lines, hold the bag at a 45-degree angle and apply a small amount of pressure so that the icing will stick to the cake. Squeeze and hold the tip slightly above the cake so that the string of icing is suspended and falls in a straight line. When you reach the end, release pressure and push tip lightly against glazed icing to break the line. Add lattice to all 4 ovals before going on to the next step.

Place a no. 16 tip on this same bag and outline the inner curves of the ovals with a rotary motion, keeping the lines close together. Decorate the outside curves with the same motion. At the bottom edge of the cake, repeat the rotary design but apply a little more pressure. For a heavier border, use a no. 30 tip.

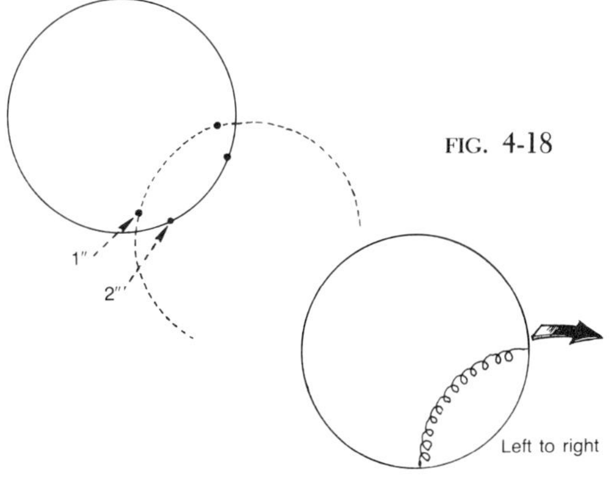

FIG. 4-18

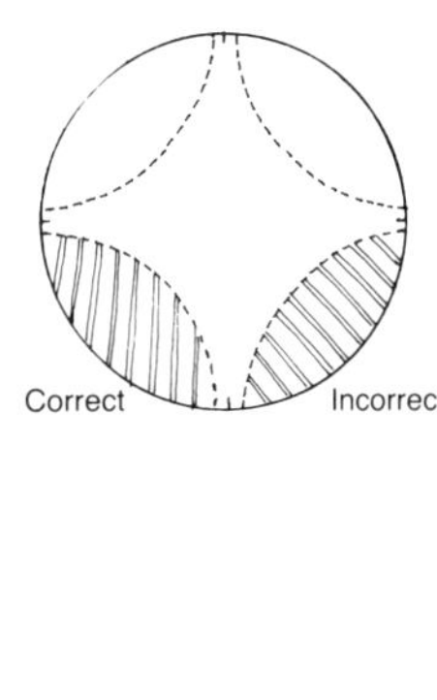

Clustered Roses

FIG. 4-19

To complete the cake, place a rose at each point where the ovals join and make 3 leaves around it. In the center of the cake, you can put a cluster of roses on a mound of icing, although you have a free hand in the placement and number of roses on this cake.

Roses can be made and applied to this kind of cake without first drying. Follow the instructions and illustrations in Chapter 3 for making the flowers. After the roses have been made on the nail or dowel and lifted off on waxed paper as directed, use the point of the scissors to pick up the rose. Slip the flower off the scissors and onto the cake, using a no. 7 nail.

Whatever frosting you have left can be saved for the next cake, or even the cake after that. This frosting does not spoil if kept in an airtight container without refrigeration. I use any screw-top jar that is odorless. (Have you ever had sauerkraut-flavored frosting? Avoid pickle and mustard jars and any container that held very strong or spicy foods.)

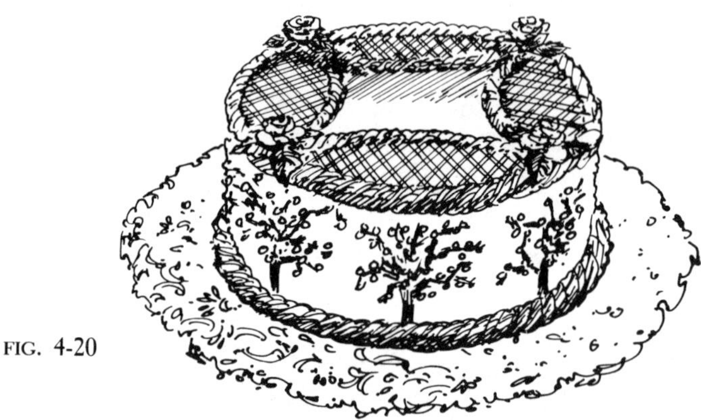

FIG. 4-20

CHAPTER 5

Ring of Roses

"Ring around the rosie/A pocket full of posies." Even nursery rhymes can provide a source of inspiration for cake decorations.

Soft pink roses frame pink lattice work on this white cake. The Ring of Roses is simple, quick, and, with the addition of candles, a delightful birthday cake.

SUPPLIES

9-inch two-layer round cake
Platter or cardboard disk with glassine doily
2 recipes Basic Frosting (see Index)
3 containers with lids
Toothpicks
Paste colors leaf green and pink
Small metal spatula
4 decorating bags with couplings
Tips nos. 22, 47, 65, 67, 104
25 to 30 roses (made on a no. 7 nail or wooden dowel)
Cleaning brush
Dishcloth

Crumbing and Glazing

While the cake is baking, make 25 to 30 roses on a no. 7 nail or a wooden dowel, following the instructions in Chapter 3. For the frosting for these roses, place about 1 cup Basic Frosting in a small bowl and, using a toothpick, add pink paste color. Mix slightly so that frosting is streaked when placed in the decorating bag. Place a generous tablespoon of pink frosting in the bag; follow it with the same amount of white icing. Continue alternating the two colors until you have a sufficient amount. Make the roses. The number of flowers you make depends on the size of the roses and the size of the cake. They should set at least 1 hour before you remove the waxed paper and arrange the roses on the cake.

When the cakes have cooled on the cooling rack, place one of the cakes on a platter, allowing at least 1½ inches of space all around. The larger the cake, the more space you should allow around it. If you use corrugated cardboard, put a small amount of icing on the board; then arrange the glassine doily. Put more icing on the doily before adding the cooled cake. This will prevent the cake from sliding.

Put approximately 1 cup Basic Frosting in a small bowl and add a few drops of cold water to thin the icing for crumbing (see Chapter 2). Frost the top of the first cake and apply the second cake. Now crumb the cake, completely covering the entire surface with icing. Crumbing keeps the cake fresher and simplifies the glazing. Let the frosting set until it is dry to the touch.

In the meantime, mix about 1 cup light pink icing to do the lattice on the top surface and the pink leaves on the lower border. This icing should be mixed thoroughly to make sure that the color is even throughout the bag. Put the pink frosting in a decorating bag fitted with a no. 47 tip.

Fill another bag with white frosting, placing a no. 22 tip on the coupling.

Mix about 1 cup green frosting, adding a touch of red color to tone it down; place it in a decorating bag with a no. 67 leaf tip.

By this time, the crumbed cake should be dry. Put a small amount of frosting in a bowl and thin it down with a few drops of cold water (see Chapter 2) for glazing. Frost the cake by holding a small metal spatula at a right angle to the plate (as shown in Chapter 2). Using long strokes, apply enough frosting to give it a white finish.

Then dip the blade of the spatula in a glass of hot water and wipe the blade dry. Go over the frosting with the hot blade to give it a glazed effect. Keep dipping and drying the blade to keep it hot.

Lattice Work Top

To form the diamond lattice on this cake, first divide the top in quarters (see Chapter 4). Mark the edge of the cake 2 inches to either side of the center line as shown in fig. 5-1. Connect these points through the center point, using a long metal spatula or a carving knife. Take the bag with pink frosting and a no. 47 tip to do the lattice. Hold the bag so that the serrated edge of the tip faces upward. To anchor the frosting, place the tip on the edge of the cake over the line and apply pressure. Continue to apply pressure and draw bag towards you, holding the tip a scant ¼ inch above the line. Continue to the opposite edge of the cake. When you reach the edge, stop pressure and push tip slightly into glazed frosting to cut icing. By holding the tip slightly above the surface of the cake, you will find it easier to make a straight line. Continue to add stripes about ½ inch apart. Do all the lines going in the same direction first; then complete the lattice.

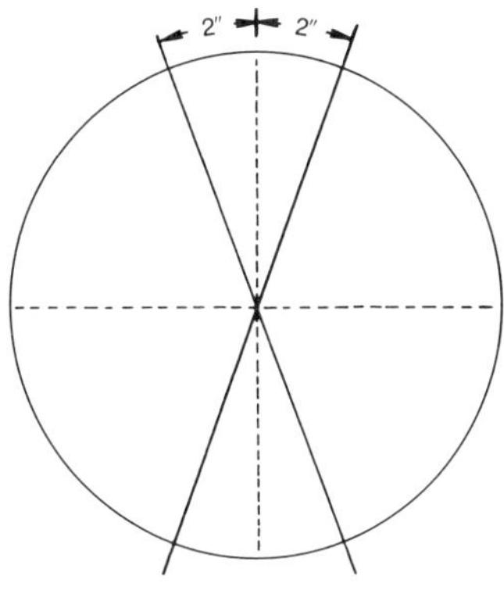

FIG. 5-1

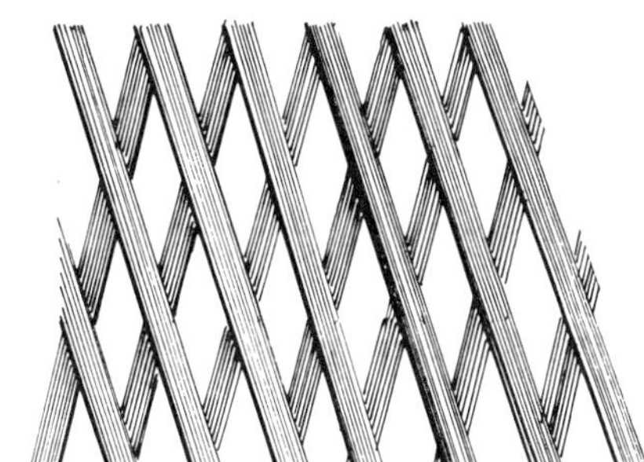

FIG. 5-2

Borders and Leaves

Take the bag of white icing with the no. 22 tip. Make a zigzag motion along the top edge of the cake about ¾ inch wide. Remove the waxed paper from the roses and place them on the zigzag border. You may place them in a uniform formation or position them irregularly.

To form the leaves around the roses, use the bag of green icing and the no. 67 tip. Insert the tip next to the rose and apply pressure to secure leaf; then raise the tip slowly and stop squeezing at the same time. The frosting will break and form a leaf. Add enough leaves, always using a clean tip, to cover the zigzag border.

For the bottom trim, take the bag with white frosting and the no. 22 tip on the coupling. Holding the bag at a 45-degree angle with the tip at the base of the cake (see lower border on Flag Cake in Chapter 2), apply a great deal of pressure so that the frosting forms a mound about ¾ inch long. Release pressure and pull away about ½ inch. Make a second mound the same size and continue around the edge of the cake.

Wash tip no. 67 and put it on the bag of pink frosting. Make a pink leaf at the joining of each mound as shown in fig. 5-3 as follows: Place the clean tip against the cake over the indentation and apply pressure. Hold till leaf is attached; then pull away slowly and release pressure. Repeat over each joining seam.

FIG. 5-3

With the no. 65 tip on a bag with green icing, make a small green leaf over the pink leaf as shown. Follow the same procedure, but make the leaves smaller so that the pink border shows.

CHAPTER 6

Harvest Cake

One of the delights of cake decorating is making all kinds of flowers. Armed with a bag of frosting, you can create an appetizing confectionery garden.

The oval Harvest Cake provides a perfect shape for an arrangement of fall chrysanthemums and ferns. In this chapter, you will add a new flower to your repertoire, as well as learn how to cut an oval from a rectangular cake. The soft orange and yellow mums against the beige background are accented with a frame of graceful roping.

SUPPLIES

- One-layer oval or rectangular cake at least 2 inches high
- 2 recipes Basic Frosting (see Index) depending on size of cake
- Waxed paper
- Cardboard disk with glassine doily or board
- 3 mixing bowls
- Paste colors golden egg yellow or lemon yellow, leaf green, and brown
- Toothpicks
- Spatula
- 3 bags with couplings
- Tips nos. 19; 67 or 68; 79, 80, or 81
- No. 7 decorating nail
- Dishcloth

Shape the Cake

Whenever decorating a cake with flowers, you are well-advised to make them ahead of time. Some setting time makes them easier to handle when working on an arrangement. Before baking a cake in a rectangular pan (12 × 7, 13 × 9, or 17 × 11 inches), trace the bottom of the pan on waxed paper. Fold the waxed paper into quarters and round off the corners to make an oval.

After your cake has baked, invert it onto cooling rack. When the cake has thoroughly cooled, use the oval paper as a pattern to trim the cake. Use a sharp knife to avoid creating excess crumbs.

Place the cake on a board and crumb in white or in yellow. Add a touch of brown to yellow coloring to get a fall shade; then glaze with the same color.

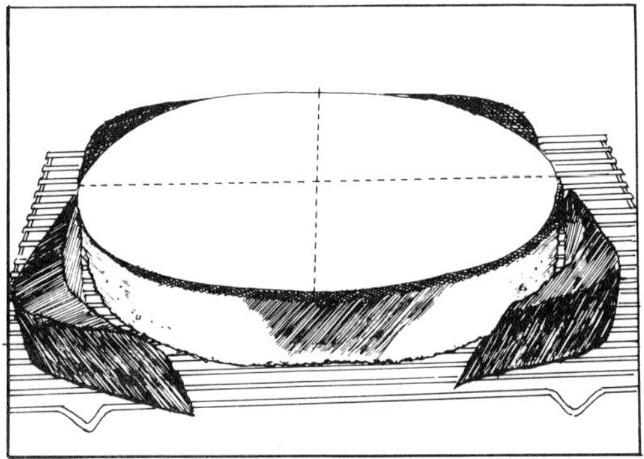

FIG. 6-1

Prepare the Colors

Mix the frosting for chrysanthemums first. A touch of brown or red added to yellow frosting will give you a pleasing color. Whenever you are mixing colors, take a little frosting to the side of your bowl to work on. When you get the right color, mix it into the remaining frosting. Fill your decorating bag and place tip no. 81, 80, or 79 (small, medium, or large) on the coupling.

A small amount of green will be needed. Mix your green frosting with a little more red than usual to make a brownish green suitable for autumn leaves. Place the frosting in a bag with a no. 67 tip. If your flowers are very large, you should make a larger leaf using a no. 68 tip.

Fill the third decorating bag with a deeper yellow (somewhat like the flowers) to do the borders. Use a no. 19 tip for this roping.

Chrysanthemums

Using the decorating bag prepared for chrysanthemums, hold it ready to make a flower with the open part of the tip facing up. Holding a no. 7 nail with a piece of waxed paper on it in your left and (see instructions for roses in Chapter 3), squeeze a mound of icing onto the center of the nail (fig. 6-3). Tip size will determine the size of the mound.

FIG. 6-2

Put the tip in the mound of icing (fig. 6-4) and squeeze to form a base. Then slowly pull outward (fig. 6-5). Release pressure and the frosting will stop flowing. Do one row of petals around base of the mound.

The second row of petals is added just above the first. Position each new petal between 2 on the layer below (fig. 6-6). The third row of petals goes between petals of the second row (fig. 6-7). As you move up on the mound, the bag will be held at an increasingly higher angle, as shown; when you reach the top, the bag will be straight up (fig. 6-8). Continue in this manner until the mound of icing is completely covered. Lift the waxed paper to remove the flower from the nail. Continue until you have as many chrysanthemums as you need. If you want a variety of sizes, use different-size tips.

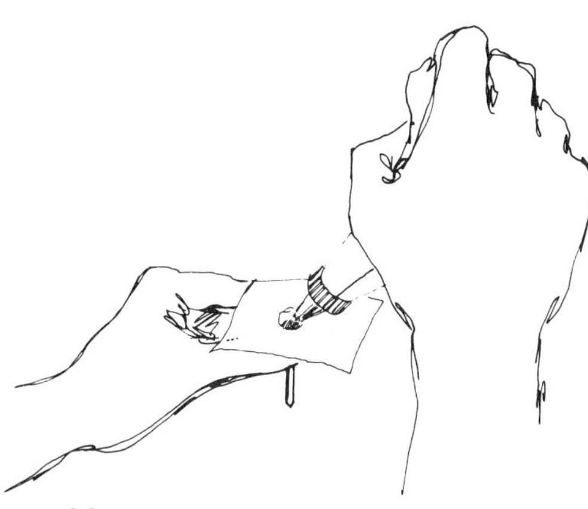

FIG. 6-3

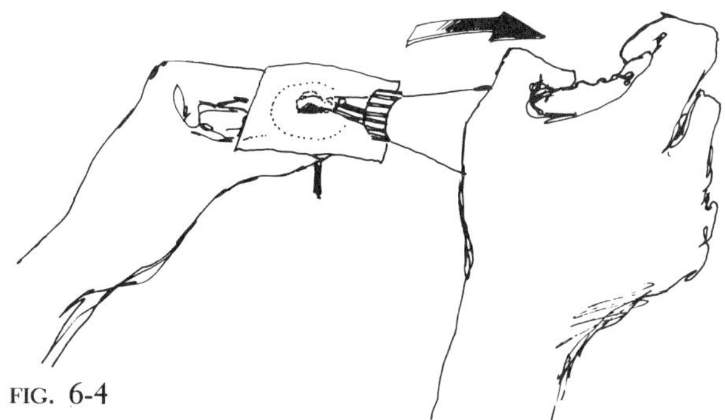

FIG. 6-4

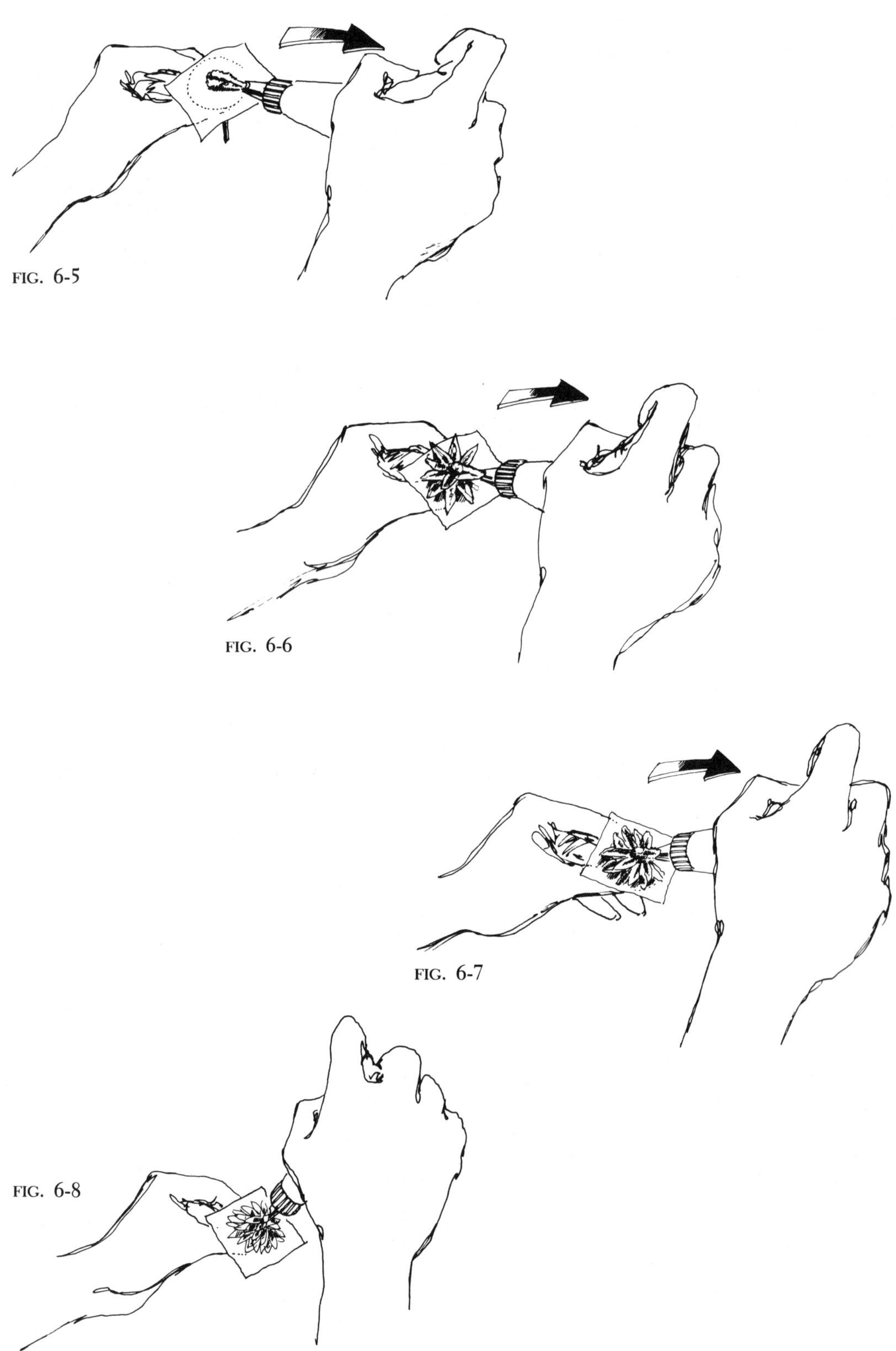
FIG. 6-5

FIG. 6-6

FIG. 6-7

FIG. 6-8

Borders and Ferns

While the flowers are drying, make the rope border around the top edge of the cake. Using the "border" bag with a no. 19 tip, hold the bag at a 45-degree angle at the edge of the cake. Apply pressure and squeeze an elongated S sideways. Place clean tip under raised mound and apply another S as shown. Continue in this manner around the edge.

Repeat the roping at the base, but apply more pressure so that it will be a little larger.

With both borders on the cake, you can now make the center design. A good rule to remember is that very seldom is a flower put flat on the cake. A mound of icing almost always goes under it so that the flower rests at an angle. For this cake, use your spatula to draw an elongated S as a guide for setting your flowers (see fig. 6-10 for floral arrangement). When adding leaves, insert leaf tip where is a leaf is desired, apply pressure, pull out, and push in very slightly to give it a heavy, rippled look.

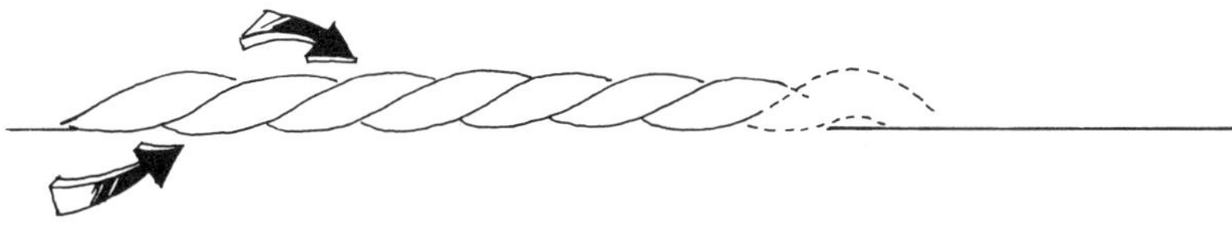

FIG. 6-9

The ferns are made with a no. 67 tip. Hold the tip in one spot; apply pressure quickly and stop. Pull away a fraction of an inch and do the same thing again. Continue, gradually reducing the pressure so that the fern will be tapered, until you have the length you want.

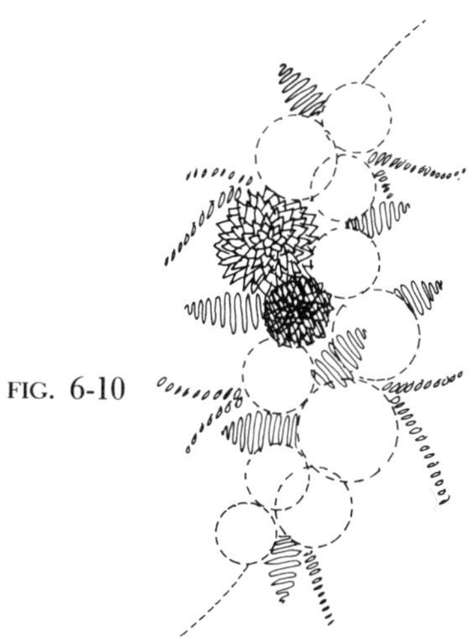

FIG. 6-10

CHAPTER 7

Basket of Flowers

A culinary tour de force completes the first part of this book. When you have finished the Basket of Flowers Cake, you can no longer be considered a beginner. The pride of self-accomplishment will make it well worth the effort and practice necessary to master basket weaving and wicker work. You will also be adding the pansy and sweet pea to your flower garden.

These cakes make wonderful confectionary centerpieces, creating a touch of romantic nostalgia.

SUPPLIES

Small round cake
2 recipes Basic Frosting (see Index)
Cake platter or cardboard disk with glassine doily
Mixing bowls or containers with lids
Paste colors brown, leaf green, lemon yellow, violet, rose pink, royal blue
Toothpicks
3 bags with couplings
Tips nos. 7, 16, 47, 67, 104
Parchment paper bag
No. 7 decorating nail
Waxed-paper squares
00 paintbrush
Small metal spatula
Pipe cleaners
Dishcloth

For best results with this cake, the flowers should be made the day before. You will need 2 batches of Basic Frosting. One recipe of frosting is used for flowers, and the other is divided in half. Color one part green for the leaves and the other brown for the basket.

For a cake 6 inches in diameter, you will need 3 to 4 dozen flowers; some of these should be roses. See Chapter 3 for instructions and illustrations for making roses.

Pansies

Pansies can be made in a variety of colors and often have two different colors in a single flower. You may use light yellow and dark yellow, light violet and dark violet, bluish violet in 2 different shades, or white with yellow or violet. This is a good time to study a seed catalog or flower book.

Mix 2 frosting colors for the first group of pansies. Place a coupling and no. 104 tip on a decorating bag. Holding the bag sideways so that the seam is in the center, take a scoop of the light shade of frosting on your spatula and insert it into the bag. Turn the spatula and wipe the frosting on the lower section of the bag, being very careful not to get any on the top section. Put more frosting in the bag in the same way and push it against the lower half of the coupling. Then put some of the darker color in the top of the bag. Push the spatula until it touches the coupling. Then, with your finger on top of the bag, push the frosting off the spatula. Continue adding more frosting, alternating colors and keeping amounts equal. When you start squeezing, you may find only a single color: This is because one color was pushed further into the coupling. Just squeeze a little more frosting out until both colors appear.

After you have made enough flowers in this color combination, turn the tip halfway and reroll your bag on the opposite side so that the top and bottom are reversed. A few flowers might be the same, but you will get a greater variety of coloration.

To make a pansy: Put waxed-paper square on a no. 7 nail. Hold the nail with your left hand; in your right hand, hold the decorating bag straight up with the thickest part of the tip down. On the upper left-hand part of the nail (fig. 7-4), make a fanlike petal with a slightly upward, then downward, motion (fig. 7-5). As you come down, stop squeezing and the frosting will break.

FIG. 7-1

Right-handed

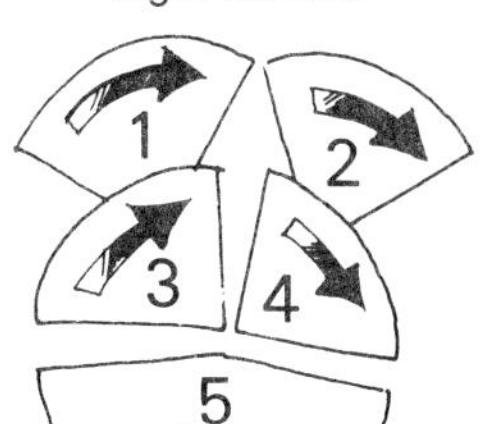

FIG. 7-2

Left-handed

FIG. 7-3

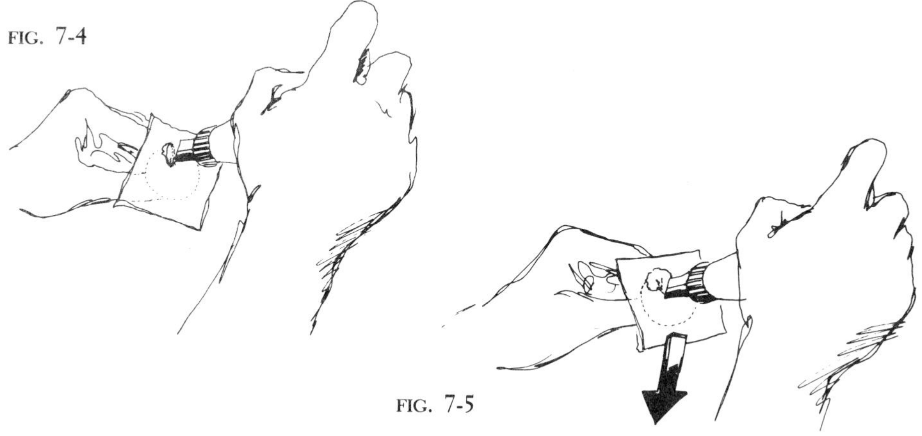

FIG. 7-4

FIG. 7-5

The second petal is added to the right of the first, just touching it (fig. 7-6).

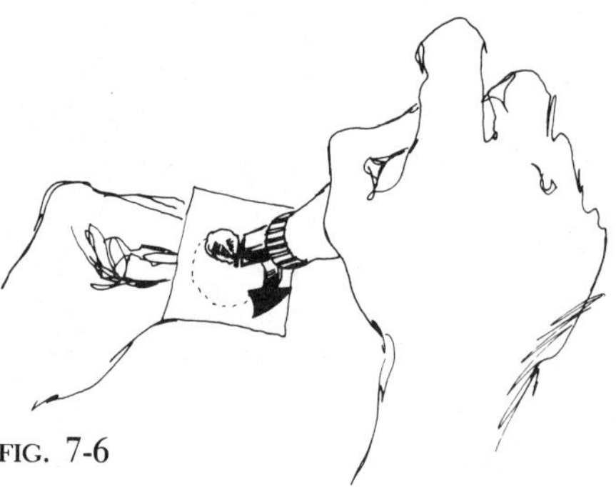

FIG. 7-6

The third and fourth petals are made on top of the first and second (fig. 7-7). This time hold the thickest part of the tip closer to the center so that the third and fourth petals will meet (fig. 7-8).

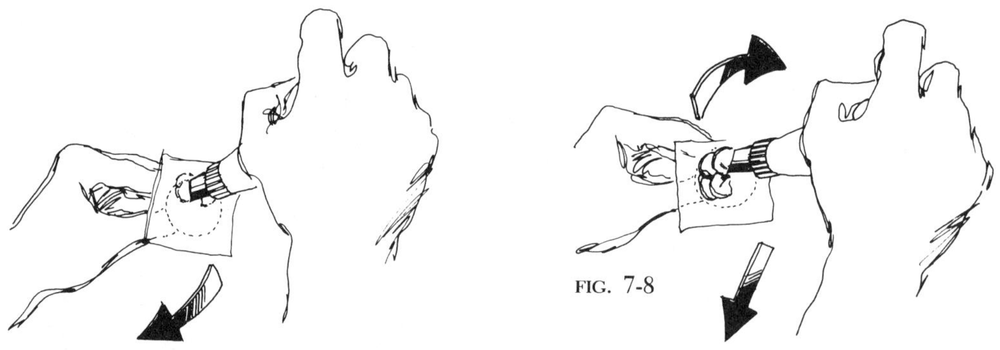

FIG. 7-8

FIG. 7-7

For the fifth and largest petal, put the thick part of the tip where the third and fourth petals begin (fig. 7-9). Squeeze the bag so that the frosting will go against the fourth petal. Pivot and swing, making one large petal ending just as it touches the third petal (fig. 7-10). As it does, release pressure; then pull tip down.

The lines for the pansy should be added with a 00 paintbrush while the flower is wet. Use violet, blue, yellow, or even orange paste colors. Dip the brush in the jar of paste color; then remove some of the paint by wiping the brush in the cover. Draw lines on the third and fourth petals very finely and in an arch (see fig. 7-1), starting at the base on the left side of each petal and working to the right.

The large petal is done the same way, starting at the base on the left side of the petal.

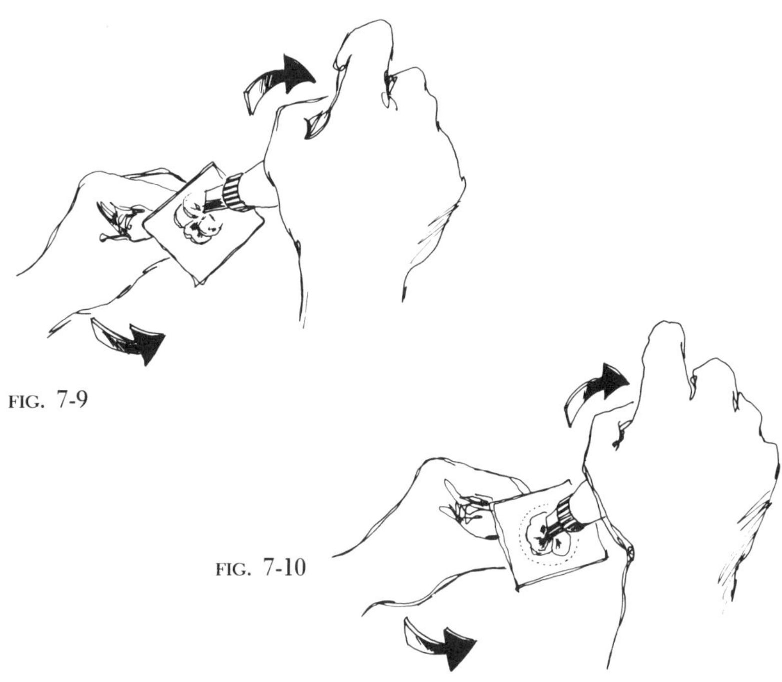

FIG. 7-9

FIG. 7-10

To complete the pansy, place a little dot of yellow in the center. Put yellow frosting in a parchment bag for this step. If you are making only a few flowers, you can use the end of the nail to put a little dab of icing on the center. These flowers take at least 24 hours to set.

Sweet Peas

The sweet pea is a fragrant flower that grows in a variety of colors. Fill a decorating bag fitted with a no. 104 tip with frosting a pastel shade of your choice. With a piece of waxed paper on a no. 7 nail in your left hand, hold the frosting bag straight up with its tip parallel to the nail. Squeeze the bag and pull up slightly so that the frosting will mound. Release pressure and break the frosting off by pulling down on the tip.

Put tip about ¼ inch below the bud on the left side. Apply pressure and raise the thin part of the tip, fanning it down slightly over the bud. Then bring the tip down and release pressure as you pull down. Do the same thing on the right side of the bud. Now remove the flower from the nail by lifting the paper, and pinch the paper at the base. Let it dry before adding to the cake.

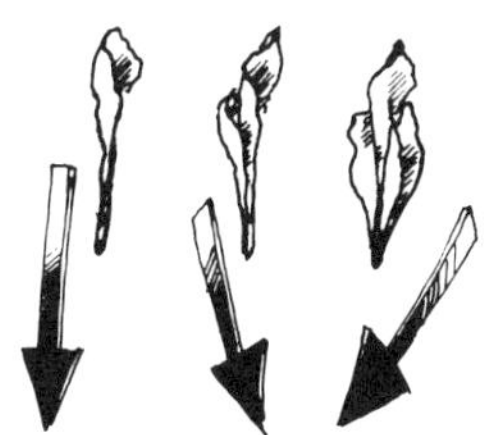

FIG. 7-11

There is another way to make a sweet pea, still using a no. 7 nail and no. 104 tip. Hold your bag at a 45-degree angle in front of the nail with the right side of the tip against the nail and the heaviest part of the tip in the center of the nail. Apply pressure to the bag and slide tip on nail for about ⅜ inch. Pivot on the thickest part of the tip and continue to apply pressure. Move down, touching the left side of the petal until the same length is reached.

Make another petal directly over this one, as shown, but make it a little shorter and slightly smaller: Hold the bag straight up against the center of the flower. Apply a little pressure; then raise tip slightly. Pull down and stop squeezing.

Remove paper and flower from the nail. Pinch the paper at the base to get the effect shown, and let the sweet pea dry at least 24 hours before removing paper.

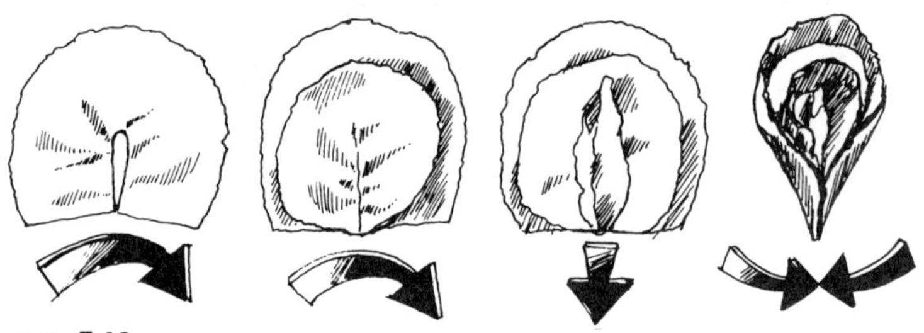

FIG. 7-12

Weaving the Basket

The following instructions are for the straight-sided basket cake with handle shown in fig. 7-21. An empty 1-pound coffee can or a candy or cookie tin makes an excellent pan to bake this cake. Grease the inside of the can, line the bottom with waxed paper, and grease the waxed paper.

After your cake has been baked and cooled, place it with the rounded top up on a doily and cardboard or on a beautiful platter. (To avoid scratching the platter, place a cardboard disk the exact size of the cake and covered with aluminum foil under the cake. The frosting will cover it.) Whatever you use, make sure that you secure the cake and doily or cardboard with frosting.

Crumb the sides of the cake the same color brown as the basket weave. If there are any spaces in the weave, they will not show as much. When mixing the brown color, cocoa may be added for flavor but not for color. Too much cocoa will make your frosting dry and unmanageable; add brown paste color to get the desired shade.

Crumb the top of the cake green. The joining of the green frosting to the brown frosting will not show when the cake is completed. If the cake

FIG. 7-13

does not have a rounded top, add a mound of green frosting. This mound will raise the flowers at the center of the decorated cake.

After you have crumbed your cake, fill 2 bags with brown frosting, using nos. 7 and 47 tips. The no. 7 tip may be placed on a parchment bag. Fill a bag with green frosting, and place the no. 67 tip on the coupling.

This is one time the crumbing layer of frosting cannot be allowed to dry. If it does, add a little more frosting or moisten the surface with a wet spatula. Dry frosting will not hold the basket weave as well.

For a basket cake with straight sides, hold your bag with the no. 7 tip up, squeeze, and make a line from the base of the cake to the top edge. This line of frosting should be round like wicker.

With tip no. 47 serrated side out at the bottom of the cake and ¾ inch to the left of the vertical line, squeeze out a horizontal line going over the vertical line and stopping ¾ inch to the right of the vertical line. Push tip into icing to break. Leaving a space the width of the tip, make another line parallel to the first. Continue until you reach the top edge.

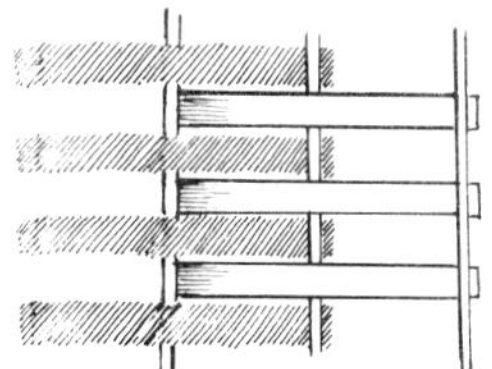

FIG. 7-14

Make another vertical line over the ends of the horizontals with a no. 7 tip. It must be over them to create the in-and-out effect of the basket weave. With a clean no. 47 tip, insert between spokes and push in. Apply enough pressure so that the frosting will stick; then bring the tip to ¾ inch beyond the second vertical line. Do this up to the top edge of the cake. With the no. 7 tip, make another vertical line over the ends of the horizontal spokes.

Continue this same procedure, working one section at a time, until you are about 2 inches from joining. Make adjustments in your vertical lines to make sure that they will end up evenly spaced.

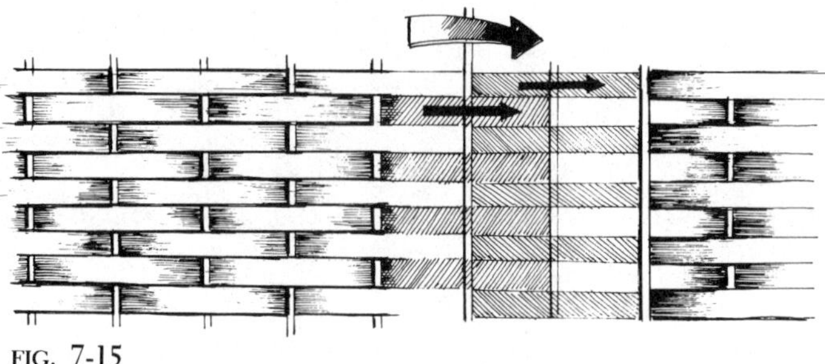

FIG. 7-15

The Round-bottomed Basket

Wicker and basket weave may be used on any shape cake. For a basket with a rounded base (see fig. 7-13), a 1-quart casserole or small bowl from an electric mixer is ideal, but any oven-proof bowl can be used. Because these round bowls cannot be lined with waxed paper, grease them and then coat them with flour. Invert the bowl and tap it lightly on the counter to remove the excess flour.

After the cake has been baked and cooled, invert it onto a flat plate or cardboard disk to do the basket weave. All cakes with round bases must be worked upside down so that the weaving goes completely under. Crumb the cake with brown frosting or whatever color you have chosen to do the wicker work. Using a no. 7 tip and the brown frosting, follow the weaving directions for the straight-sided basket cake. The vertical lines must be at right angles to the countertop or table, but the lines will be closer together on the top (when turned right side up, the bottom of the cake), see fig. 7-16. Make sure you weave high enough on the cake so

FIG. 7-16

that when it is turned over, the cake does not show. You may use a round tip that is smaller or larger than the one specified, but keep in mind that the smaller the tip, the closer the lines, and the longer it will take to complete the project.

When the weaving is completed, center doily and cardboard disk or tray on cake bottom. With one hand over the tray and the other under the cake, invert the cake carefully onto the tray.

Frost the top of the cake with green frosting. If the mound is not high enough to show the flowers attractively, add more green frosting.

You may wonder why a cake that is completely covered needs to be crumbed. For one reason, frosting seals the cake, acting as a preservative. For another, if your basket weaving has spaces, they will not be as noticeable with the same color of frosting underneath.

Flowers

Remove waxed paper from the flowers. To one side of your basket, make 10 to 12 leaves in a small group with a no. 67 tip. Among these leaves, insert sweet peas with the fine pinched point in the frosting (see figs. 7-11 and 7-12). Above this grouping, put a mound of frosting and place a rose or a pansy on it. Start from one side of the cake and work over the top to the other, keeping an uneven line around the edge and placing some flowers lower than others.

FIG. 7-17

Leaves

To apply the leaves, fill a bag with a no. 67 tip with green Basic Frosting. Insert the tip between the flowers and apply pressure to form a heavy base; then stop squeezing and pull up. If the leaf does not form a point, the frosting may be too dry: Remove frosting from bag, mix in a few drops of water, and try again. You may pinch the end of the leaf with your thumb and index finger to get a point. Insert as many leaves as you think are necessary.

Handle with Care

If you want a handle on your basket, you will need 4 pipe cleaners if they are short, 3 if they are the longer decorative cleaners. Color does not matter since they will be completely covered with frosting. Find 2 spots on opposite sides of the cake that would be appropriate for the handle. Sometimes a flower has to be removed.

Carefully study the sketch of the handle. Take 2 pipe cleaners and place them as shown; twist them together tightly, adding a third cleaner when you complete twisting the first 2. Do not leave spaces between them. On each end, where there is a single wire, twist it around a round toothpick and insert it into the cake as shown in fig. 7-19.

FIG. 7-18

With brown frosting and a no. 16 tip on the decorating bag, work on one side to cover the twisted wire as shown. Turn the cake and repeat. Avoid going over a spot as it will make the handle heavy and may cause it to droop.

If you wish, you may add a few leaves and/or flowers where the handles are attached to the cake.

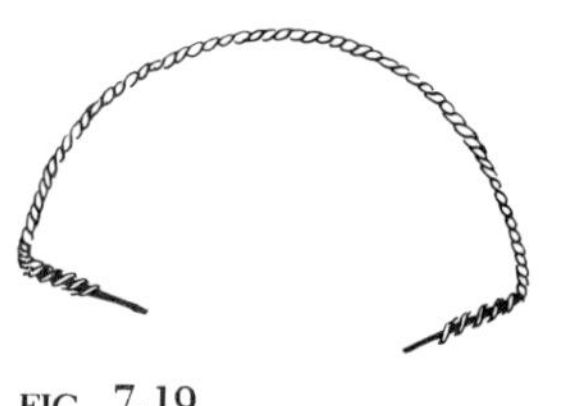

FIG. 7-19

FIG. 7-20

FIG. 7-21

PART II

More Advanced

Cakes for special occasions demand special decorations—touches of creative elegance that turn your most delicious efforts into feasts for the eyes. The decorations in this section are made with Royal Icing, which gives them a crisp, clean, and fragile look and allows them to be applied separately, giving a light and airy appearance to your cake.

In addition to flowers already described in the preceding chapters, we will work with the lily and daisy shapes, which add such variation and beauty to your arrangements. The Royal Icing leaves covered in Chapter 10 lend a wonderfully realistic effect when tucked around the various flowers.

Chapter 11 covers all types of decorative ornaments that can lend great distinction to any cake. You can make all sorts of garlands to festoon the sides of a cake as well as delicate lattice panels and fragile sugar fences with whimsical little birds to perch on them.

An excellent item I have found to add an interesting texture to my designs is grape clusters. Small ones decorate garlands and cascades, and large ones create interesting borders around the base of a cake. Also included in this section are bows and streamers that present a very feminine touch when applied as accents.

For your more grandiose efforts, wonderful carved-looking scrolls add an architectural look when combined with lattice work panels.

Chapter 12 deals with the intricacies of assembling a wedding cake. Sometimes working out a compromise between the weight of the cake and the concept of the design can try the patience of an engineer.

As you can see from the photographs in this book, I have a decided preference for floral arrangements on the tops of cakes, which I refer to as sculptures in sugar. I believe that any devoted cake decorator is an artist at heart and these sugar sculptures are a delightful opportunity to give vent to your creative urgings.

An urn of sugar filled with dozens of Royal Icing flowers will evoke endless comments that will do wonders for your ego. After all the time and effort you have spent creating these masterpieces—believe me—you deserve them.

CHAPTER 8

Bell-shaped Flowers

This chapter is primarily devoted to Royal Icing ornaments and decorative flowers, which are a must for an elegant cake. A variation of shapes can create an illusion representing many flowers. Once you have mastered these shapes, you will be able to make all of the cakes shown in this book.

I have tried many versions of Royal Icing and have found the following recipe to be the most successful. It can be doubled, if needed, if you have a powerful mixer. A hand-held mixer is not recommended. For superior results use good-quality meringue powder, which can be kept in a grease-free, airtight jar indefinitely. Do not refrigerate. Frosting will also keep in a grease-free, airtight jar 2 to 3 weeks without refrigeration, although the frosting is likely to set and separate. Before using be sure you mix it thoroughly with a spatula.

ROYAL ICING
1 pound plus ½ cup confectioner's sugar
5 tablespoons meringue powder
½ teaspoon cream of tartar
½ cup less 1 tablespoon water
Few drops white flavoring to taste (I prefer mint)

Make sure all utensils and equipment are free of grease. Place all ingredients, except the ½ cup sugar, in a bowl; mix at low speed. With a rubber spatula, scrape the bowl so that the icing will not stick to the bottom or sides. Add the remaining ½ cup of sugar and mix thoroughly. Beat at high speed until frosting is stiff and creamy, about 5 minutes.

Cover the bowl immediately with a damp cloth to prevent the frosting from drying, or place it in a grease-free glass jar covered with a piece of waxed paper before screwing on the cover.

Use only new bags or bags that have only been used with Royal Icing; keep them separate from the bags used with shortening in the frosting.

The amount of sugar depends on the degree of stiffness you need in the icing. A rose requires stiff icing; run sugar does not. Use this recipe of Royal Icing unless otherwise stated.

If possible, do not make Royal Icing flowers in humid weather as the frosting will dry in a powdered form and the flowers will break very easily. During humid conditions, use an air conditioner or a dehumidifier, or wait for a good dry day.

Cile's Stephanotis

My version of a stylized stephanotis is a 3-petal flower with a round trumpet (see Fig. 8-16). Not being able to round the base, I have it come to a point. The flower is very delicate and attractive. It takes a little longer to make than a rose, but the final results are well worth the effort. For this kind of flower, Royal Icing must be used.

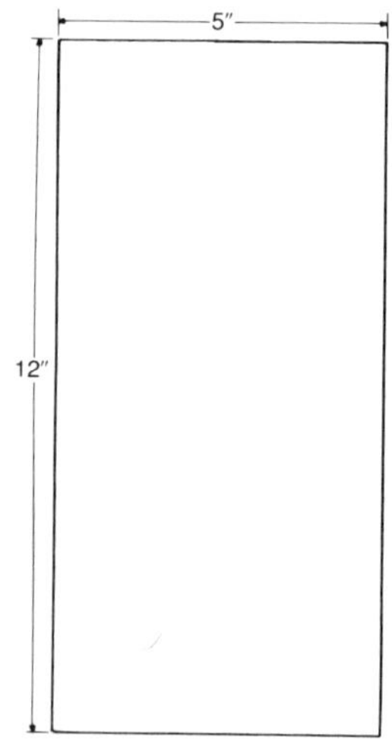

FIG. 8-1

To make a paper cone for this flower, tear a piece of waxed paper 5 inches wide using the serrated edge of the box (fig. 8-1), and proceed as follows: Fold in half (fig. 8-2); fold again; crease and cut at the folds, 5 × 3 inches (fig. 8-3); cut paper halfway on the longest edge (fig. 8-4). Overlap (fig. 8-5) and keep pushing the cut section until the paper resembles a miniature dunce cap (fig. 8-6). At this point the paper is not quite tripled, leaving about ½ inch before cut sections join (fig. 8-7) as you can see through the 2 layers of waxed paper.

Place both thumbs inside the cone and cup fingers lightly on the outside edge about halfway up on the cone (fig. 8-8). With your fingers, slightly gather paper (fig. 8-9). Turn the top edge to form the brim (fig. 8-10), as on a dunce cap (fig. 8-11). Be careful not to make creases or folds in the cone that will catch the icing and break the flower when the waxed paper is removed. Also avoid a sharp crease on the "fold-over" that will act as a knife on the petals.

I try to keep a few hundred cones folded and ready to be used as the preparation is very time-consuming. I cut the pieces of waxed paper complete with slits and keep them in a box. While watching TV, engaged in a long phone call, or on a long car trip I make my cones. I store them in a brown shopping bag marked to identify the size, and then seal the bag with a clothespin or paper clip to keep them free from dust (fig. 8-12). The papers must be folded properly or they will fall apart before

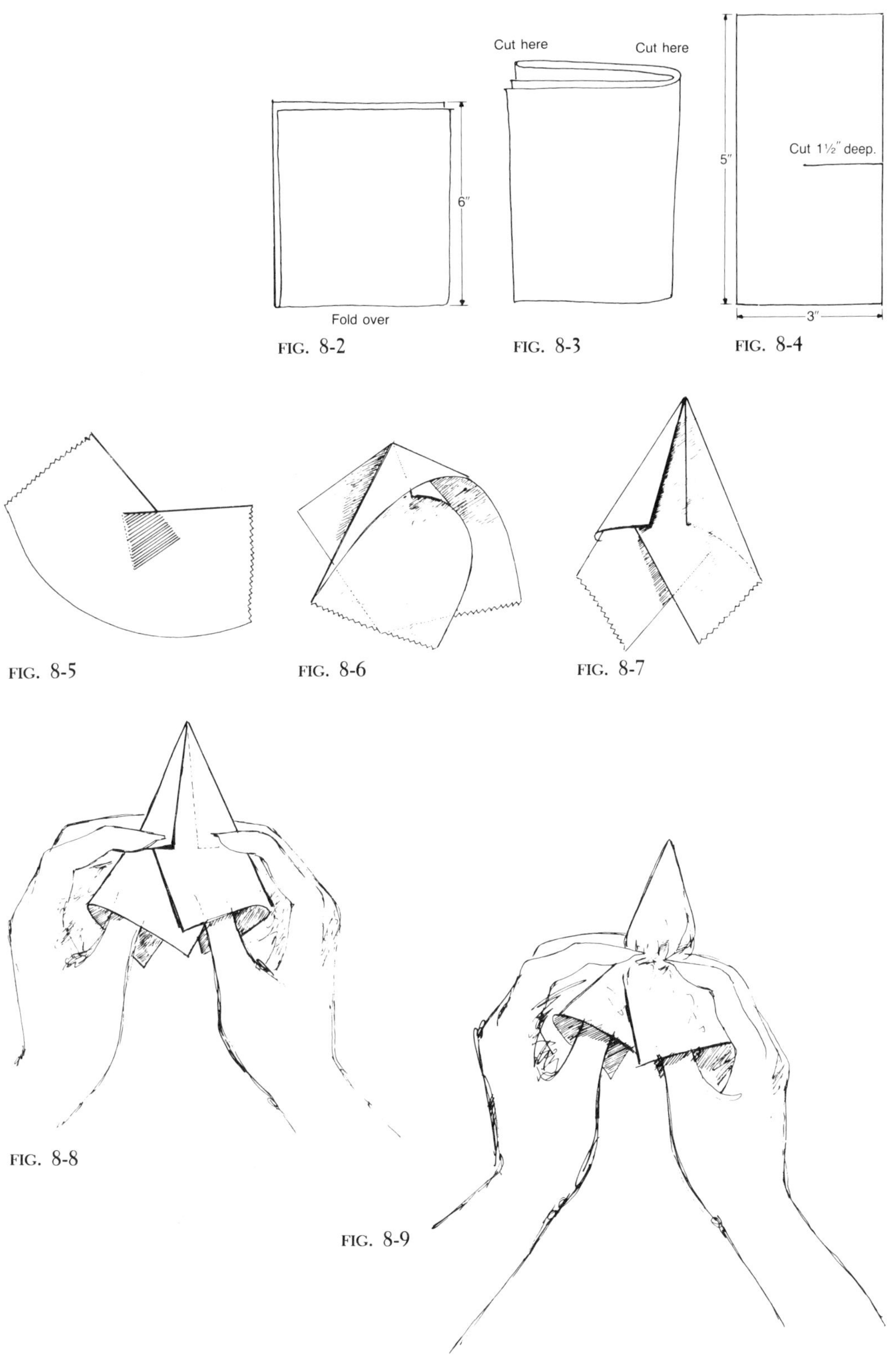

FIG. 8-2

FIG. 8-3

FIG. 8-4

FIG. 8-5

FIG. 8-6

FIG. 8-7

FIG. 8-8

FIG. 8-9

the flowers are made. Getting the papers ready takes longer than making the flowers.

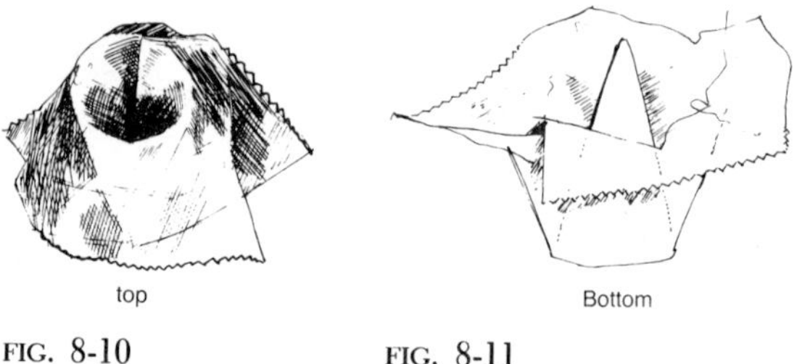

FIG. 8-10 FIG. 8-11

FIG. 8-12

After putting the coupling into your grease-free bag, fill it with Royal Icing any color you wish. Use tip no. 67 or 68 depending on the size flower desired. To give life and highlights to your flowers, mix a small amount of colored Royal Icing in a grease-free bowl (avoid soft plastics). Fill the bag by putting into it a rounded teaspoonful of white icing, then a rounded teaspoonful of colored icing. Do this until the bag is two-thirds full. Do not overfill. If necessary see Chapter 2 for instructions on folding the bag. Keep tip against a wet towel until you are ready to use it as the icing hardens very quickly if exposed to air.

A no. 12 decorating nail can be used to make these flowers, but I prefer just holding the paper cone in my left hand and rotating it. If the nail is used, place a small amount of icing on the nail cup and make sure the pointed section of the cone is secure before starting the flower.

Hold the brim of the cone in the left or right hand with your thumb on the outside and your index finger on the inside of the brim (fig. 8-13). Hold the bag of icing in the opposite hand in an almost upright

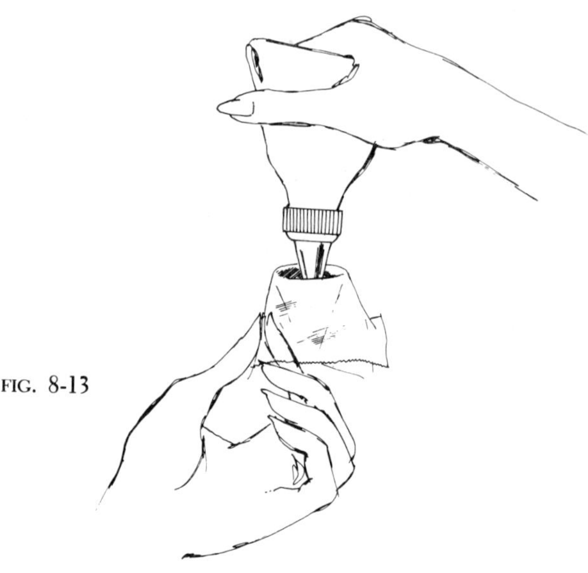

FIG. 8-13

position with the tip directly against the bottom and the flat part of the tip on the inside wall of the cone. Apply pressure and raise bag slowly, making a petal. The lower half of these petals should be fairly heavy but not too thick; if they are too thin they will break easily. Release pressure just after you have passed the top ridge of the cone but continue petal till frosting breaks. Make three petals in this fashion, evenly spacing them in the cylinder (fig. 8-14). Four petals also makes an artistic shape (fig. 8-15). Practice will eventually give you petals of the same thickness and length. If the petal does not end with a point, pinch the end between your thumb and index finger. A little softer icing will sometimes help put points on the petals. If a petal is too long it is more likely to break when the waxed paper is removed; you can pinch off the excess length.

FIG. 8-14

FIG. 8-15

When you are no longer able to squeeze any more icing from your bag, do not scrape out the bag. Carefully add a small amount of a complementary color, and continue to make flowers. This will give you another shading and add variety to your flowers. For example, if the icing is a soft pink, you can use a deeper pink or white.

When your flower is completed, put in 2 stamens (fig. 8-16). In the past few years, stamens have been very difficult to find. If your cake-decorating store or craft shop does not carry them, go to a millinery supply house that produces bridal headdresses. There you will find a pearlized stamen that will enhance any flower.

Most stamens have pearls on both ends; you can cut them in half and use both ends. If they are merely folded, they seem to spread apart and spoil the beauty of the flower.

When the flower is completed, allow it to dry 3 to 4 days, depending on the dryness of the room, before removing the paper.

Remove the waxed paper by pulling the cut outer edge (fig. 8-17) on the underside of the cone until it is free from the flower. If the flower is thoroughly dry, you can sometimes push on the hard tip of the cone, and the waxed paper will just peel off. Do not remove the waxed paper until you are ready to use the flower.

FIG. 8-16

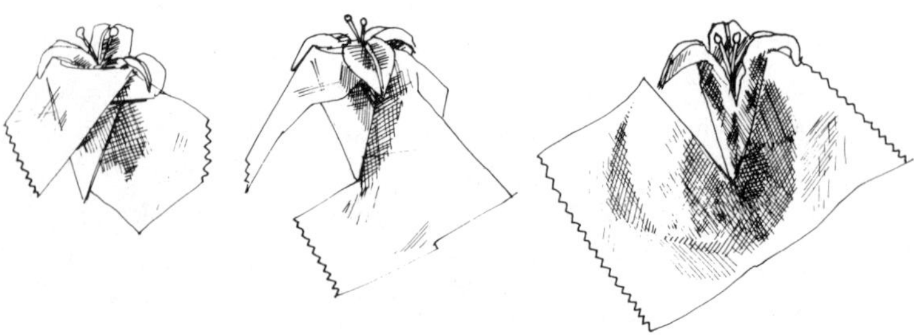

FIG. 8-17

These flowers will keep for some time in a cardboard suit box stored in a dry place. Never put them in an airtight plastic container.

Shown is another pronged flower that is very similar to Cile's Stephanotis but with another dimension (fig. 8-19).

You make this flower with a parchment cone. Check Chapter 4 for folding instructions. Make the waxed paper cone a little smaller than the one for the previous flower by twisting the paper until it is tripled and the cut sections meet, one on the inner side of the cone and the other on the outer edge. Turn the brim down in the same way.

Make sure the tip of your parchment cone is tight without an opening. Fill the bag with Royal Icing. Cut the cone tip with the icing in it.

Hold the bag flat on its side and cut the cone on an angle on one side about ⅜ inch from the tip (fig. 8-18); then do the same on the other side. The point of the paper cannot be too long as it will bend and not make the groove in the icing. Do not use a large piece of parchment paper as the cut tip does not hold up. The parchment bag will have to be replaced if you plan to make many flowers.

Make the petals exactly the same as for the stephanotis by holding the bag (fig. 8-13) with the flat section on the inner edge of the paper cone and the cut pointed piece of paper directly in the center of the petal, forming the line that creates the leaf effect (fig. 8-19). These petals are a little thicker and not as uniform. Place 2 stamens in the center and allow to dry completely before removing paper. Follow same directions for removing waxed paper as for the stephanotis.

FIG. 8-18

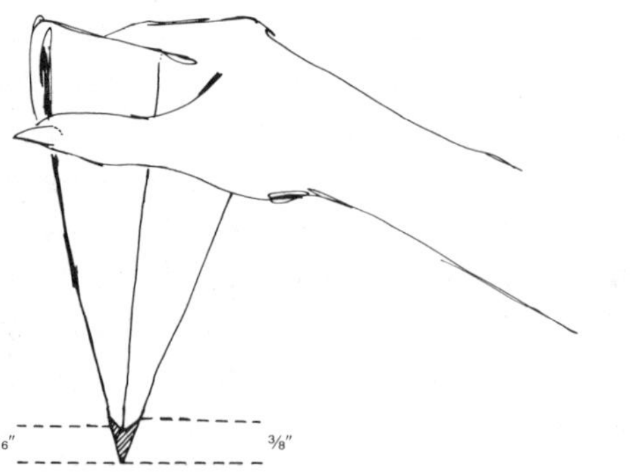

FIG. 8-19

The Lily

A few devices for making the lily are available, but I have found, through experience, that the paper cones might take more time but the end results are very rewarding and the lily far more realistic.

To make the cone: Tear a piece of waxed paper about 6 inches wide using the serrated edge of the box. Fold this paper in thirds and cut so that each piece is 6 × 4 inches. On the 6-inch side cut a slit 2 inches deep. Overlap paper on this 2-inch slit and keep tightening until you have a 2½-inch overlap (fig. 8-20). Turn down the brim (see preceding instructions on the stephanotis).

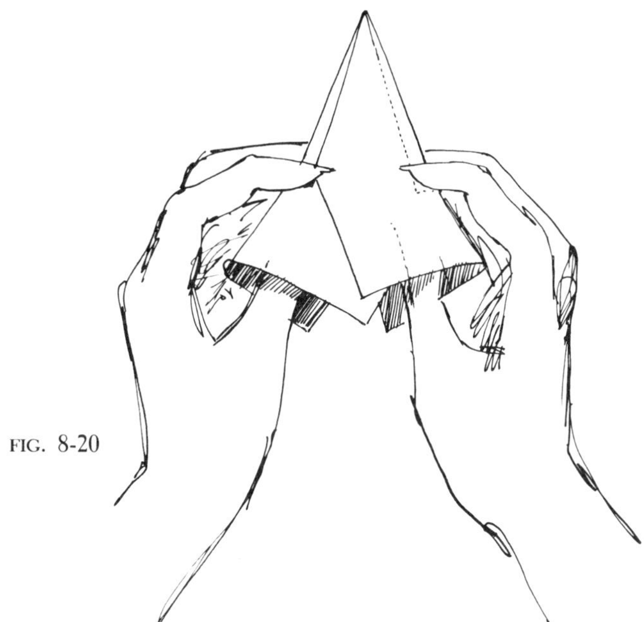

FIG. 8-20

The lily is also made with Royal Icing with a tip no. 67 or 68. Use white or the variegated colors described for the stephanotis.

Do not use the nail for this flower. Holding the brim section of waxed paper (see fig. 8-13) with the right or the left hand, make petals as you would for the stephanotis. Apply pressure and pull up along the inner cone of the paper, making the leaflike petal a little heavier on the lower half of the flower. As you get to the top edge, release pressure. There should be enough frosting to extend the petal another ¼ to ⅜ inch. Do not make these petals too long or they will flop over and break. Make 3 petals in the cone, evenly spaced (fig. 8-21). If the no. 68 tip is used, the petals will probably touch one another. (If a larger flower is desired, make the opening of the cone bigger.) Now make 3 more petals in between the first 3 (fig. 8-22). On these last petals keep the same pressure from

FIG. 8-21

FIG. 8-22

the beginning of the petal to the end. The heavy base to strengthen the flower was done in the first 3 petals. After the flower is completed, add 3 stamens, and let dry at least 3 to 4 days, again depending on the dryness of the air.

Stems and Sepals

You may put stems on these conelike flowers so that they may be arranged in a cachepot or an urn placed on top of the cake (see Chapter 13).

Toothpicks or fabric-coated millinery wire make the most satisfactory stems. Millinery wire is sometimes available in green. I prefer the rounded wooden toothpicks with the sharp ends; the decorative plastic toothpicks are not successful. To color the toothpicks green, place a few tablespoons of water, depending on how many you are coloring, in a shallow plate with green paste color and a dash of red. Mix thoroughly. Stir the toothpicks with a fork so that they are stained evenly. Place them on a paper towel to dry. If the color is too dark, quickly dip them in water and let dry. If you leave them in water too long, the color will fade out. Cut the fabric-coated wire to the desired lengths and tint them in the same way. These stems are good for all the pronged flowers.

Cut the point off of the waxed paper cone just enough so that the green toothpick can be inserted tightly into the hole (fig. 8-23). Push the toothpick through until ⅝ inch remains inside the cone; the remainder forms the stem.

Make the flower as directed and insert the stamens. Carefully place the toothpick in Styrofoam; allow at least 5 to 6 days to dry the flower before removing waxed paper. The toothpick and flower will part company if not completely dry when the paper is removed.

After the waxed paper is removed, take a bag of green Royal Icing with a no. 3 tip and add the sepals. Holding the bag at a 45-degree angle and starting at the toothpick, apply pressure as the icing comes out of the tip.

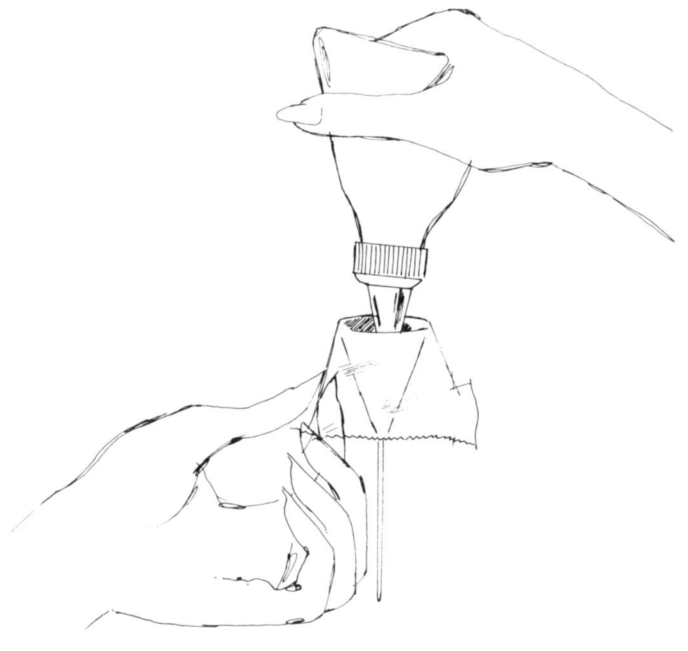

FIG. 8-23

Hold the bag so that the roundness of the icing is flattened against the base of the flower. Flatten sepal for about ½ inch; then release the pressure and pull away. This will give a flattened sepal with a rounded pointed extension (fig. 8-24). Make 3 or 4 sepals depending on the base of the flower.

Place flower again in Styrofoam and let dry before doing your floral arrangement.

FIG. 8-24

Lily of the Valley

If you want a lily of the valley piped directly on a cake, you first make a curved green line using tip no. 2, 3, or 4, depending on the size desired. See fig. 8-25. Using a 67 or 68 tip, make a long tapered leaf and/or one that is folded over.

The flower part can be piped directly on the cake with Basic Frosting or made separately on waxed paper with Royal Icing. On the cake or waxed paper, use white frosting with a no. 2 tip. Holding the bag at a 45-degree angle, start with a dot; then apply a little pressure forming a little spiral that gets bigger as you go around (fig. 8-26). As the little

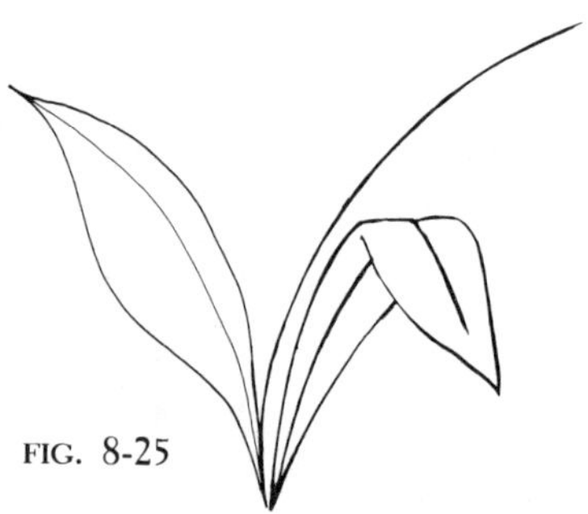
FIG. 8-25

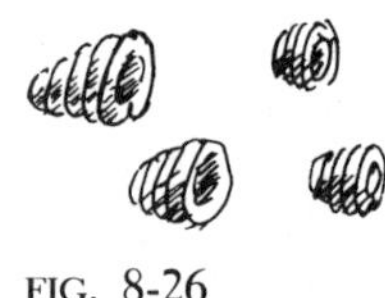
FIG. 8-26

petals go up the stem they get a little smaller, sometimes ending in just a dot. If these bell-like flowers are large enough, a little touch of yellow icing may be placed in the center with a no. 1 tip or a parchment bag.

If the flowers are made separately and applied to a stem of frosting, put the flowers on as soon as the stem is made; if the stem is dry, it will break. I find tweezers are a help in doing this.

For a wired lily of the valley that will stand upright on the cake, the fabric-coated wire is excellent but also very difficult to find. The paper-covered wire is second best. If you can find green, you don't have to do the next step. Mix paste color and a little vodka (dries quickly), and paint the wire green with a paintbrush. Avoid harsh colors when working with food.

When the wire is dry, place it on waxed paper that is placed over a cookie sheet. Using a no. 2 tip and white Royal Icing, place a little dot about 1/4 inch away from the wire stem at the top end (fig. 8-27). Allowing 1/2- to 5/8-inch spaces between dots along the length of the stem, place as many dots as you wish to have flowers. Do not place them too low on the stem as they will break off when you use it. Now place the wire over these little dots of icing. Make a little bell-like flower directly (fig. 8-26) on the inside curve of each of these little dots, keeping in mind that the larger bells are at the base and the smallest at the tip. The dots of icing under the wire and the bell-like flowers encircle the wire with icing, which makes the flowers stay on better (fig. 8-28). Do all of this as fast as possible as Royal Icing sets very quickly. Dry thoroughly. Do not remove from waxed paper until you are ready to make the floral arrangement.

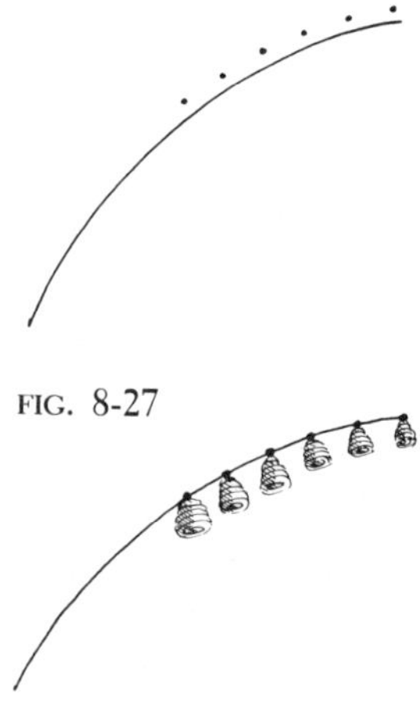
FIG. 8-27

FIG. 8-28

One disadvantage of using wired arrangements is that they are very difficult to transport. The wires swing and tend to break the sugar flowers.

CHAPTER 9
Daisy Family

Basic Daisy

Prepare 2-inch squares of waxed paper as you did for making roses (Chapter 3), but this time cut a slit halfway through the square as shown in fig. 9-1. Fill the grease-free bag with white Royal Icing and add a no. 104 tip to start. You can get other variations by using straight (nos. 101 to 104) or curved (nos. 59 to 61) tips.

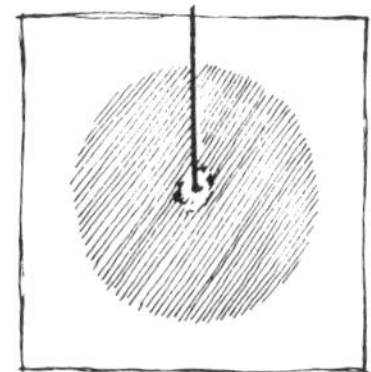

FIG. 9-1

Put a small amount of icing on a no. 7 nail, and place the waxed paper with the slit at 12 o'clock. Holding the bag in your right hand at a 25-degree angle, place the heaviest part of the tip at the end of the cut and the thin section directly at the cut (fig. 9-2). Apply pressure in an upward rounded motion, then down, as shown in fig. 9-3. As you come down, stop squeezing and the icing will break. Make 4 or 5 more petals in the same fashion, leaving a small space about the size of another petal (fig. 9-4). (If icing collects in the center you are applying too much pressure. Try again.)

Put a little dab of icing over the space (fig. 9-5) and overlap the paper so that petals meet (fig. 9-6). Press against dab of icing to make the paper stick. You now have a cupped flower. Let flowers dry on a tray or a cookie sheet with sides for 24 to 48 hours, again depending on the weather.

Another method for drying that I have found to be very effective is to place the completed and cupped flower on the reverse side of an egg carton (fig. 9-7). This is especially good for very large daisies made with a no. 104 or 61 tip. The petals fall in the grooves, which creates a very

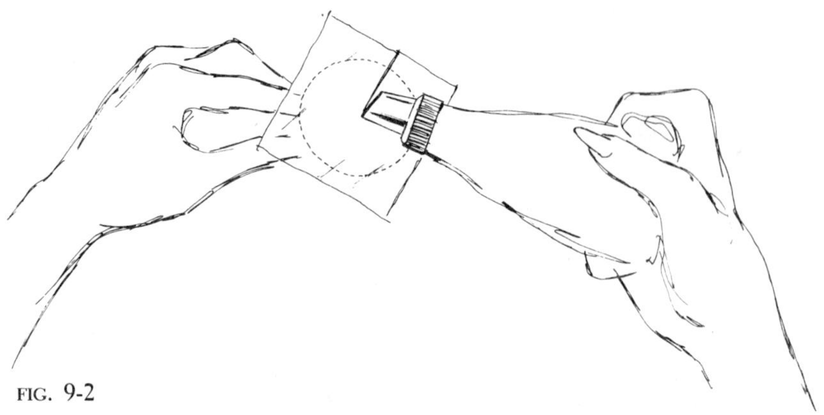

FIG. 9-2

FIG. 9-3

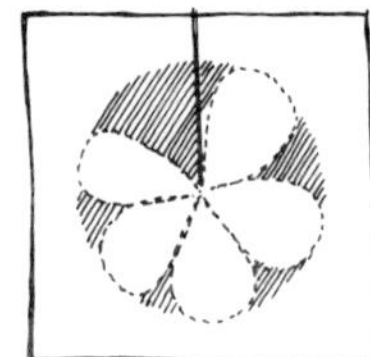

FIG. 9-4

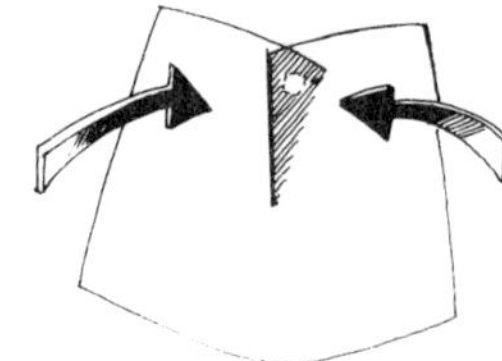

FIG. 9-5

FIG. 9-6

realistic flower (fig. 9-8). By using many egg cartons side by side on a very large sheet pan, you not only have the grooves of the individual cartons but also in between each box as well. The 2½-dozen egg crate is also good if you can find it.

Whenever you are using a Royal Icing bag, always leave the tip against a damp towel to prevent the icing from hardening.

Some of the daisies may be made flat if you like; just continue the circle of petals until they join (fig. 9-9). Avoid letting icing collect in the center of the flower. If this happens, you are not stopping the pressure soon enough.

Painted daisies may be made in the same way in a variety of pastel colors.

FIG. 9-7
This is how the flowers look in the egg carton.

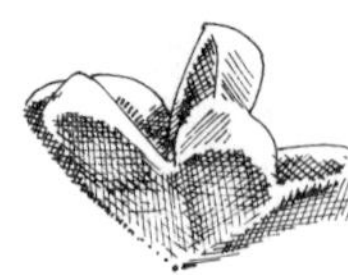

FIG. 9-8
This is how they look after they have dried.

The no. 104 tip makes a large petal. The no. 7 nail can be used with large flowers but a larger working surface is easier. In an emergency, I used the bottom of a 10¾-ounce soup can. However, since then, I have had a 3½-inch stainless-steel disk welded to a stainless-steel rod; I find it very effective for large flowers.

FIG. 9-9

The smaller the tip on the bag, the narrower the petal, and the more petals you need to complete a flower. Petals can be long or short; unfortunately, the longer and finer petals break easier.

Here is another variation using any of the tips mentioned for the daisy and a bag of variegated icing: Follow the same method in making the petals flat or cupped but do it with your hand shaking or using a vibration motion. This will give you wrinkled lines in the flower creating another texture (fig. 9-10). If the lines are not definite or do not hold their shape, your icing is not stiff enough; add more confectioner's sugar.

FIG. 9-10
These are some of the different shapes you can make using the same vibrating motion.

Daisy in 3 Dimensions

Step 1. Place a no. 101 tip on a bag with Royal Icing. Put a small amount of icing on a no. 7 nail and place on this a square of waxed paper with a slit cut in it (fig. 9-1). With the thick part of the tip at the end of the cut and the remainder along the cut edge, apply pressure, holding the bag at a 35-degree angle, and make a long thin petal as explained for the daisy. Make these petals about ⅛ inch smaller than the no. 7 nail. Make as many petals as you wish to form a half circle (fig. 9-11). The thinner petals are more attractive and delicate, as well as fragile. Place icing on waxed paper and overlap. The first and last petal join to make a very deep cupped flower. Make as many flowers as desired. It is always best to make more than is needed. You can use this flower in this size on any cake, or you may go on to make a 2- or 3-layer flower. In either case, let it dry completely before you continue. Remove the waxed paper by slowly pulling the under cut section until the paper is completely removed (fig. 9-12).

FIG. 9-11

FIG. 9-12

Step 2. Using tip no. 102 and a cut piece of waxed paper on a no. 7 nail, make petals in the same manner the same length as the circle of your no. 7 nail. This time make enough petals to form a two-thirds circle (fig. 9-13). Overlap paper and join. Now remove the waxed paper from the dry flower in Step 1. Place in center of Step 2 flower, arranging so that the petals do not lie directly on top of each other (fig. 9-14). Allow to dry before going on to the next step.

FIG. 9-13

Step 3. Using tip no. 102 and a fresh square of waxed paper, make petals the same as in Steps 1 and 2 but this time a little longer than the no. 7 nail. Leave about ¼ inch before the slit (fig. 9-15) for a flower with a slight cup (fig. 9-16), or make the flower flat (fig. 9-17). Remove the waxed paper from the dry Step 2 flower, and place it in the center (fig. 9-18).

FIG. 9-14

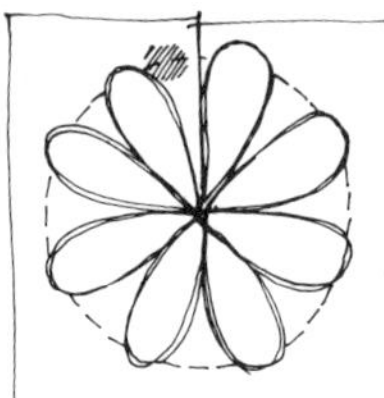

FIG. 9-15

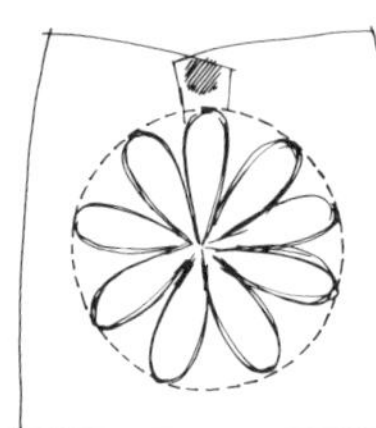

FIG. 9-16

FIG. 9-17

FIG. 9-18

Allow your flowers to dry at least 48 hours before you put in the yellow centers. Mix a small amount of bright yellow icing, and place it in a tightly folded parchment bag with an even opening or a canvas bag with a no. 2 or 3 tip, depending on the size of your flower. Put a small mound of icing in the center of each flower. Hold your flower, still attached to its waxed paper, over a small bowl of granulated sugar. Using a teaspoon, put some sugar over the wet yellow mound. Smooth the mound with your finger. Turn the flower upside down over the bowl and tap it with your finger to remove excess sugar. Fig. 9-19 shows the completed flower. If the sugar sticks to the petals, your flowers should dry a little longer. Do not attempt to do this on a humid day no matter how dry your flowers are because the sugar will stick to everything.

On a very elegant pink and white cake, yellow centers detract from the beauty; use white centers on the dark colors and pink on the soft-colored or white flowers. All white flowers also look splendid. Use sugar on these centers too.

Another center treatment that is also very effective is using a no. 13 tip to make the rounded mound in the center of the flower.

Do not remove the waxed paper from any flower until you are ready to use it. The paper protects it from breaking.

FIG. 9-19

Stems for Daisies

You can make stems for cupped and flat flowers if they are not too large. Fill a parchment or canvas bag with Royal Icing tinted green. Remove the waxed paper from the completely dry flowers to be used. Turn flower over and place a no. 4 tip against the center bottom of a flower; apply pressure and pull up slowly so that the icing forms a ball (fig. 9-20). Lightly push a green toothpick into the center of the ball being careful not to break the flower.

Let these flowers dry upside down 12 to 24 hours. They may be placed next to a box or high pan so that the toothpicks are supported. If some of the toothpicks fall over, it could be just another interesting angle. Too soft icing can yield a more than acceptable number of interesting angles.

Remember when making any flower with Royal Icing high humidity prevents proper drying; the flowers will break when you remove the waxed paper.

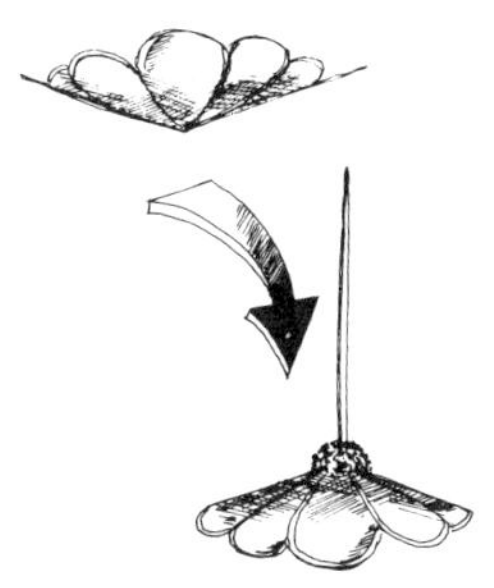

FIG. 9-20

Daisylike Chrysanthemums

If made large (use Basic Frosting), these are flowers for a man's cake because the size gives a very masculine look. They can also be made small and delicate (use Royal Icing); the different shape adds character to a cake.

Using a no. 80 tip, put a dab of frosting on a no. 7 nail and a 2-inch waxed-paper square on top of it. If you want a very large flower, use the no. 79 tip with a larger piece of waxed paper on a larger nail.

Place a mound of frosting in the center of the paper. The amount would depend on the size of the flower. Hold the frosting bag at a 25-degree angle with the open part of the tip facing up (fig. 9-21). Place

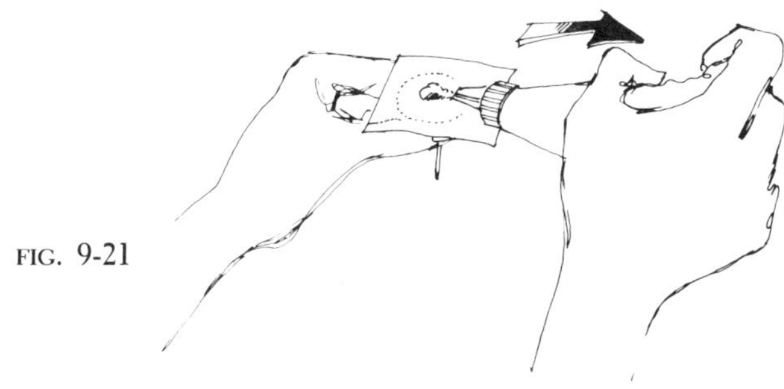

FIG. 9-21

FIG. 9-22

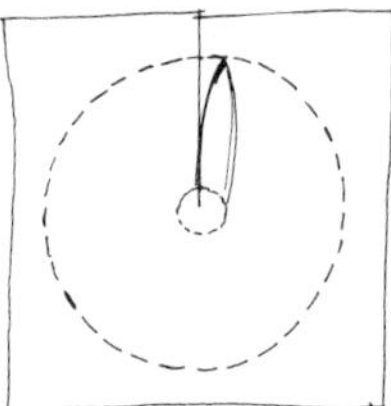

FIG. 9-23

the tip in the mound of frosting and apply pressure. As the pressure builds up, pull out and release pressure just slightly before you want the petal to end. As you stop pressure the frosting will break. Make petals all around the mound. On the next row, make the petals over but in between the previous ones. Make these petals a little shorter. Make a third row of petals. In the center, using a no. 13 tip and bright yellow frosting, make a mound of frosting and place tiny stars very close together (fig. 9-22).

For a similar but interesting shape, place a square of waxed paper with a slit halfway through on the nail. Leaving the center of the paper without frosting, start the petal along the slit (fig. 9-23). Make petals all around leaving a space of about ½ inch before the slit (fig. 9-24). Make another row over it with the petals the same length as the first. If the petals are thick and close together, 2 rows are sufficient. If not, make another row with petals of the same length. Now place a dab of frosting next to the slit (fig. 9-25) and overlap paper. You may let these dry before applying yellow centers. Using a no. 13 tip, mound icing and cover with little stars very close together (fig. 9-26).

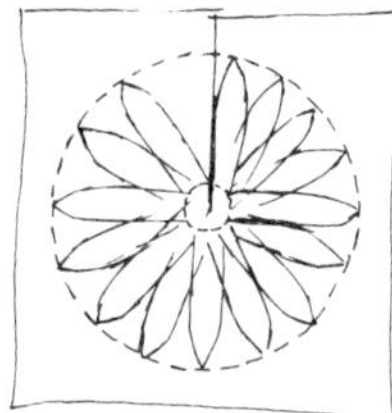

FIG. 9-24

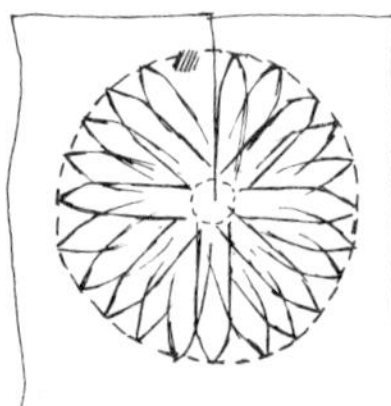

FIG. 9-25

FIG. 9-26

Narcissus and Daffodils

Narcissus and daffodils are made somewhat alike except for the center sections. These flowers can be made with Basic Frosting, but I prefer using Royal Icing.

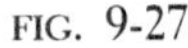

FIG. 9-27

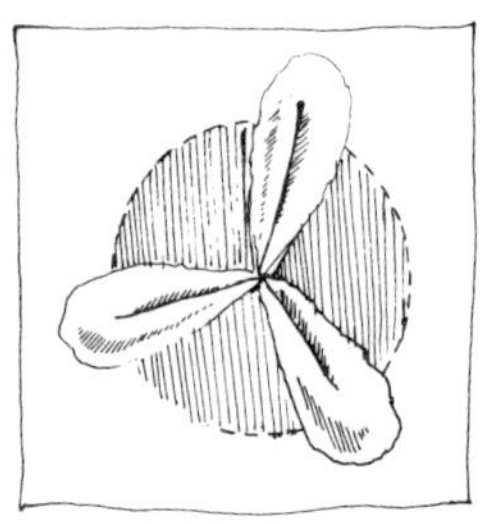

With the no. 103 tip on the decorating bag, put a dab of white icing on a no. 7 nail; place a 2-inch waxed-paper square on it. Hold the bag at a 25-degree angle with the thickest part of the tip down. Starting in the center of the nail, pipe a long narrow petal extending beyond the edge of the nail. Make 3 petals evenly spaced like the old-fashioned airplane propeller (fig. 9-27). Make 3 more petals in the same way. Dip your thumb and index finger in cornstarch and pinch the end of each petal so that the edge rolls and the end comes to a point (fig. 9-28). With yellow icing and a no. 3 tip, place a yellow dot in the center of these petals. Make a small circle around this dot and continue in a spiral with the circle coming up and getting a little bigger (figs. 9-29 and 9-30). Place bright yellow icing in a parchment bag and cut the end to make a fine opening. Place the point of the bag in the center of the spiral and pipe a small dot. The top edge may be painted a reddish brown with a dry fine brush dipped lightly in the covers of the red and brown paste colors; brush color sparingly in an outward motion.

FIG. 9-28

For daffodils make the petals with a no. 104 tip the same as for the narcissus except wider and a little longer. Bright yellow is the usual color. After the petals are completed, wait a minute for the icing to set; then pinch the ends of the petals without using any cornstarch.

FIG. 9-29

Using the same tip, make a trumpet in the center of these six petals: With the thickest part of the tip against the petal and the thin part straight up, apply pressure and make a standing circle. As you are about to join the ring, release pressure and the icing will break.

FIG. 9-30

Change to tip no. 59° and, with the thickest part of the tip against the trumpet, form a ruffle around the top edge (figs. 9-31 and 9-32).

With the no. 2 tip and the same color icing, make 3 pistils in the center of the trumpet: Hold the bag still, apply pressure to give it body, then release pressure as you pull out. Or, if you wish, place three short yellow stamens in the center.

A jonquil, a more delicate flower, is made very much in the same way except smaller and lighter in color.

FIG. 9-31

FIG. 9-32

CHAPTER 10
Leaves

Leaves Made on the Cake

The green leaves are the final touches to your floral arrangement. Basic Frosting may be used to pipe the leaves directly on your cake. Add a slight touch of red paste color when you mix the green frosting to tone the color down and give it a grayish tint. If you add too much red, you will get a dirty brown. Fill your bag and place a leaf tip on the coupling. No. 67 is a good size for an average cake; for a cupcake, no. 65 will give a better proportioned leaf. Try all the tips nos. 65 through 70 and see what works best for you.

To make the leaves, slip the tip in between the flowers, hold the bag in an upright position, and apply pressure. Let the frosting build up, not ripple, to form a base. Pull up slowly and release pressure. The frosting should then break off. If the leaf does not end in a point, pinch it with your thumb and index finger or thin down the icing slightly. If the frosting is too thin, the leaf will collapse completely.

Leaves Made on Waxed Paper

I found another method of doing leaves that gives excellent results; these must be made in advance and can be stored for future use. Mix green Royal Icing with a tint of red to enhance the color. Fill the bag and use tips nos. 67 and 68 for two different sizes. Place a piece of waxed paper on a cookie sheet. Holding your bag at a 45-degree angle with the tip touching the waxed paper, apply pressure and pull to the length desired. Stop squeezing just before you pull away. Either the beginning or the end should form a point. If the leaves have no points, your icing is too stiff. Make these in different lengths to use on a variety of cakes (fig. 10-1). They will dry in 24 hours.

If you have a place to keep the leaves while they dry, you can make many sheets using various shades of green. As soon as you empty a bag, mix a slightly different shade of green and fill the same bag. The icing that adhered to the bag gives highlights to the next color. When the leaves are dry, carefully place them, one sheet over another, in a cardboard box. Do not store them in a plastic container.

When you are ready to use the leaves, just pick them off the waxed paper and insert them where they are needed.

FIG. 10-1

Leaves Made on Toothpicks

The toothpick leaf is made on a green toothpick colored as for the stem flowers (Chapter 8). Place a no. 5 tip on a bag with green Royal Icing. Insert the toothpick about ¾ to 1 inch into the icing tip and pull out. The icing that covers the toothpick will help to hold the leaf. Put toothpicks on a sheet of waxed paper that has been placed on a cookie sheet. Do about 6 or 7 toothpicks and then change to a no. 67 or 68 tip. Use 2 bags if you are making many leaves. Holding the bag at a 45-degree angle, place the tip on toothpick where the icing begins. Apply pressure and pull along the toothpick, following the toothpick with the vein part of the tip (fig. 10-2). Extend leaf about 1 inch beyond toothpick. Do not allow icing to ripple. For a thin narrow leaf use a no. 67; for a thicker heavier leaf use a no. 68. To make a sturdier leaf, I have inserted a paring knife between the prongs of a tip and opened it a little more. Sometimes you must do this to the tip if the leaf separates at the vein.

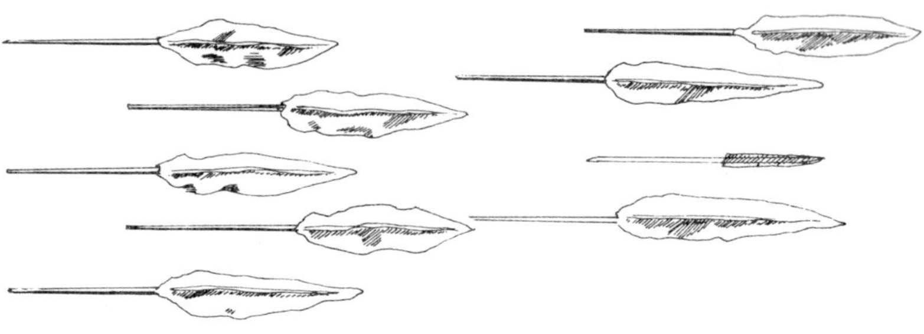

FIG. 10-2

Leaves Made with Parchment Bags

If a heavier looking leaf is desired, make a parchment bag with a tight point. If you wish, a piece of transparent tape may be wrapped at the point to reinforce the paper. Fill the bag with either Basic Frosting or Royal Icing, with the joining section of the bag in the upper center. If you want a small leaf, cut the tip to form a point as shown in fig. 10-3. For a larger leaf, cut as shown in fig. 10-4. Keep in mind that this is paper and if the point is too long, it will not make a good indentation in the frosting. Put the flat side of the tip against the surface and hold the bag at a 45-degree angle. As you apply pressure, raise the bag slightly and pull away; release pressure and keep pulling until frosting breaks. If the leaf does not come to a fine point, the frosting is too stiff. Thin it down with just a drop or two of water and try again.

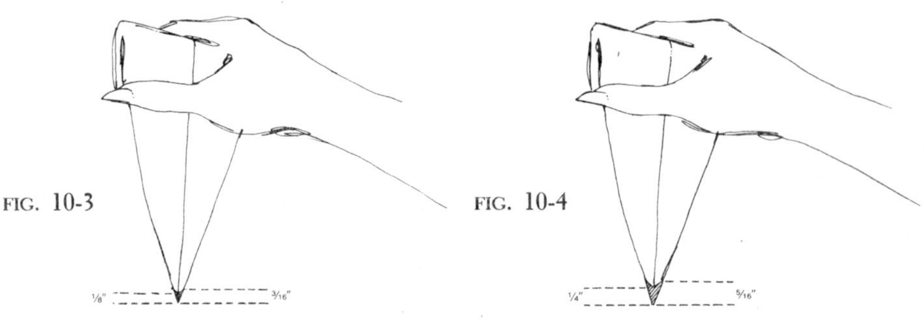

FIG. 10-3

FIG. 10-4

White Lace Wedding Cake

New York Cake

Wedgwood Cake

Les Belles Fleurs

Victorian Wedding Cake

Octagonal Wedding Cake

Gift Box Cake

Swan Cake

Manchester Wedding Cake

Bride's Magazine Cake

French Terrace Cake

Rose Noel

Cachepot Cake

Terra-cotta Tier Cake

Daisy Cake

Christmas Strawberry Cake

Flower Swag Cake

Pink and Blue Basket Cake

Victorian Fan

Long-stem-flower Cake

Gateau Chinoiserie

Name Cake

The Heart

Mom's Birthday Cake

Fondant Cake

Boot Cake

Telephone Cake

The Drum

Car Cake

Butterfly Cake

"80"

Book Cake

Holly Leaves

Whenever I make a Christmas cake, I like to use many varieties of holly leaves. Here are a few methods that I have found to be very successful. Using the parchment bag previously mentioned, start the leaf as explained for fig. 10-1. For holly leaves apply pressure, pull a short distance, release pressure, and stop. Do this 2 or 3 times; then break the frosting leaving a point on the leaf (fig. 10-5). A fine brush dipped in hot water can be used to pull out the points. If Basic Frosting is used, you can pipe directly on the cake. With Royal Icing and tip no. 67 or 68 on waxed paper, you can make leaves that stand at different angles for a more realistic appearance.

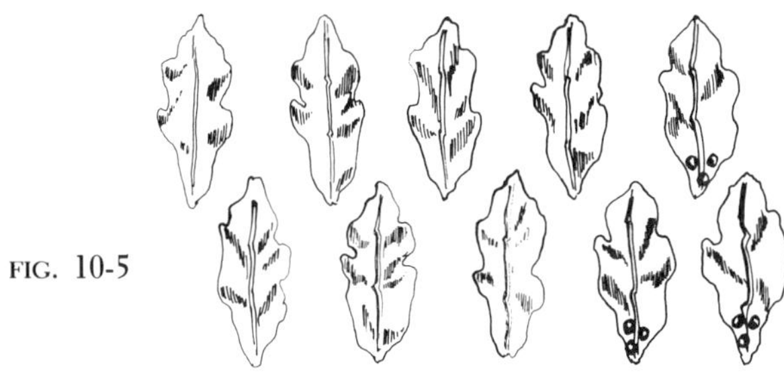

FIG. 10-5

Another method that I have found very effective is to make the leaves as in fig. 10-1 using Royal Icing and the no. 68 tip; then make curved lines on the leaf with a cake tester as shown in fig. 10-6. The tester cuts the icing so that when the leaf dries and is removed from the waxed paper, the excess icing falls off.

A few holly berries made with red icing depending on the size berry desired will enhance the leaves. To make the berries, place a tip no. 2, 3, or 4 at the stem end of the leaf and apply pressure to form a ball.

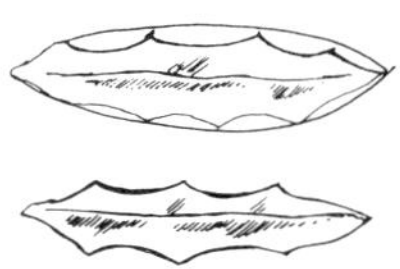

FIG. 10-6

Ferns

Ferns are very effective with a spray of flowers on a cake. For this leaf, tip no. 65, 66, 67, or 68 is preferable. Realistically a fern would be coming from behind a floral arrangement; so place your tip next to a flower to give it the same appearance. Squeeze just a small amount of frosting, stop, pull away, squeeze again, this time with a little less pressure, and go on ending with a dot (fig. 10-7).

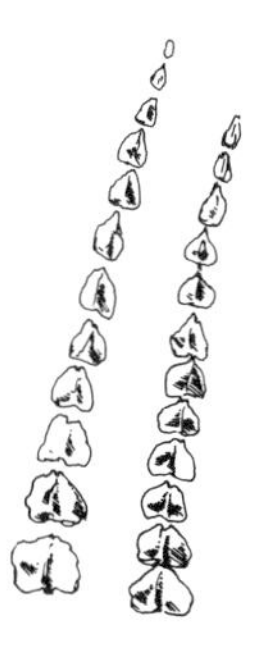

FIG. 10-7

Leaves Made on Wires

To make a leaf to go with a wired arrangement, use fabric-coated millinery wire for best results. The wire should be cut to the length you need for your floral arrangement. If you use wire leaves or ferns to go with a toothpick arrangement, cut the wire 5 inches long. Tint the wire green with vodka and food color as explained in Chapter 8. Straighten out the wire so that it will lie flat. Make the leaf as you made it on a toothpick (fig. 10-2). After it dries, the wire stem can be bent to form a curve.

To make a curved leaf, cover a large can with waxed paper. Bend the wire over the can. Keeping the wire curved, push the end of the wire about 1 inch into a no. 4 tip on a bag of Royal Icing. Place the wire on the can. The icing on the wire will hold it in place. Make the leaf over it as you did on the toothpick (fig. 10-8). Allow to dry thoroughly before removing it.

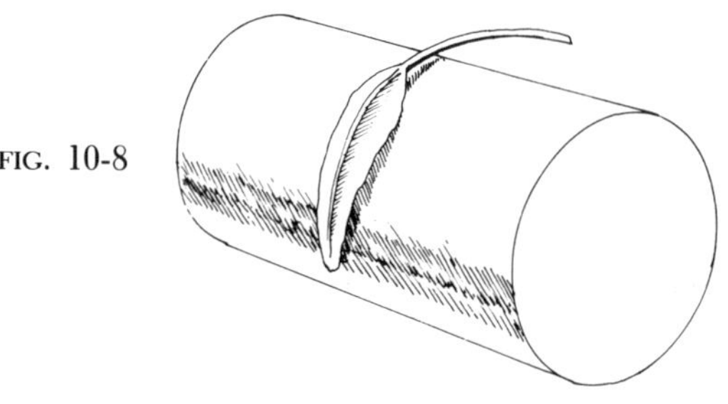
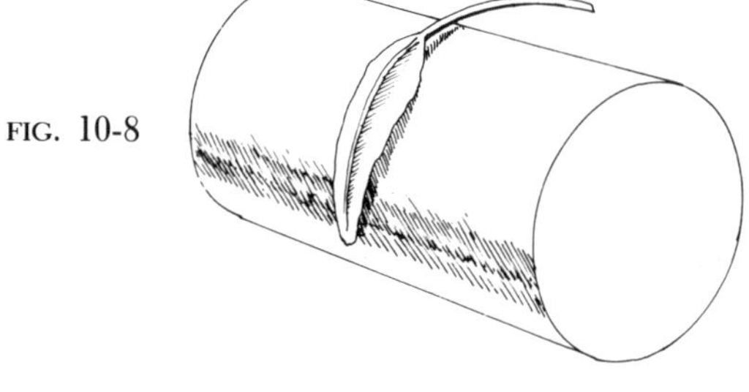

FIG. 10-8

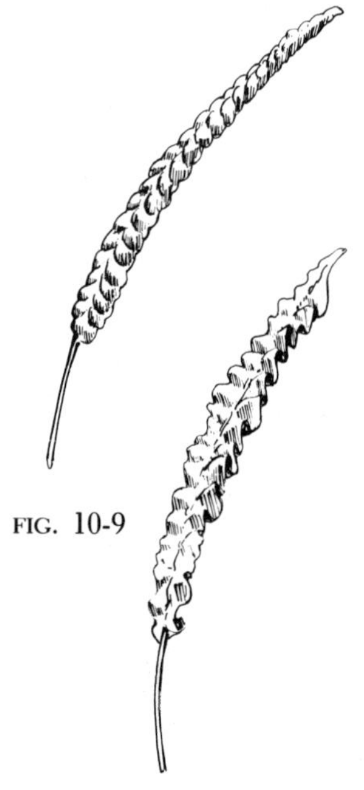

FIG. 10-9

FIG. 10-10

You can also make ferns on straight or curved wires. Put a tip no. 4 or 5 on a full bag of green Royal Icing. Insert the wire into the tip leaving about 1½ inches so that you have something to hold. Apply pressure to the bag and at the same time move your hand from left to right. Continue as you slowly pull out the wire. As you go up the wire make the fern smaller by not squeezing as much (fig. 10-9). You can make a fern on a toothpick if you allow enough space on the lower edge for you to insert it in Styrofoam to dry.

Another method for making a fern on a wire is done with a full bag of green Royal Icing with tip no. 68 on the coupling. Insert the wire into the tip leaving about 2 inches exposed. With your left hand, hold this piece of wire. With your right hand, apply pressure and slowly pull out, trying to keep the groove of the tip on the wire. The leaf will ripple slightly. As you get to the end of the wire, ease up on the pressure so that the leaf will be tapered (fig. 10-10). Insert it in Styrofoam to dry.

The Ateco no. 352 (imported) tip also makes a very good leaf. It is an excellent substitute for tips nos. 67 and 68.

CHAPTER 11

Decorative Ornaments

Birds

FIG. 11-1

Two little birds sitting on a Royal Icing fence is a charming and whimsical feature on a cake. Use Royal Icing and any tip with a plain hole to pipe a bird. The smaller the tip is, the smaller the bird will be.

Holding the bag of icing at a 45-degree angle, apply pressure on waxed paper until you have a rounded mound. Then raise your tip and reduce pressure to form the neck and the head, pulling forward to complete the beak (fig. 11-1).

Make a whole row of birds in this manner about 1 inch apart. Then make the wings by placing the tip against the side of the bird. Apply pressure and pull the tip towards the back forming a pointed wing (fig. 11-2).

FIG. 11-2

Bows

A bow is a delightful feminine touch on a cake. There are several different types that I use. Here are the basic methods. Measure the width of the bow desired; then draw a pattern (fig. 11-3). Tip nos. 44 and 45 are the ribbon tips, but you can also use any of the rose tips. Place a piece of waxed paper over the pattern and start in the center where the knot would be. If you are using a ribbon tip, it does not make any difference which end is up; if using a rose tip, the fine end is up. Hold the icing bag at a 45-degree angle and follow the line of the ribbon around and back to the center knot; then go down to make a short streamer. Do the left side in the same manner (fig. 11-4). One side is always very awkward to do. This bow may be made in any size. The larger the bow is, the larger the tip should be.

FIG. 11-3 FIG. 11-4

If you want to have rounded streamers, make your template with rounded lines (fig. 11-5).

FIG. 11-5

Another method of making a bow (usually a much larger one) is to start in the center at the knot and make a figure 8 (fig. 11-6). The streamers are made separately on a piece of waxed paper. Take a paring knife and cut the ends of your icing ribbons on an angle, or cut double angles with the clean point of blade (fig. 11-7). As long as the icing is cut, it can remain; when it is dry, it will break away easily.

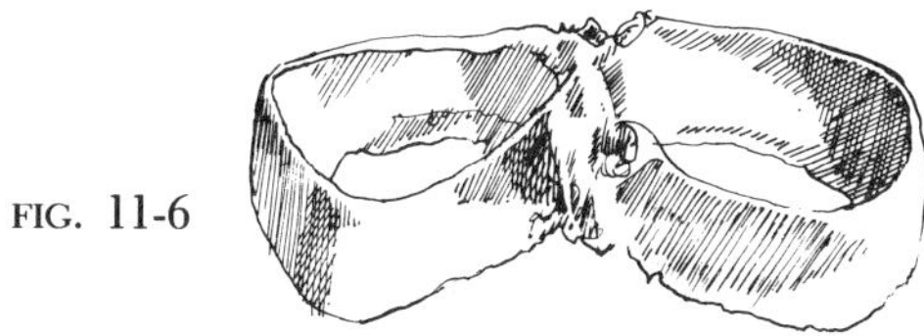

FIG. 11-6

The part of the streamer that will be tucked under the bow can be cut into a point in the same manner.

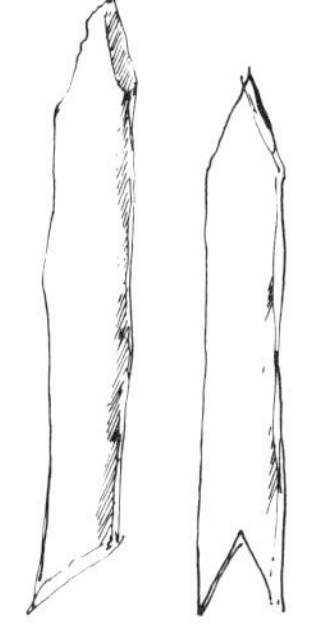

FIG. 11-7

To make a multi-looped bow out of icing (fig. 11-8), use a no. 104 tip with any color Royal Icing. Holding the bag at a 45-degree angle with the heaviest part of the tip down on waxed paper, make a loop ending with the icing coming to a point (fig. 11-9). Make about 25 to 30 loops of different shapes and lengths. Ten to twelve of the longest loops will form the base of the rosette. The others should vary in size. Let the loops dry.

To assemble, place a mound of Royal Icing on a piece of waxed paper. Form a circle with the larger loops around the base; then fill in with the remaining loops. Let set until completely dry. Remove waxed paper and place a small amount of icing on the cake where you want the bow.

By using different-size rose tips and making different length loops, you can get bows of many sizes.

FIG. 11-8

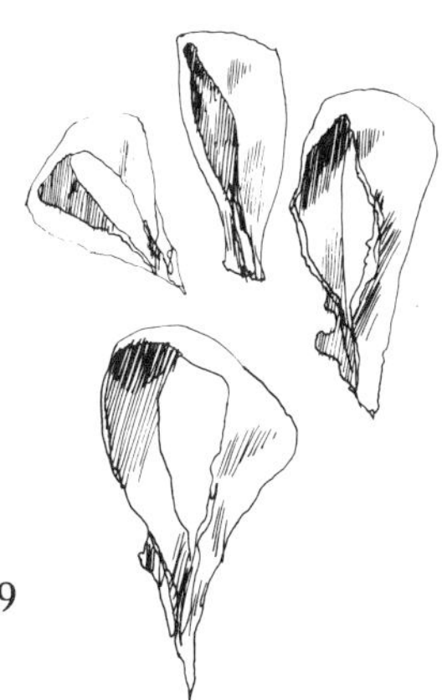

FIG. 11-9

Garlands

Garlands on the sides of the cake can be that final touch to complete an elegant cake. If the cake is octagonal, your problem of spacing the garlands evenly is solved. If the cake is round, you will need to make a paper pattern as described in Chapter 4. Fold the waxed paper into as many parts as you want garlands, either six or eight. Notch the paper on the creases. Open up the pattern and place it on a dry cake that has been crumbed and glazed. Place a toothpick at every notch. When you have a cake of many layers bring the toothpicks down to mark each layer (fig. 11-10). If you would like to have the swags alternating on each layer, mark the notches on every other layer; then turn the waxed paper so that the notch is halfway between 2 existing marks and mark the other layers (fig. 11-11). You must next decide how low the swags will be. I have found that a little less than half the length of a layer is a graceful dip. To mark it, use a kitchen ruler placed halfway between the toothpicks (fig. 11-12). If your cake is 4 inches high, mark the swag at 1¾ inches by making a line with a toothpick. After these marks are done all around the cake, mark the complete swags with a toothpick (fig. 11-13).

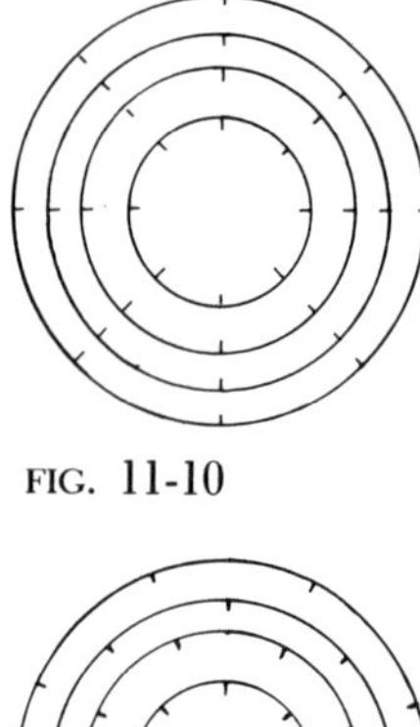

FIG. 11-10

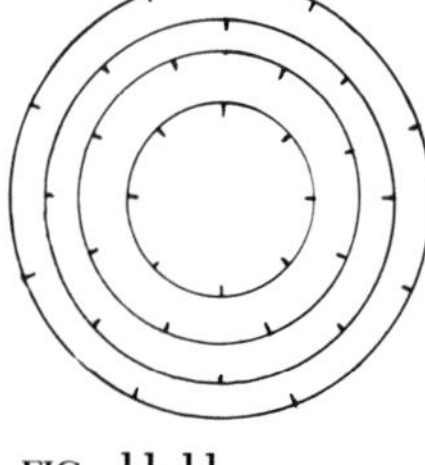

FIG. 11-11

Garlands may be made in 2 or 3 layers, graduating from the largest to the smallest tip. For example, in making a 3 layer garland, 22, 20, and 19 are a good combination. Using basic frosting and starting at the top of a garland, apply pressure and move the tip with a slight up and down motion. See fig. 11-14. As you go down on the swag, make the frosting a little heavier and wider. Decrease pressure, narrowing the swag as you come up to the toothpick. All the garlands may be done twice using the same tip and making sure that you push the tip into the icing to keep the swags from falling off. The third row should be done with a smaller tip (no. 14 or 15) to make the zigzag a little narrower. These garlands are very pretty like this, but grapes and flowers may be added as an additional decoration.

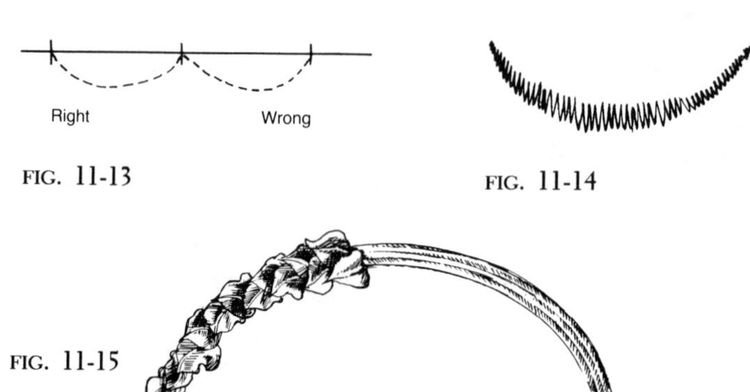

FIG. 11-12

FIG. 11-13

FIG. 11-14

FIG. 11-15

You can also make a garland covered with leaves falling to the left and right (fig. 11-15). For a heavier garland, do a swag with tip no. 16 to 20, depending on how thick you want it. Make leaves over it with tips nos. 66 to 68, again depending on the size desired.

If you want a cascade between the swags use tip no. 19 or 30 (light or heavy). Begin by holding the bag filled with Basic Frosting at a right angle to the cake and start at the bottom of the cascade. Apply pressure until frosting mounds. Keeping your bag at the same angle, pull up to complete the pear shape, and slowly release the pressure (fig. 11-16).

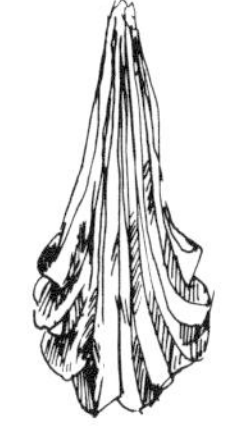

FIG. 11-16

If the cascade is long, go over it with a smaller tip making several cascades, each a little shorter (fig. 11-17). I find tip nos. 30, 19, or 16 make good-looking cascades.

For the garland with a leaf motif, continue the leaf design in between the swags. Starting at the lowest part of the drop, apply a leaf in proportion to the swags; then overlap it with the same size or smaller. Make 2 or 3 more in graduated sizes to join the swags (fig. 11-18).

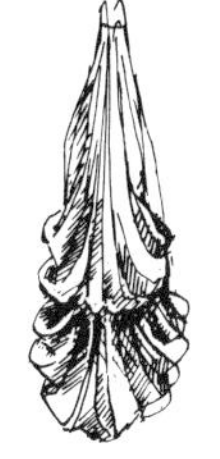

FIG. 11-17

FIG. 11-18

Grapes

I find grapes in various sizes a wonderful decorative feature, especially when tucked into leaf garlands.

Either type of frosting can be used for the grapes, but I find the Royal Icing is far superior. Any plain hole tip may be used, depending on the size and where the grapes are to be displayed.

Line a cookie sheet with waxed paper. With the tip in, hold the icing bag at a 45-degree angle. Apply pressure until a nice rounded mound forms; release pressure and pull away. Make another mound to the left, release pressure, and pull away. Make another to the right of the first, another between the second and third, and so on (fig. 11-19).

Make clusters side by side using different tips for variety (fig. 11-20). They may be left on waxed paper and kept in a cardboard box until ready to use.

FIG. 11-19

FIG. 11-20

Lattice and Fencing

Before you can do any lattice or fencing, your cake has to be baked in order to get the proper measurements.

A square, rectangular, or octagonal cake is the simplest for lattice work. Plan where you want the lattice on the cake and the type of lattice; then start measuring the space to be covered. Accuracy is most important. Place your ruler directly on the cake and measure the height and width. Avoid having to make very large pieces, at least on your first attempt.

Make a pattern with a piece of paper. Use any type of squaring device to make your pattern, an L-square preferably. A magazine, book, or paper with a ruler will also work. Whatever type of lattice, diamond or square, fine or bold, the format is the same.

When you have drawn an outline to the measurements of the cake, measure and mark the same distance at the top and bottom edges (fig. 11-21). This is a must, to keep your design from going on an angle (fig. 11-22). Try a different measurement, and it will give you a different angle. For example, if you have a 4-inch square, 2 inches will give you a diamond shape (fig. 11-23) and 4 inches will give you a square (fig. 11-24).

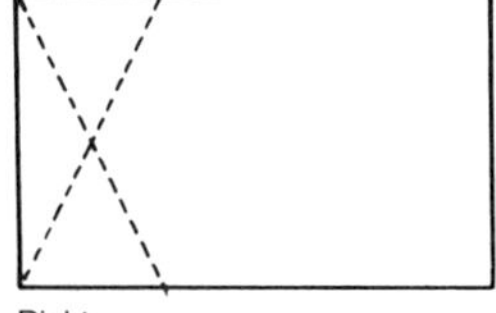

Right
FIG. 11-21

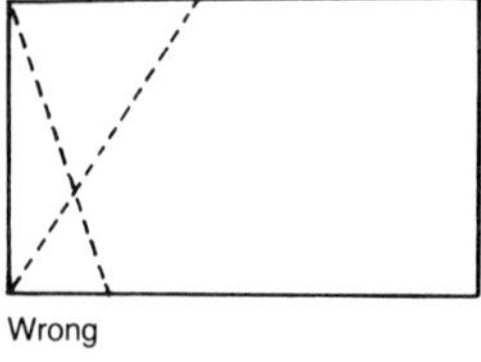

Wrong
FIG. 11-22

The closer the lines are made, the smaller the squares will be. The smaller squares look more delicate on the cake, but the lattice is actually sturdier. If you make the lines far apart, the lattice will be done faster, but it might not have enough icing to hold it together, nor is it as pretty.

Figs. 11-23 and 11-24 show you how to place your ruler. Be accurate in measuring. The size tip you plan to use will determine how far apart you draw your lines. When I use a no. 4 tip, I make the lines ¼ to ⅜ inch apart.

FIG. 11-23

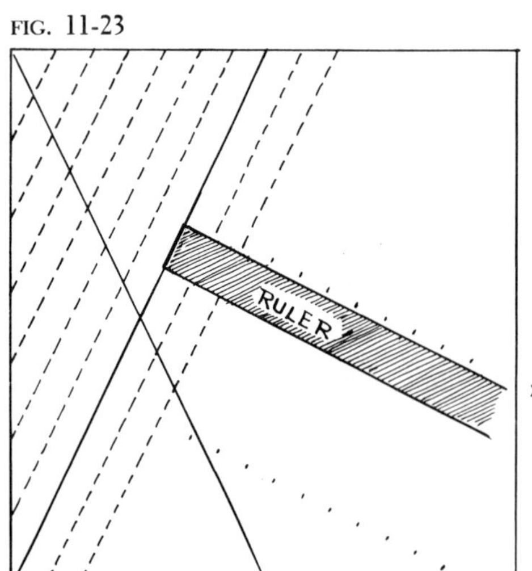

FIG. 11-24

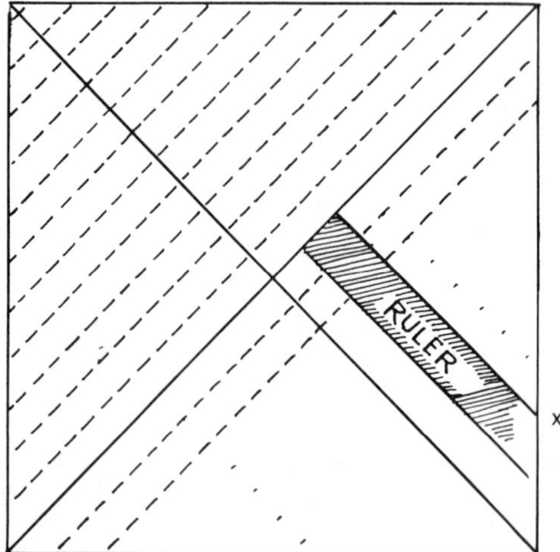

Fill your bag with white Royal Icing. Make sure the icing is smooth with no air bubbles because a bubble will break the string of icing.

Place your pattern on a flat cookie sheet. Cut a piece of waxed paper about 1 inch larger at each edge, and place it over the pattern.

With your left hand hold the waxed paper in place. Hold the bag with a no. 4 tip at a 45-degree angle; place the tip at the upper edge of a line and apply a little pressure so the icing adheres to the waxed paper. Raise your tip a little, and continue to apply pressure while you slowly go down the line. Do not drag the tip when you are doing this type of lattice. The line should look like a smooth rounded string. When you reach the bottom edge, release pressure, push the tip against the waxed paper, and the string will break (fig. 11-25). Do all the lines going in the same direction first; then do the lines going in the opposite direction. If you start the first lattice with lines going from left to right, continue doing those lines first on all the lattices. Do not allow your lattice to extend beyond the pattern (fig. 11-26). It's a good idea to make one or two extras of the same size in case of breakage. Allow 24 hours to dry.

FIG. 11-25

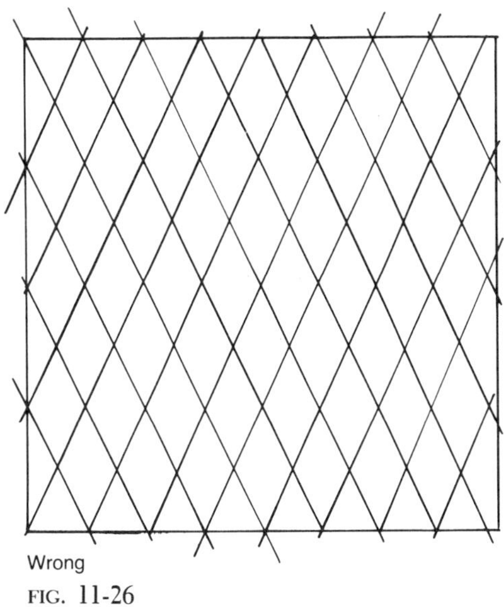

FIG. 11-26

The lattice made with Royal Icing must not touch the Basic Frosting on the cake. The vegetable shortening in the frosting will soften the lattice making it crumble.

You can crumb and glaze your cake with Basic Frosting; then make a frame for the lattice with Royal Icing and a no. 10 tip (fig. 11-27). Turn the dry lattice over carefully and peel off the waxed paper. Place the waxed-paper side on the icing frame on the cake. Do the next sections the same way.

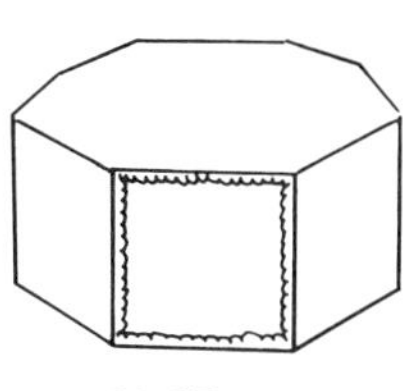

FIG. 11-27

I have found that I have to make a new pattern for every cake, as each seems to differ slightly.

Fencing is done the same way as lattice. The cake has to be first baked before you can get exact measurements. The lattice in fig. 11-25 may be used, or you might like to try something a little different. The fences in figs. 11-28 and 11-29 will give an oriental effect. To do one of these designs, make a pattern and follow the numbers in fig. 11-30 or 11-31. When you do any line with icing, wherever the line begins, insert the clean tip slightly into the icing to make it stick as well as give the appearance of a continuous line. Where the line ends, have another line going over it. When the lines are completed, go around the entire piece of fence with the same tip to reinforce it.

FIG. 11-28

FIG. 11-29

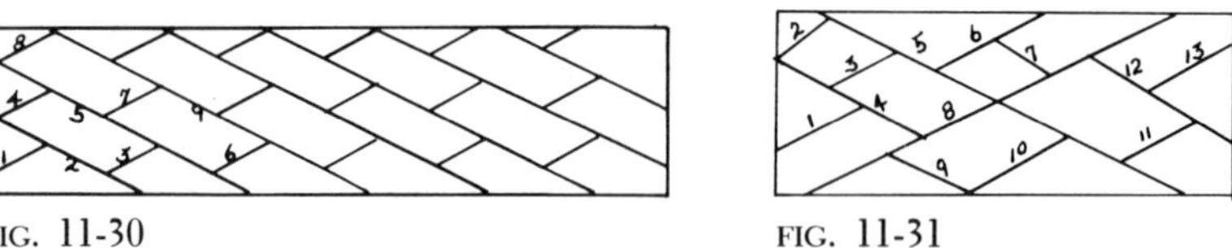

FIG. 11-30

FIG. 11-31

Whatever type of fence you use, do not make it more than 1⅛ inches high or more than 6 to 7 inches long. The fence can be straight or wavy (fig. 11-32).

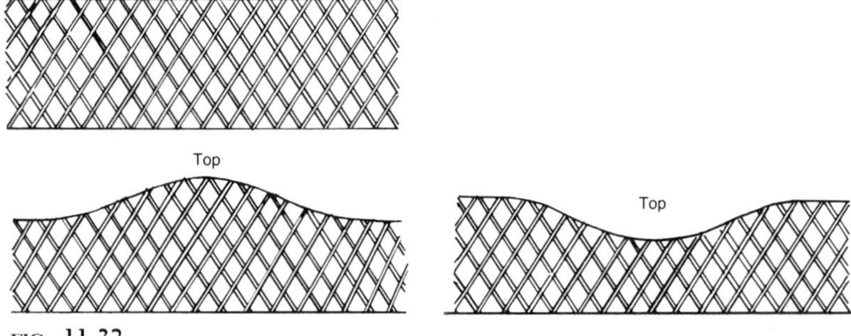

FIG. 11-32

Once the icing on the fence has set, make one of the following to complete the top edge. All must be done using Royal Icing.

Fig. 11-33 illustrates a design made by centering tip no. 65 or 66 on the fence and piping a leaf going to the right, then the next leaf over it but pulling to the left, then to the right, and so on.

Fig. 11-34 shows a beading design made on the top of the fence with tip no. 5, 6, or 7, depending on the size of the fence. Hold the icing bag at a 45-degree angle and apply pressure until the icing mounds to the desired size; stop squeezing and pull away about ¼ inch; apply pressure again until you get the same size mound. Continue in this fashion until the border is completed.

Fig. 11-35 illustrates a mock roping made by using a no. 5 tip. Hold the bag at a 45-degree angle, apply pressure, and make a rotary motion.

Fig. 11-36 shows a similar roping done in the same way as for fig. 11-35 but with a no. 13 or 14 star tip.

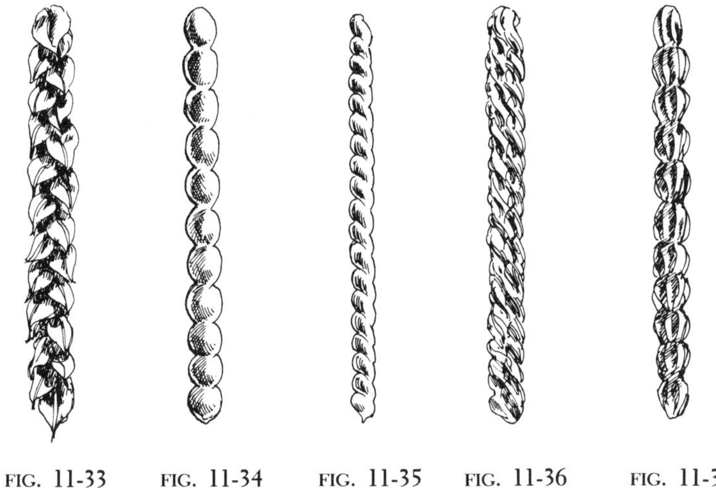

FIG. 11-33 FIG. 11-34 FIG. 11-35 FIG. 11-36 FIG. 11-37

Fig. 11-37 illustrates a small puff done with tip no. 15 or 16. Holding the bag at a 45-degree angle, apply pressure until icing mounds to the desired puff, stop squeezing, and the icing should break. Pull away and squeeze to form the next puff. Allow all these edgings to dry thoroughly, about 24 hours, before using.

After your cake is crumbed and glazed, let the frosting set for a short time. On the top edge of your cake where the fence will be, make the same border in Royal Icing that is on the top edge of the fencing. Turn the fence over on a paper or dish towel and carefully remove the waxed paper; then insert it in the center of the border. Toothpicks may be inserted to help support the fence until it dries if they are not put in Royal Icing. (The icing will dry on the toothpick and you will not be able to remove it.)

Join the fencing together with the same edging as is on the top of the fences.

Run Sugar

The name run sugar is very descriptive as the icing is soft and flows readily. Icing lines outline the design and act as a barrier to enclose the body of the design.

Coloring books are excellent sources for run-sugar designs. Any line drawing that appeals to your creative eye may be used, but try something small for the first project. You can buy numbers or letters of different sizes and shapes; emblems and logos are also excellent. Or you can create your own design. The colors used are primarily a matter of choice, as is the design and where it is going to be applied.

FIG. 11-38

To do run-sugar decorations, place a design on a cookie sheet and put waxed paper over it (fig. 11-38). Do not use wood as it holds moisture and your run sugar will not dry properly.

You will need Royal Icing for run sugar. I do not reccommend using an egg-white recipe; the meringue-powder recipe is far superior. Icing will keep in a grease-free, airtight jar 3 to 4 weeks without refrigeration. I cannot stress enough the importance of grease-free utensils when working with Royal Icing. A trace of grease in the icing is the main cause of failure.

The basic recipe for Royal Icing is of the proper consistency for making the outline barrier for your design. If you are doing numbers or letters, outline the outside as well as the inside of the figures. Hold a bag with a no. 4 tip at a 45-degree angle so that you will have a fully round line. Outline the design and join all lines so that when the soft icing is applied it cannot flow out.

The run-sugar icing has to be much softer in order to fill in the space between the barrier lines. In a glass bowl (grease free, no soft plastics), place white Royal Icing. The amount depends on the design. Add color, if you want it, and, mixing icing very slowly so that you do not create any air bubbles, add a few drops of water. Run a spatula through the mixture. If the icing separates and soon fills in again, you have reached the correct consistency. If not, mix in a few more drops of water and try again.

The smaller the design, the smaller the tips should be for the run sugar. You must also use a small tip if the design is very detailed. When filling in, I prefer using a tip rather than a parchment bag opening. If the tip is too large, the frosting will flow out so rapidly that it will be almost impossible to control.

Place a no. 3, 4, or 5 tip in a canvas or parchment bag; then place the bag in a high narrow glass and pour in icing. Work quickly because the icing will flow out of the tip. Immediately pick up the bag and put your finger on the tip to stop the flow. Carefully fold the top and place the tip against a wet cloth if you are not ready to use it. When you start running your sugar icing, work quickly. Try not to let one area set before you have finished with it. If you are doing a design with many colors, let each color set before starting another. Avoid very dark colors as they do not seem to dry; evidently there is too much liquid in the paste color.

To apply the icing, place the bag with your finger over the tip in a position to allow the icing to flow between the barriers. Remove your finger and push the icing against the holding wall. A toothpick will help get icing into the corners. Do not allow icing to overflow.

Experiment with this; each time you do it, your technique will improve. When your design is completed, you can go over the outline and features if necessary.

Allow the design to dry completely. The length of time depends on the size and thickness of the icing. When you are ready to use the design, place it face down on a paper towel and slowly peel off the waxed paper. If the icing is not completely dry, your design will break. Place a small amount of Royal Icing on the back of your design in order to secure it to the Basic Frosting on your cake.

Scrolls

Scrolls must be made with Royal Icing. If you know where you plan to place them, you can find a suitable size. Make a template (fig. 11-39) and trace it so that you have a left and right side. Place the pattern on a flat cookie sheet and put waxed paper over it. Using tip no. 19 or another size tip in proportion to your scrolls, start by doing a rotary motion at the other end (fig. 11-40). If this scroll was done from left to right, the opposite scroll must be done from right to left. Let dry completely, at least 24 hours, keeping the sides separated as it makes it easier to assemble.

FIG. 11-39 FIG. 11-40

Remove the waxed paper from left-to-right scrolls and invert them. Using tip no. 15, start at one end, and using very little pressure, do a left-to-right motion until the back side of the scroll is completely covered. Place the corresponding scroll over it, sandwiching the filling. Do not squeeze it together as the filling will bulge. The scroll should look as if it were a whole piece.

Complete all scrolls and let dry thoroughly before using.

If you wish, you may decorate the scrolls with tiny flowers and grapes.

Sugar Molds

Working with sugar molds is as easy as making mud pies—and sometimes as messy, if you are not careful. Clear a space to work where the molds can dry before they are moved. Once dry, they very seldom break unless they are dropped. (The broken pieces are fine for your morning coffee.)

I have been very successful in using 1 cup of granulated sugar to a scant 3 teaspoons (equals scant 1 tablespoon) of ice cold water to make the sugar molds. The finer the sugar granules are, the better the results will be. If the air is humid, I use a little less water. This recipe can be reduced to ⅓ cup sugar and a scant teaspoon of ice water or doubled and tripled.

Any type of container may be used for a sugar mold—that is, anything you can fill and invert keeping the shape intact (see Chapter 13). I use different-size cereal bowls, candy dishes, and even Waterford crystal for small urns. There are many molds on the market made especially for this purpose. For something more individual, look in flea markets and garage sales.

It is a little difficult to know the exact amount of sugar you need to make a mold because it packs down when dampened. Whatever mold you choose, fill it twice with dry sugar. Then measure the sugar to determine how much water needs to be added. Place the sugar in a bowl (preferably not metal); to keep the sugar from spilling while working with it, use as wide a bowl as possible. There is nothing more annoying than sugar on the counter and floor. After you have made quite a few sugar molds, you will reach a point when you will not have to measure the water; you will know the correct moisture level that will give you the best results.

Measure the required amount of ice water into a small glass. Pick up a dab of color paste with a toothpick and dissolve it in the water before adding the water to the sugar. If you are using colored sugar, make sure you mix enough because it is very difficult to mix the exact color the second time.

For white sugar molds, just mix sugar with water. Doing this with your hands gives better and faster results. Mix thoroughly until all sugar and water is blended.

Your molds must be clean and dry when putting sugar in them. Fill one and press on the surface so that the mold is filled solidly. Clean excess sugar off the edges and place an index card over the mold. Invert it onto a flat surface. Holding the mold, gently pull out the card; then remove the mold. If there are any cracks or blemishes in the form, scoop up the sugar with your card, place it back in the bowl, and start again.

Some of the commercial molds have left and right pieces. They can be made separately and cemented together later with Royal Icing. It does not take any longer to make these molds in one piece, but it does require a little more care. Holding the right or left section in the palm of your hand, fill it, mounding the sugar. Place the mate of the mold over it, making sure that they are well matched. Squeeze it as much as as you can; then remove the top mold and scrape off the excess sugar around the edge. Place the mold over it again and squeeze. Then turn the mold over, remove the other side, and clear away excess sugar. Keep doing this until the two sections meet. Using the end of a paring knife or a small spatula, remove all excess sugar to make a clean edge all around. Remove one side of the mold and let stand. When it is dry enough, turn the form over into a clean matching mold and let the other side dry completely before using.

CHAPTER 12

Assembling the Wedding Cake

Research is very important in trying to find new techniques and ideas for decorating. Books on architecture, interior decorating, and even wallpaper design are excellent sources. If you have an artistic mind, whatever you look at will be stimulating.

How Many Layers

Some novice decorators become quite hesitant when considering making their first tiered cake. If you do not think of it as a large cake but rather as many small cakes on top of one another, you may feel calmer.

Before you design a cake, you must know how many people the cake is required to serve. I have found the scale of servings per pan on the chart below to be quite accurate.

6-inch round pan serves 10	6-inch square pan serves 20
8-inch round pan serves 25	8-inch square pan serves 35
10-inch round pan serves 35	10-inch square pan serves 50
12-inch round pan serves 50	12-inch square pan serves 75
14-inch round pan serves 70	14-inch square pan serves 100
16-inch round pan serves 100	

Any cake pans larger than this would require a commercial oven. If you have a different-shaped pan, fill it with water and empty the water into one of the pans above to determine how many servings of cake it will hold.

By the time the frosting is placed on these cakes, each tier should be between 3½ and 4 inches high whether the tier is 1 layer or 2. If I want a 4-inch high cake, I prefer baking it in 2 layers. The baking time is shorter; therefore, the texture is finer. Fig. 12-3 shows basic cutting charts for the round and square cakes.

Take out your cake pans and arrange them in different combinations of 16 inch, 12 inch, 8 inch, and 6 inch (fig. 12-1) to see which is more pleasing and graceful. You will find that using 12-, 10-, 8-, and 6-inch pans (fig. 12-2) make a thicker shape. As you may sometimes need all the cake, you may have to use all the pans; if the arrangement looks thick to you, you can make the base section look larger with an interesting placement of flowers around it.

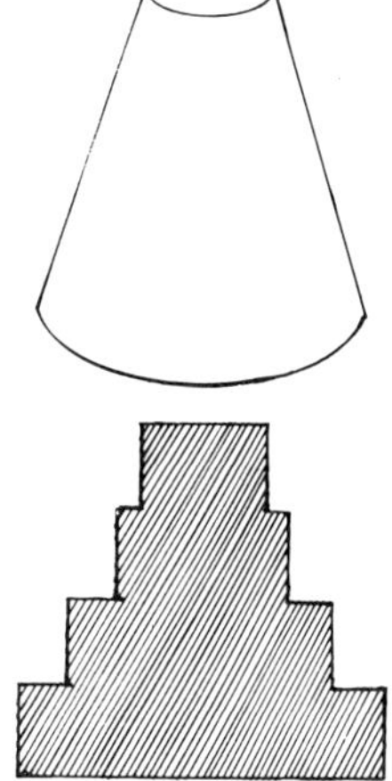

FIG. 12-1

Using a cake-decorating comb to make lines going up the cake will give an illusion of height. The secret to using this comb is to apply a heavy layer of frosting over the dry crumbed cake. This frosting does not have to be glazed, but it should be fairly smooth because the comb lines will accent any indentations. Frost a small section at the base of the cake; then dip the comb in hot water and slowly pull up on the frosting. Wipe off excess frosting and do the same thing over again, being careful when you overlap the sharp lines that they are kept straight.

It is almost impossible to tell you how much batter to use in any baking. Every recipe varies. A good rule to remember is to fill the pan ⅔ to ¾ of the height of the cake you want.

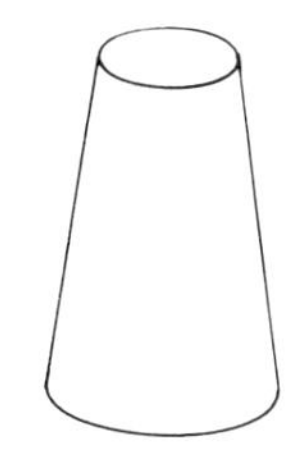

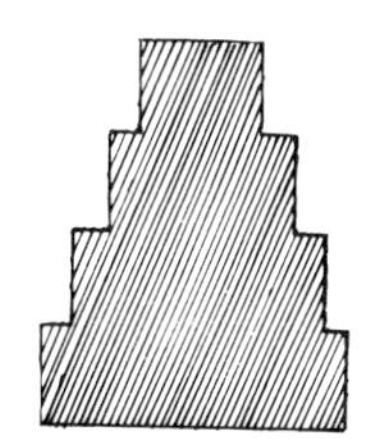

FIG. 12-2

Just before you place your cake in the oven, weigh it and note the weight. If there is any adjustment to be made later, you will have a figure to work with. Place the cake in the oven and note the baking time. After it is baked, check the thickness. If the layer is too thin, try it again with a little more batter until you have the correct amount. Different cake batters will vary in weight. If you keep notes on the batters you work with, you will have less guesswork.

Once your cakes are baked, you can trim off some of the rounded sections with a long sharp knife, and then turn over onto a cooling rack. If you are planning tiers with 2 layers and you find the cakes have baked too high, trim off the extra cake now. When the layers are completely cooled, frost the tops with just enough Basic Frosting to make the layers stick. If you use too much frosting, the top layer will slide. If you want a heavy filling, make a 2-layer tier only. When you place the next tier onto your cake, make sure that it is level on top before you turn it over. If anything needs to be measured and trimmed, do it now. Place the assembled cake in a plastic bag and freeze it. Try to get as much air as possible out of the bag before you seal it.

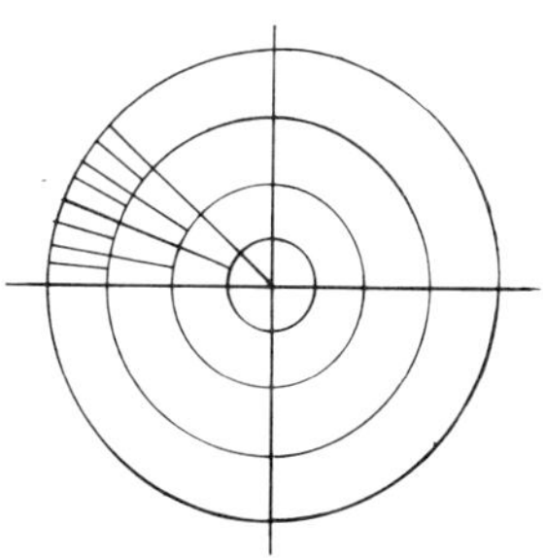

FIG. 12-3

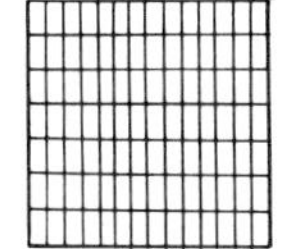

Crumbing and Glazing

Your cake should be crumbed as soon as it comes out of the freezer to ensure freshness. If frozen, leave a few places on the cake without frosting to allow some of the frozen moisture to escape; then seal it with frosting. The length of thawing time will depend on the size of the cake. If in doubt, use a cake tester to see if the cake is completely thawed.

The cake can be glazed as soon as the icing is dry to the touch, or it can be done the next day. The crumbing layer will seal in the moisture so the cake remains fresh.

The cake is now ready to be decorated. The instructions for the cake in the following chapters will tell you how.

If you need to mark for decorating, the glazing layer will have to be completely dry before you begin.

If making a small wedding cake (serving 50 to 100), have all the frosting, flowers, and decorations made ahead of time.

Seventy-two hours before the cake is to be served, start baking. As soon as the cake is completely cooled on a cooling rack, you can begin assembling. A very elaborate cake with lattice, scrolls, and flowers can take 2 to 3 weeks to complete. This type of cake would have to be baked first in order to get the right specifications for your decorations. The cake is baked, measured, and then frozen as soon as possible.

Supports for the Cake

A silver tray is ideal for a small wedding cake. Wrap a piece of corrugated cardboard the exact size as the cake bottom with aluminum foil and secure it on the tray with a small amount of frosting. This will prevent your tray from being scratched when the cake is cut.

A piece of ½-inch Plexiglas any size, round or square, is excellent for a cake. It gives the appearance of the cake just hovering over the table with the lace or colored tablecloth showing through. The Plexiglas can be placed on a book about ½ inch thick. This allows you space to slide in fresh ferns or greens of any type as a setting for the cake.

The thin plastic commercial supports that are inserted into the tiers to support the next tier are not worth the risk of disaster. Use ⅜- to ½-inch wooden dowels to be safe. Insert a dowel in your cake, mark it just at the level of the cake, and then saw it off. Use fine sandpaper to smooth off the edges; then wipe them thoroughly with a damp cloth. Four supports are sufficient for a 10- or 12-inch cake. If you have a larger cake, use 6 or 8 dowels.

You can make a cake that has round or square extensions (fig. 12-4); the small cakes can be made of carrot or chocolate cake. The cakes are inserted under a special support table of plywood that will support the main cake. This table is made of ¼-inch plywood and is 1½ inches larger than the cake it will support with ½-inch dowels for legs (fig. 12-5). Measure the height of the extended cakes and add ⅛ inch to determine how high the legs should be. After the dowels are cut, they are glued and nailed to the plywood. The larger the support table is, the more legs it will need. The wood must not come in direct contact with the cake; cover the plywood with aluminum foil using tape to hold the foil in place underneath the table.

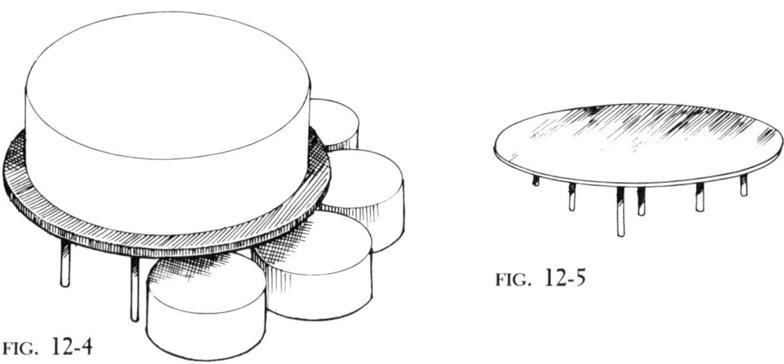

FIG. 12-4

FIG. 12-5

Assembling the Cake

Make a large container of Basic Frosting. If you have a large enough mixer, make a double recipe. The frosting can be made softer by adding an extra tablespoon water to each recipe to make it easier to frost the cake. Keep the mixer at a low speed so that you do not create any air bubbles. The consistency of this frosting is too soft to use for decorating. Keep frostings in separate airtight containers and mark them. Fig. 12-6 shows how the cake is assembled: 12-6a plexiglas, 12-6b cake, 12-6c rounded piece of foil, 12-6d corrugated cardboard wrapped in foil, 12-6e cake.

The cardboard covered with aluminum foil is placed between each tier so that when the tier is cut, the layer below is not interfered with. Let us say that your cakes are 6 inches, 10 inches, and 14 inches. The 14-inch cake is placed top side down on ½-inch-thick plexiglas, 24 inches in diameter. The cake is inverted so that you will have a flat surface with right angle edges to work on.

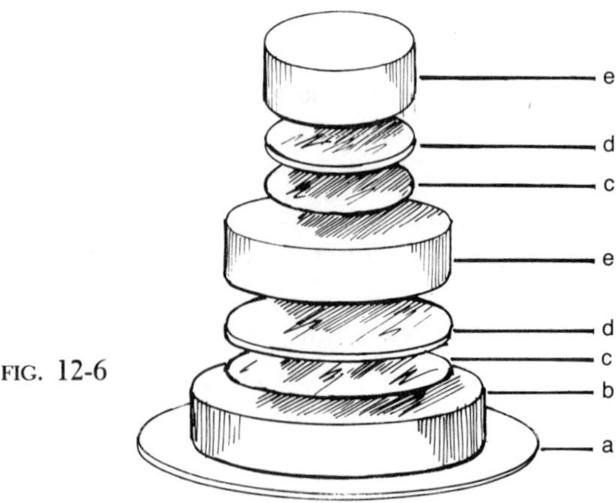

FIG. 12-6

Crumb the top and sides of the 14-inch cake with a double thickness of frosting on the top. You need the extra frosting on top because the aluminum foil on top of it will be peeled off, when the top cake is ready to be cut, taking some of the frosting with it.

Outline your 10-inch and 6-inch baking pan on corrugated cardboard. Now do the same thing on aluminum foil (fig. 12-7). Cut out all these circles. Wrap pieces of foil a little larger than the circles around each one (fig. 12-8).

FIG. 12-7

Put supports into your 14-inch cake; they should sink down into the frosting. You want some of the weight on the cake, otherwise the top layer will slide.

Center the 10-inch piece of foil on your 14-inch cake. Place the 10-inch disc with the smooth foil facing up on top of it. Invert the 10-inch cake onto the cardboard and crumb with a double thickness of icing on the top. No supports are needed here. Now do the same thing with the 6-inch cake and crumb.

Concerning the top layer, when the cake is assembled in this manner a small section of the decorative edging may be broken away just enough for you to insert a spatula in between the two layers of foil (See fig. 12-6c and d). Then with care the top layer of cake may be removed and frozen for the first anniversary.

If your cake has been frozen, you should leave spaces without frosting in order for some of the frozen moisture to escape. If you seal it completely, your frosting might bubble. Sometimes you can insert a hat pin or a fine toothpick in the bubble to release pressure and smooth it over with a hot spatula. However, it is not always that convenient.

FIG. 12-8

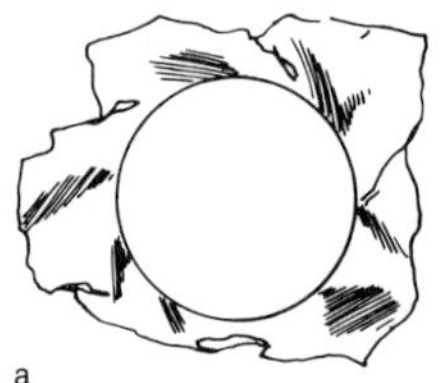

a

b

c

Pillar Supports

Pillar supports are used between the tiers of cakes to create an illusion of height. Plastic supports are available, but I believe that everything on your cake should be edible. (The exception is the pearl stamens in the pronged flowers, although these, too, have been eaten more than once.) I make the pillar supports out of molded sugar. These sugar molds are very strong and can support 1 or 2 tiers of cake, although I do not recommend transporting them in this manner. Place your top layer of cake on after you have arrived at your destination. The molds are available through Maid of Scandinavia. This mold is in 2 sections, but make them as one as described for sugar molds in Chapter 11. Always make extras.

The pillar supports are placed on top of a cardboard divider; another divider is placed on the pillar supports. Look ahead to fig. 12-17. The size of the dividers will depend on where they are placed on the cake. If you want the pillars between the 6- and 10-inch cakes, make the cardboard circle 8 inches in diameter. If you want them between the 6- and 8-inch cakes, make the circle 7 inches. Cut 2 circles out of heavy corrugated cardboard. Trace 1 circle on waxed paper and 2 on aluminum foil; then cut these out. Cover each of the 2 cardboard circles with another piece of foil, using Royal Icing to secure the foil (fig. 12-8). The aluminum-foil circle will be used later when assembling the cake. The waxed-paper circle is used as a pattern for the placement of the sugar pillars. If you plan to use 8 pillars, fold the waxed paper pattern very accurately in half, then fold in quarters, then in eighths. Always have the paper in a wedge shape. For detailed drawings see Chapter 4. On the folded edges notch the creases. When the paper is opened, you have a pattern for the exact placement of the pillars (fig. 12-9). If you plan to have 6 pillars, fold the paper in half, then in thirds.

By the time you reach this point, the sugar molds should be completely dry. If you plan to decorate the pillars with vines of leaves and grapes, it should be done at this time (fig. 12-10). If the design is different on each end of a pillar, make sure that the designs are all going in the same direction. Let dry completely before starting to assemble.

Lattice can be made on the outside (fig. 12-11a and b) or the inside (fig. 12-11c and d) of the pillars. The pillars are placed ¼ inch from the edge of the cardboard. Using a pencil, outline the placement of the sugar pillars (fig. 12-11e), marking the center of the cardboard with a + (fig. 12-11f). If the lattice is to be outside, measure from a to b for the width. The height would be the length of your sugar mold pillars less ⅛ inch. See section on lattice work in Chapter 11.

Whether you have a lattice or not, you need something in the center. A small urn (fig. 12-12) or a cluster of flowers (fig. 12-13) is perfect. Do not make it too large. Allow enough space around it so that you can see

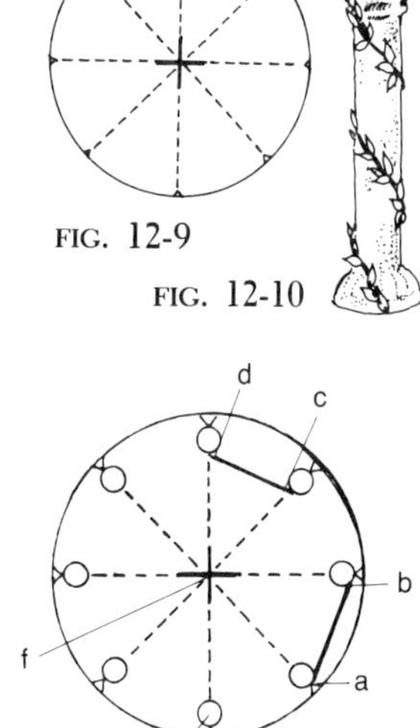

FIG. 12-9

FIG. 12-10

FIG. 12-11

FIG. 12-12

FIG. 12-13

through. Whatever the decorations, all should be completed and dried before you start assembling the dividers. Once you begin, it is best to work fast to keep the icing from setting.

Before assembling sugar pillar dividers, look at fig. 12-17. Start on 1 covered cardboard circle at the line between figs. 12-11c and 12-11d, using tip no. 67 and white Royal Icing. Make leaves all around with the leaf extending slightly up and to the outer edge. Keeping the leaves close together continue going around the circle, covering all foil. Continue making leaves until just the very center remains. Place a dab of icing in the center and apply sugar urn (fig. 12-12) or place more icing and make a flower cluster (fig. 12-13). Make sure the center ornament is secure; once the pillars are placed it is almost impossible to reach inside.

Place a few leaves where the pillar is to be applied and put the pillar on. After the placing of the second pillar, you will secure the inner lattice to the pillars (fig. 12-14). With tip no. 7 add a small amount of Royal Icing to upper and lower parts of the pillars to support the lattice and put a small amount of icing along the sides of the lattice. Join the lattice to the pillars. Add the third pillar and join the next lattice, if it is part of the design. Do not put icing where the pillars are to be placed until you are ready to place them. The icing will dry and they will not adhere properly. Place pillars and lattice at the designated places; then continue the leaf design from the outer edge going in toward the center (between 12-11c and 12-11d).

If you want the lattice on the outside of the pillars (fig. 12-11a and 12-11b), place the leaves as previously mentioned but work in between one set of pillars. When 2 pillars are set, carefully apply the lattice (fig. 12-15). Icing sets very quickly so if lattice is placed immediately it will sink into the icing. Apply a small amount of icing to top and bottom of pillars and a small amount to the sides of the lattice and then join them. For an outside lattice, the pillars are plain.

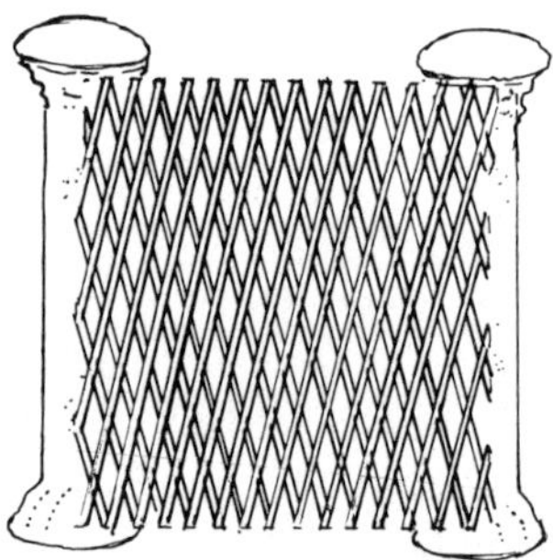

FIG. 12-14

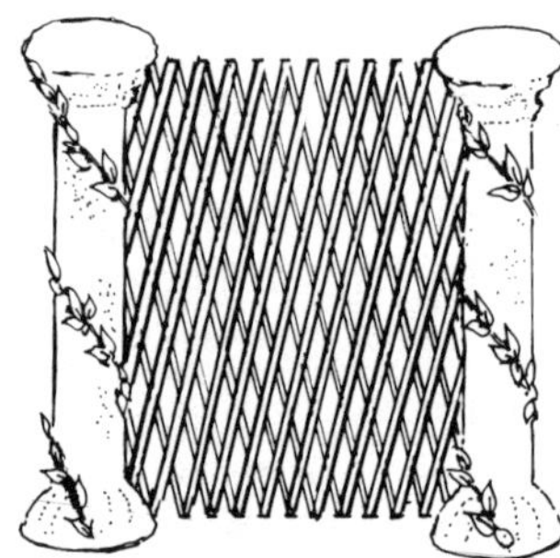

FIG. 12-15

On the other cardboard circle covered with foil, start from the outer edge of the unfinished side of the disk and apply leaves in a circle until the whole disk is completely covered. Immediately place over pillars. Check to make sure all pillars are at a right angle. Press lightly so that if you have any lattice it should be attached completely. If not, apply a few leaves to connect all pieces. By this time the joining of the lattice along the pillars has set. Add small leaves and grapes to complete the supports (fig. 12-16). Allow to set without placing anything on it for at least 2 to 3 days.

To add the cake with dividers to the wedding cake, follow steps as shown (fig. 12-17): 12-17a is cake, 12-17b foil, 12-17c dividers, 12-17d foil-covered corrugated cardboard, and 12-17e cake.

A wedding cake should never be transported with anything on top of the dividers. Additional cakes should be put in place after you arrive at your destination.

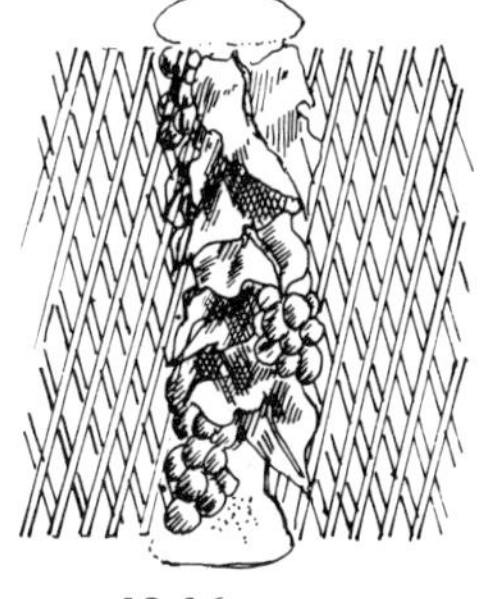

FIG. 12-16

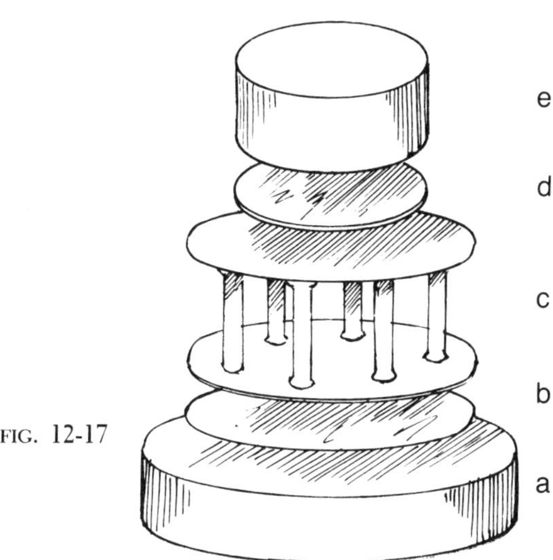

FIG. 12-17

Top of the Cake

The top layer of the wedding cake is often kept intact for the bride and groom. The top layer is sometimes their favorite cake; traditionally, it is a fruitcake with the almond-paste covering.

The fruitcake may be made 3 to 4 months in advance and left in a crock to ripen, wrapped in cheesecloth saturated with brandy. When the time comes to assemble and decorate the cake, process apricot jam with a little water in a blender until it forms a thick paste. Using a spatula, cover the fruitcake completely with a very thin coating of the jam. The jam coating is not necessary but it does help the almond paste adhere to the cake and keeps the paste and cake together when the cake is cut and served.

The following recipe for almond paste is also used for the making of marzipan.

ALMOND PASTE MIXTURE (MARZIPAN)

8 ozs. almond paste, room temperature
¼ cup egg whites or 2 medium egg whites
1 pound confectioner's sugar
½ teaspoon almond flavoring

Mix the almond paste and egg whites thoroughly, kneading it by hand. Mix in sugar a small amount at a time also by hand. Add flavoring and mix thoroughly. Keep refrigerated in an airtight container.

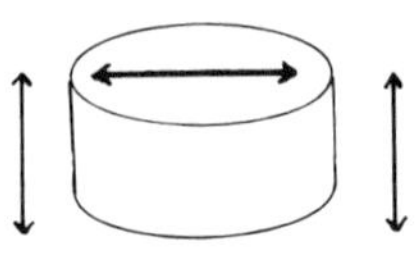

FIG. 12-18

Measure the top of your cake plus both sides (fig. 12-18). Take 2 pieces of waxed paper this size and sprinkle confectioner's sugar in between the paper and rub together. Place the almond paste mixture between the sugared waxed paper and roll it out to the thickness of pie crust. Remove waxed paper on one side and center the paste over the cake. Remove the top piece of waxed paper and mold the almond paste to the cake until it is smooth. Crumb and glaze as you would any other cake.

Another method of getting the almond paste on the cake that you might find easier is to apply the rolled-out paste in 2 sections. Place the bottom side of the pan that the cake was baked in onto the rolled-out paste and cut around it. Now measure the height of the baked cake and also the circumference (fig. 12-19). Roll out a long strip of almond paste using the waxed paper and sugar as previously mentioned. Using your kitchen tape measure or ruler, cut the paste to your measurements. A pattern can be made ahead of time and placed onto the rolled-out paste.

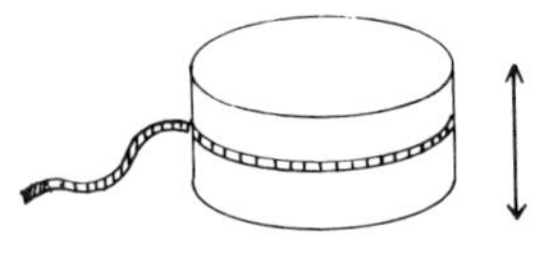

FIG. 12-19

Place the circle of almond paste on the cake and remove the waxed paper. For the side piece, cut off the extra waxed paper around the paste, leaving about a 1-inch border to make it easier for handling. Place the strip around the cake and slowly remove paper. It will stick to the thin layer of jam. Pinch the side seam and then the top and side together. With your fingertips, smooth out the paste. If necessary, dip your fingers in water to help smooth the seams. This cake is now ready for crumbing and glazing.

CHAPTER 13
Cake Tops

The *pièce de résistance* of any cake is the top decoration, the crowning glory, so to speak. I have always felt that everything on a cake should be edible including the top that is removed for the bride to keep forever. Basically the top decoration is made out of sugar, but to eliminate some of the weight a piece of Styrofoam is used for the mound in the center. Sugar may be used for this mound if you are going to place flowers directly on it. If toothpick or wire stems are used on the flowers, you have no choice but to use Styrofoam.

Sugar Molds

To make an interesting container for your arrangement of sugar flowers, you will need a mold. Look in your cabinet and see what you can find. Garage sales, flea markets, and florist shops are also excellent sources of different shapes. You may use any container that is larger at the top; however, it should not have any indentations or curved ridges. Fig. 13-1 shows some of the molds that I have accumulated.

To find the right-size mold for your cake, stack the pans you will be using for the cake. Place different molds on the top to find the size that pleases you (figs. 13-2 and 13-3). At this point you must be able to visualize the completed cake. When the cake is frosted and decorated, it will look much larger.

FIG. 13-1

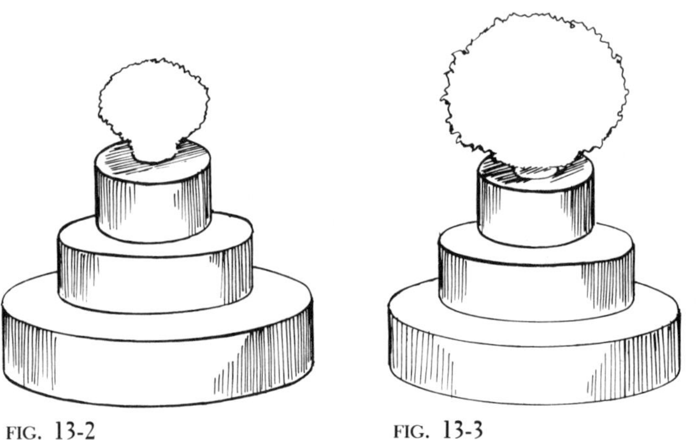

FIG. 13-2 FIG. 13-3

These cake tops or sugar ornaments will keep for many years if not exposed to dust or humidity. I have a friend, Daniel J. Foley, who wrote *Easter the World Over* in 1971. He still has a panorama egg that I made for that publication. It has been kept in a breakfront away from the bright sunlight. The colors have faded a little but it is still in good condition after all these years.

A glass dome or breakfront is ideal if it's not in direct sunlight. Under no circumstance should the cake tops be refrigerated or frozen.

Once you have decided on the proper cake top, check Chapter 11 for information on sugar molds. Make the sugar mold and let it set for 12 hours. If the air is humid, it might take longer. Turn the mold over when it's dry, and, with a teaspoon, scoop out the center leaving a very thick base and sides (fig. 13-4). This will lighten the mold. If the weight will not be a problem, do not bother scooping out the center.

FIG. 13-4

If the mold is to be decorated, it should be done at this time. All the decorations for the top of the cake must be done with Royal Icing in order to preserve it. To divide the mold for garlands, trace the top edge on a piece of waxed paper. Cut out the circle; fold in half and then in quarters marking 4 equal parts. If you have a large mold, fold the paper into sixths or eighths depending on the design of the cake. Notch the creases, unfold, and lightly place on the mold. Mark the mold at the notches with a little touch of icing and proceed. See Chapter 11 for garlands. Save this paper pattern to later determine the size of the top disk. The decorations on the sugar mold should be dry before you go on to the next step.

If your mold has a sugar base, place a ring of icing on the base and apply the mold. Do not add so much icing that it oozes out. Check carefully to make sure the mold is level on all sides (fig. 13-5). (A small level is often useful in cake decorating.) Let the mold dry thoroughly.

FIG. 13-5

To make wicker or basket weave on the mold, check Chapter 7 for detailed instructions. Before you start your weaving turn the sugar mold bowl over and center the sugar ring (base) on it. Using a pencil, mark the circle where they join (fig. 13-6). This gives you the line to start the weaving. If you cannot judge the center, measure up the same distance around the mold to make the circle (fig. 13-7). Start the weaving just slightly away from the pencil mark. Complete the weaving as soon as possible before the icing has a chance to set. Take your sugar ring base and center it over the mold (fig. 13-8). If the weave has started to set, place a little icing on the ring before attaching it. Push down to join the mold and base, and let dry before turning it over. If the frosting has set, be gentle when placing the base for the weaving will break.

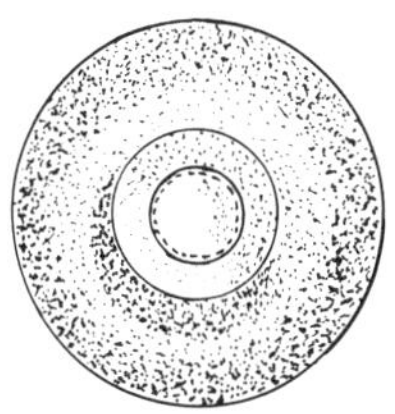

FIG. 13-6

To make the disk to support your sugar ornament, use the same waxed-paper pattern or the mold. Trace it ¼ to ⅜ inch larger all around onto cardboard. If the mold is large, make the cardboard ½ inch larger.

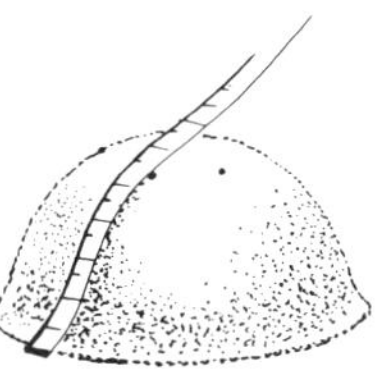

FIG. 13-7

Place this cardboard on a piece of waxed paper. Using tip no. 17, 18, or 19, depending on the size of disk, with Royal Icing, make a zigzag pattern around the edge with the design just cupping over the edge (fig. 13-9). Immediately invert the mold centering it on the zigzag. Press down and let set for about 12 hours until dry (fig. 13-10).

FIG. 13-8

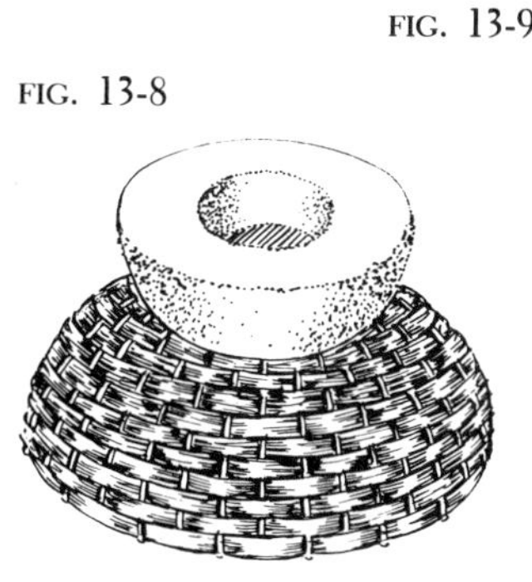

FIG. 13-9

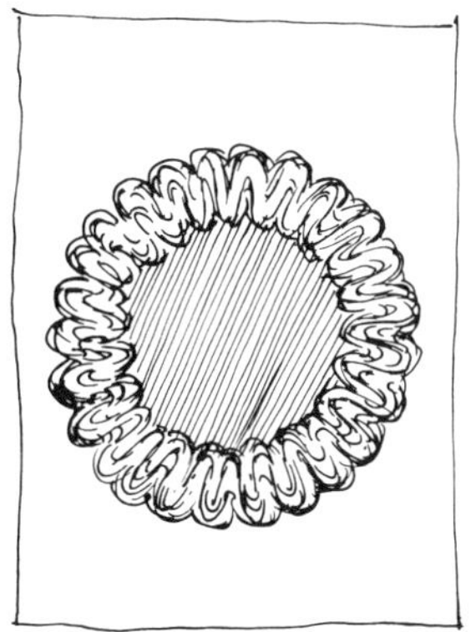

FIG. 13-10

Turn the mold right side up and remove waxed paper. The next step is to make a mound to raise the flowers. There are many different-size Styrofoam balls to choose from. Pick one that is in the proper proportion to your sugar base (figs. 13-11 and 13-12). Keep in mind that when the flowers are added, it will look much larger. If your disk is 5¾ inches, the ball should be 4 inches in diameter.

Using an electric or serrated knife, cut the Styrofoam ball in half. Put a small amount of icing in the center of the cardboard disk (fig. 13-12); fasten the flat side of the ball to the icing and let it set.

Plan about 75 flowers for a 4-inch half-ball. It is very difficult to estimate the number of flowers for a cake top, as each cake top is different.

If your urn is small or you cannot find a Styrofoam ball, use crinkled-up aluminum foil to make your mound (fig. 13-13).

Garlands or basket weave are not necessary on the molds (fig. 13-14). The Styrofoam ball can also be used without the corrugated disk (fig. 13-15). Without the disk, the decoration is smaller; therefore, you do not need as many flowers.

FIG. 13-11

FIG. 13-12

FIG. 13-13

FIG. 13-14

FIG. 13-15

Placing the Flowers

Remove all waxed paper from the flowers that you plan to use for the top ornament. If you intend to use daisies, make sure that all the centers have been put in place.

All equipment must be free of grease so that the arrangement will dry properly.

With tip no. 22 or 32 and white Royal Icing (green may be used), go around the edge of disk with a zigzag motion first; then cover the entire mound in the same manner (fig. 13-16).

Starting at the lower edge, apply your flowers, having some hanging over the edges and some higher than others. Add a few leaves (see Chapter 10) in between the flowers. Complete the flowers at the edge of the mold. The lowest row of flowers acts as a support for the arrangement. If the flowers start to slide off, your icing is too soft. At this point it is best to scoop it all off, thicken the icing, and start again.

I have had success supporting the first row of flowers with small glasses or jars until the flowers set (fig. 13-17).

FIG. 13-16

FIG. 13-17

Proceed filling in with flowers and leaves until the whole mound has been filled.

Voila. You have created a sugar sculpture to be treasured forever!

These beautiful arrangements should not be placed directly on the frosting on top of the cake. If the urn is large and heavy, cake supports of any type must be placed in the top layer of cake, especially if it is a carrot or chocolate cake.

With or without supports, a cardboard disk must be placed under the sculpture. Cut a disk about 1 inch larger than the base of your urn out of corrugated cardboard. Cut a piece of foil exactly the same size and another piece about 2 inches larger. Wrap the large piece of foil around the disk, and secure it under the edge of the foil with a little Royal Icing. Frost this side with Royal Icing; then glaze it with a hot spatula so that it is a smooth flat disk.

When the top layer of cake is frosted and glazed, the small circle of foil is centered on the top of the cake. If the frosting is dry, secure it with a dab of fresh frosting. Now place the frosted disk over it. It need not be completely dry as it will dry before the urn is placed on it. Make the same border around the disk to match the borders on the cake.

Cachepot

This cachepot is a container made of run sugar; you can make a cachepot in just about any size as long as it is in proportion to the cake. Draw a 4-inch square on a piece of paper (fig. 13-18); measure in ⅝ inch all around. Join the lines to complete the frame (fig. 13-18a). Measure in ½ inch from the inside corners and mark it (fig. 13-18b). Take a small round object (a nickel is excellent) and round off the corners (fig. 13-18c).

Using a no. 4 tip and Royal Icing, outline the frame (fig. 13-19) on both outside and inside edges. See Chapter 11 for instructions on run sugar. Use tip no. 8 for filling in the frame with run sugar. Make 5 or 6 frames. Always make extra in case of breakage. When making run sugar, air bubbles will form on the surface; sometimes they will break and disappear if pierced with a hatpin.

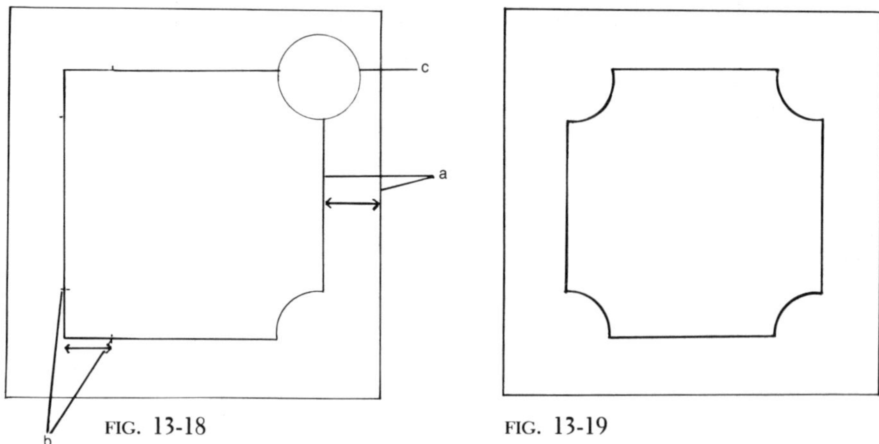

FIG. 13-18

FIG. 13-19

Outline a 4-inch square with the no. 4 tip and fill in with run sugar to make the base of the container.

Now you need to make backings for all your frames. The backings must be ⅛ inch smaller on all sides. If the frame is 4 inches square (fig. 13-20a), your backing will measure 3¾ inches high and 3¾ inches wide (fig. 13-20b). If you would like a different color for the backing, you would color your run sugar now. The outline for the run sugar can be white as it will be hidden behind the frames. Make 5 or 6 solid pieces of run sugar for the backings. Dry thoroughly.

The lattice for the frames may be in a diamond shape or square (fig. 13-20c). Chapter 11 gives detailed instructions on making lattices.

Before you make the lattice, all the frames must be thoroughly dry.

FIG. 13-20

FIG. 13-21

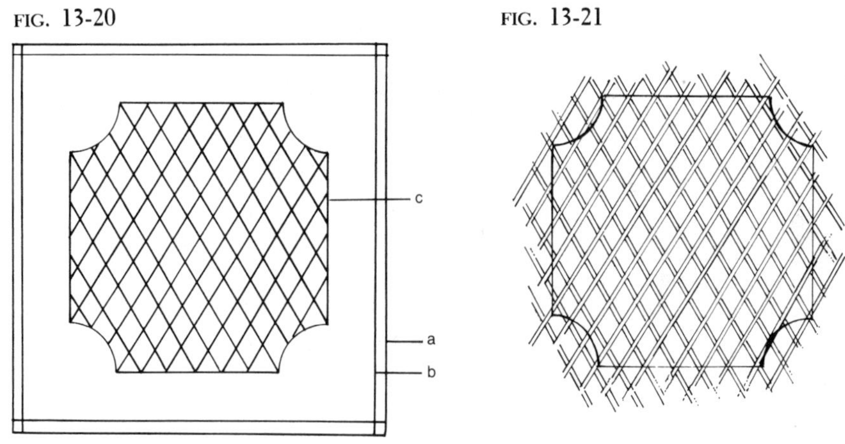

To remove the waxed paper, turn frames over onto a paper towel and gently pull off the paper. If any icing sticks to the paper, let the frames dry longer. Place a piece of waxed paper over the lattice pattern and make the lattice using tip no. 4, extending the lines at least ¼ inch beyond the inside of the frame. As soon as the lattice is completed, place the frame directly over the lattice and gently push down. Complete the 5 best frames. Let dry thoroughly before going on to the next step.

The lattice can also be made separately at the same time the frames are made. Let all the pieces dry completely before assembling. Turn the frames over with the wrong side facing up (waxed-paper side). Using tip no. 5 or 6 and Royal Icing (not run sugar), outline the inner edge of the frame about ¼ inch in (fig. 13-22). If the icing is too close to the edge, it will ooze out. Center the frame, with the waxed-paper side down, evenly on the lattice. Check the lattice to make sure all the pieces are going in the same direction before you add the backing.

FIG. 13-22

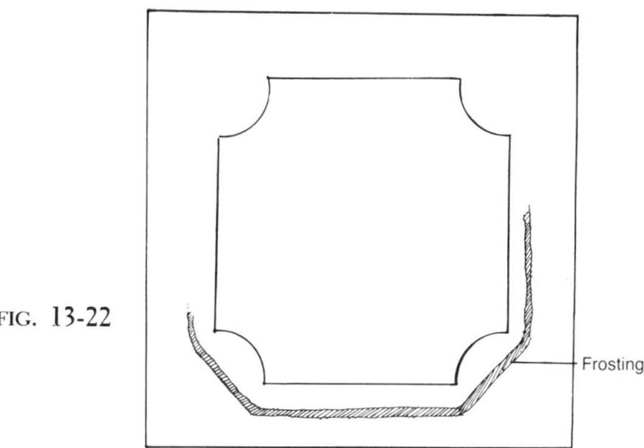

The backings may be attached at the same time the *dry* lattices and frames are joined. If the frame was attached to wet lattice, wait until it dries before attaching the backing. At the top edges, the backing and frame are even. The backing should be ⅛ inch smaller at the sides and the bottom should be ¼ inch shorter.

Attach the backing to the frame with Royal Icing as described for the dry lattice, except that the icing is piped between the inside and outside edges of the frame. When everything is completely dry, you can start assembling the container.

Tear off a 6-inch piece of waxed paper and place it on a cookie sheet or a flat tray. Place on it the 4-inch bottom piece of run sugar with the right side up. This piece may also be colored, but I prefer keeping it white. Remove waxed paper from a side piece. You have made 1 or 2 extras so that you can pick the best-looking pieces. You also have an extra in case one breaks.

An extra pair of hands for the next step is very helpful, but, with care, you can do it alone. With tip no. 8 or 9 and white Royal Icing, pipe around the 4-inch bottom square applying a little pressure. Take the side piece and place the bottom edge against one of the edges of the square. With your tip, pipe up the inner edge of the frame square with icing; then join the next frame. Connect all 4 sides to complete the container. The outside frames will not meet. Make sure the pot is square. Let dry completely before you pick it up or go on to the next step.

With the no. 4 or 5 tip and white Royal Icing, fill in the spaces at the top edges between the frames and the backings by going side to side with the tip. Wait a minute and smooth it out with your finger (like mortar between bricks). Complete all 4 corners. Let dry completely.

To place the footing on your cachepot, place your fingers on the corners and carefully turn it upside down. Fill in the spaces around the edges if there are any and smooth it off with your finger. Place a sugar cube at an angle at each corner. Put a dab of icing under each to make it stick and place another cube in the center to reinforce the base (fig. 13-23). If you turn the container over before the sugar cube dries completely, the cachepot will level itself.

Now for the trimming. I have tried many different designs on cachepots, but I have found the leaf and grape border to be the most outstanding.

First study the grapes in Chapter 11. Using tip no. 4 make at least 40 grape clusters, each ½ to ⅝ inch long. Wait until they dry to assemble.

With tip no. 67 and white Royal Icing, start at the lower edge of one corner of the pot and make a leaf in the center that pulls to the right; the next one pulls to the left, and so on until you reach the top edge. Insert about 5 grape clusters (fig. 13-24). Complete all corners.

The top edge is decorated the same way. Do not let the leaves or grapes hang beyond the inside of the frame. When the center arrangement is completed, it is lowered into the cachepot. At this point, the container is completed.

The inside measurement should be 4 × 4 inches. If you take a 5-inch Styrofoam ball and cut off about ½ inch on 4 sides, it should slide in easily (fig. 13-25). Do not force it in. If you think that the ball

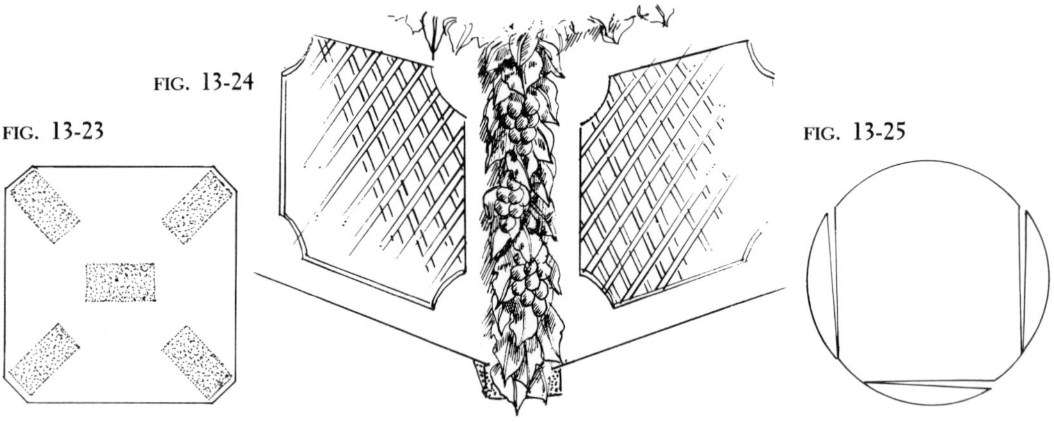

FIG. 13-23

FIG. 13-24

FIG. 13-25

should stand a little higher, take a piece of the Styrofoam that was cut off and place it in the base of the container (fig. 13-26). If you want the ball lower, cut a piece off the bottom.

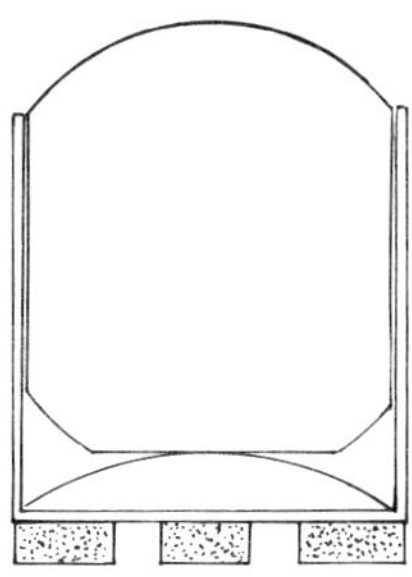

FIG. 13-26

Another method that might be easier for the novice is to take a block of Styrofoam 3½-inches square and as high as the container or to make a block of just pieces (fig. 13-27). Top it with a 4-inch half-ball. Whatever method you choose, you will need about 60 to 70 toothpick flowers (Chapters 3, 8, and 9), depending on the size of the flowers and about 4 dozen toothpick leaves (Chapter 10) to make the arrangement.

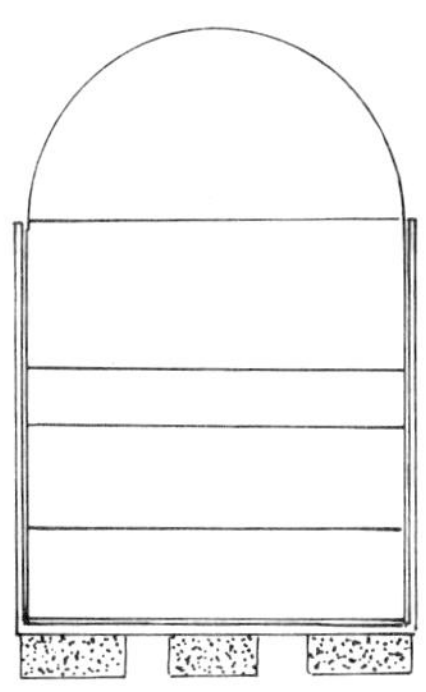

FIG. 13-27

Place the Styrofoam in a bowl or container to start your floral arrangement. You may cut off a little of the rounded base so that it will stand flat. I prefer frosting the top white, although it may be done in a soft green.

Start putting the toothpick flowers on the top first with leaves in between. Apply flowers on both sides at the same time using both hands (fig. 13-28) to keep the Styrofoam from moving around. The whole arrangement may be completed this way and then placed in the container. Place a little dab of Royal Icing on the Styrofoam block, if you are using one, so that the pieces of Styrofoam stick together. I prefer to work about halfway down the ball, then place it in the container, and fill in the corners with Royal Icing before arranging the remainder of the flowers and leaves.

The cachepot must stand on a cardboard base. The base may be round or square, but I prefer the square for the cachepot. Measure the base of the cachepot at the outside edges; each one seems to vary. If it is 4½-inches square, make the corrugated cardboard 6-inches square, ¾ inch bigger on all sides.

Cut out the cardboard and a piece of foil the same size. Cut another piece of foil about 1 inch larger on each side (8-inch square). Cover the cardboard with the larger piece of foil and secure the foil with a little Royal Icing under the edges. Frost this side with Royal Icing and glaze it with a hot spatula until it is smooth. Center the foil on top of the cake and place the glazed cardboard on top of the foil. The base may be outlined with grapes and leaves or whatever border is on the cake. Place cachepot on base for final touch.

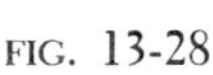

FIG. 13-28

Sugar Swans

Sugar swans supporting an urn of flowers makes a very decorative cake top. The swan molds are available through Maid of Scandinavia. See Chapter 11 for details on sugar molds. The urn may be made by using a bell-shaped candy dish or the individual salad ring with a cereal bowl. The sugar urn should be completely dry before going on to the next step. For the base, use a piece of Styrofoam, 8 inches round and 1 inch high.

Trace an 8-inch circle on a piece of aluminum foil and a piece of waxed paper. Cut them out. Take another piece of foil and wrap it over the Styrofoam disk, securing it with Royal Icing on the edges. Mold the foil in your hands tightly against the Styrofoam placing the smooth side down. Fold the waxed-paper circle in half, then in quarters. Notch the creases and place it on the Styrofoam. With tip no. 2 and white Royal Icing, mark the notches (fig. 13-29a). Mark the center with a cross and draw a circle around it the same size as the bottom of the sugar urn (fig. 13-29b). These 4 rectangles mark the placements for the swans (fig. 13-29c). At the notches, measure an area ⅝-inch wide and 1½ inches long. Place a 10-inch piece of waxed paper on a cookie sheet; place the 8-inch Styrofoam over it.

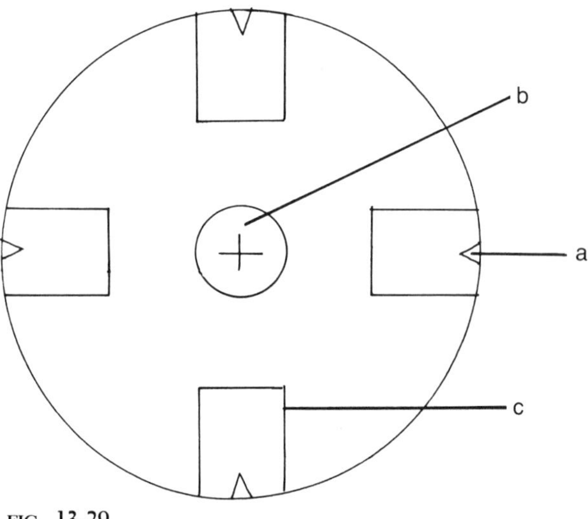

FIG. 13-29

Fill the white Royal Icing bag and place a no. 68 tip on the coupling. With the tip held approximately ½ inch up from the base, apply pressure and pull down to form the leaf (fig. 13-30). Fill in the sides and surface of the base with clusters of leaves except the sections marked for the urn (fig. 13-29b) and swans (fig. 13-29c). Fill in the center and place the urn. Do the notched areas and place the sugar swans one at a time. Done this way, the icing does not have a chance to set. When the icing is completely dry, the waxed paper will peel right off the bottom. I recommend using the swan decoration on a 10-inch cake. Place the 8-inch piece of foil, which was cut earlier, on top of the cake first.

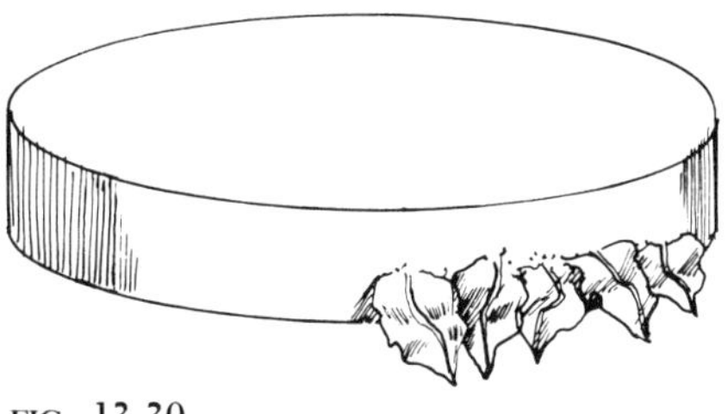

FIG. 13-30

Hovering Daisies

Cut 50 pieces of millinery wire, 2 to 5½ inches long. Make 80 to 100 white daisies in assorted sizes. Fill in the yellow centers and sprinkle the centers with sugar when the flowers are dry. Instructions for making daisies are in Chapter 9. When the centers have dried, remove the waxed paper and attach the wires as shown in Chapter 9.

Place an 8-inch pan over a piece of ¼-inch-thick Styrofoam, and cut around it with a paring knife. Trace this disk onto a piece of aluminum foil and cut it out. Cut another aluminum-foil circle 1 inch larger than the disk at the edge.

With tip no. 3 and Royal Icing, pipe in a zigzag motion around the edge of the Styrofoam disk that has been placed over the larger circle of foil. Pull the foil up over the icing and adhere it completely. Place the smooth side of this disk on a piece of waxed paper. With a no. 30 tip, pipe roping around the edge.

With the no. 30 tip and the Royal Icing, cover the entire surface of the disk to the roping with stars. Immediately arrange the wired daisies on the disk, starting in the center and working out to the edge. Between the wires, place some daisies directly on the icing. Add a few white leaves to complete your cake top.

PART III

Cakes of All Types

The following pages demonstrate a collection of cakes that I have created over the years. They range from a pair of western boots for the fiftieth birthday of a boot manufacturer to a towering gift-box cake tied with ribbons of Royal Icing to a small group of elegant confections designed expressly for the windows of Tiffany's in New York City, June of 1983. Naturally, wedding cakes occupy many pages; these splendid creations are crowned with floral sugar sculptures or romantic Victorian summer-houses. These fantasies in frosting represent the perfection of one's craft and many hours of work, often sustained only by a love of what one is doing.

Each cake is explained in detail in order that you might reproduce any one of them, but I believe that any art form should be the personal expression of the artist's talent, ability, and creativity. I hope that in studying these cakes you will be inspired to strike out and create wonderful and beautiful fantasies on your own. Nothing quite equals that inner glow of accomplishment when you stand back and say, "I did it my way."

CHAPTER 14

Very Elegant Cakes

White Lace Wedding Cake

SUPPLIES (serves 100)

Cakes:
- 16- × 12-inch oval
- 11½- × 8-inch oval

Top Ornament:
- sugar mold from an oval container, 7 × 3½ × 3¼ inches

Flowers:
- 80 toothpick flowers
- 150 small white roses
- 200 small daisies
- 100 cupped daisies
- 125 to 150 assorted flowers (roses, daisies, lilies, and stephanotis)

Leaves:
- 50 toothpick leaves
- 100 of assorted lengths

Grape Clusters:
- 225, ⅝ inch, using tip no. 4.
- 75, ¾ inch, using tip no. 5

Lattice Fans

The design of this cake came from the border of a piece of Venice lace. The cake is one of five cakes designed for the windows of Tiffany's on Fifth Avenue in New York City.

Make all the flowers and decorative pieces first. Make the cupped daisies with Royal Icing using tip no. 60 with petals ⅛ inch smaller than the nail.

Because many of the grape clusters (Chapter 11) have to be the same size, make patterns by drawing parallel lines ⅝ inch and ¾ inch apart (fig. 14-1). Place a piece of waxed paper over these and use as guides for the grapes.

FIG. 14-1

To make the top ornament, an oval sugar mold is needed that is in proportion to the cake (see Chapter 13 for details). Before you do anything to the sugar urn, trace the base on a piece of cardboard, being careful not to dirty the sugar. Keep this for the completion of the cake. Next turn the mold upside down, and with a little Royal Icing attach the sugar cube feet (fig. 14-2). Let set on its feet.

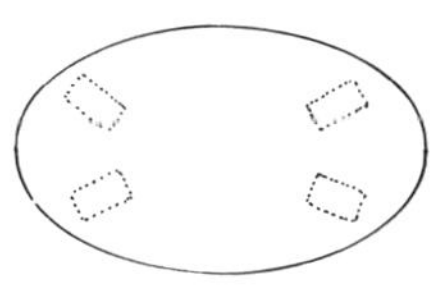

FIG. 14-2

Divide the mold into 6 equal parts and mark 6 arches around the mold (fig. 14-3). Make a line of Royal Icing following the outline of the arch using tip no. 16. Apply the flowers as shown in fig. 14-3. Use tip no. 65 for the leaves.

FIG. 14-3

Around the very top edge of the urn pipe a line of Royal Icing using tip no. 16. Place a grape cluster about every ½ inch, and then do a left-and-right leaf motif in between (fig. 14-4).

FIG. 14-4

With the toothpick flowers and leaves, complete the flower arrangement in the urn.

To make the lace fan motif for the sides of the tiers, use a no. 3 tip and Royal Icing for all the steps. Make the lattice (fig. 14-5a). Pipe a zigzag motion to fill in the space at the top of the lattice (fig. 14-5b). Starting at the center, place 3 grape clusters evenly spaced on one side (fig. 14-6). Put another 3 clusters on the other side (fig. 14-7). With a no. 3 tip make a mock roping to hide the insert of the grape clusters. Make the same roping on each side of the lattice.

To determine how many of these fans you need, measure around the pans you will be using and be sure to make extras. You can be more accurate when you measure the baked cake later. There should be a little space in between each fan to place a daisy (fig. 14-8).

Bake the cakes. If you do not have the correct size pan, read Chapter 6 on how to make an oval from a rectangular cake.

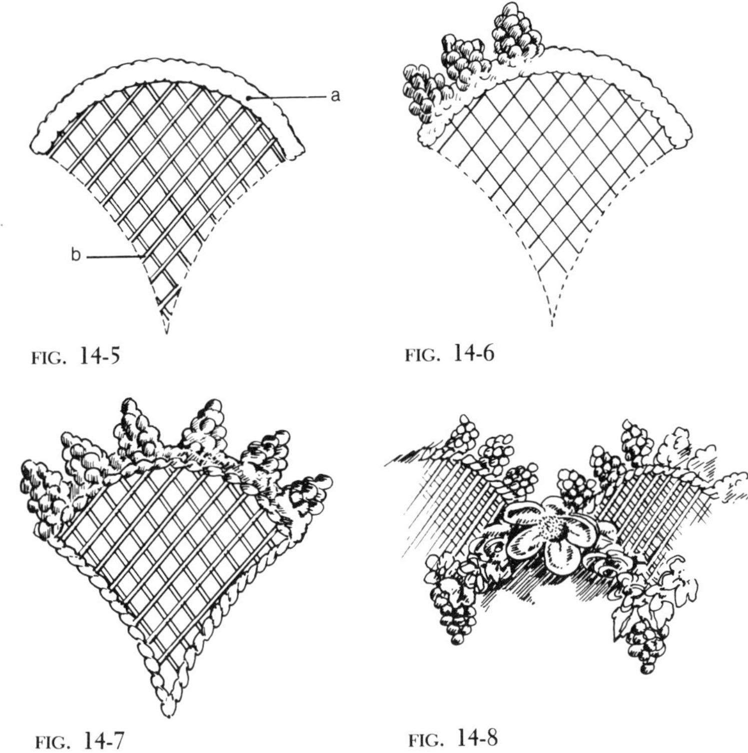

FIG. 14-5 FIG. 14-6

FIG. 14-7 FIG. 14-8

I would suggest putting supports in these cakes because of the weight of the urn and its arrangement.

After the cakes are cool, place them on Plexiglas and assemble as shown in Chapter 12 on wedding cakes.

When the cakes are glazed and dry, take a bag of Basic Frosting and tip no. 19 and make a slight zigzag line on the bases of both tiers of cake. Make an arrangement of white flowers and leaves.

With your tape measure, figure out the exact spacing for your lace fans on both tiers. If you can work quickly when placing them, they will not have a chance to set and you will be able to adjust them.

Start on the lower tier and apply a little Royal Icing with tip no. 7 at the three points of the fan (fig. 14-9). Place the 2 upper corners against

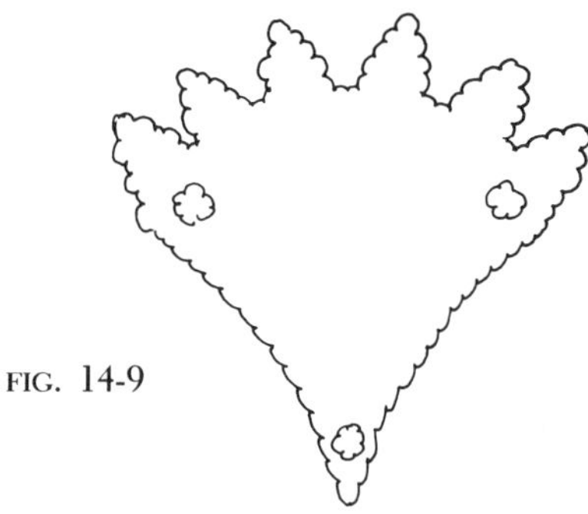
FIG. 14-9

the top edge of the cake. You must leave at least ½ to ¾ inch in between each fan (see photograph).

When this tier is completed, allow it to set before you place a beading around the inside against the fan using tip no. 7 and Royal Icing. The beading helps support the fans and makes a neater finish. This should be done before you place the fans on the top layer.

Attach the fans on the top layer in the same way. Do the beading behind the fans.

Using a no. 7 tip and Royal Icing, make a slight zigzag motion over the lower edge of the fans following the arch, and apply the roses, daisies, and grapes as shown in fig. 14-8.

The cake makes a very elegant presentation in the classic tradition of the white wedding cake.

New York Cake

SUPPLIES

(serves 230)

Cakes:
- one 14-inch octagonal, 3¾ inches high
- four 8-inch square, 4 inches high
- two 6-inch square, 4 inches high

Sugar Molds:
- 16 small bells
- 1 medium bell

Bows:
- 30 bows, 1 inch wide

Flowers:
- 300 assorted multicolored flowers
- 150 assorted white flowers
- 25 small cupped daisies
- 8 tiny five-petal flowers

Leaves:
- 50 white leaves
- 150 green leaves

Grape Clusters:
- 50 small, ½ inch long
- 75 medium, ⅝ inch long
- 12 large, ⅞ inch long

Dome:
- half of an 8-inch Styrofoam ball

Lattices:
- 10 French doors
- 10 lengths of fencing
- 10 framed lattices for base (includes 2 extra of each)

Read all instructions before you begin. The gazebo section of this cake is made over a Styrofoam shape so that the bride may cherish it forever.

Start by baking the 6- and 8-inch square cakes. When cooled, measure the sides of the 8-inch cake for the 10 frames and lattice (see Chapter 11). Make the frames as for the Cachepot in Chapter 13. Let set to dry. Keep the cakes frozen until it is time to assemble your masterpiece.

To make the dome, take an 8-inch Styrofoam ball and cut it in half; then glaze it by adding a little water to a small amount of Royal Icing. If the icing is too soft, it will just run off. Allow to dry completely.

To form the octagon structure under the dome, cut out three 8-inch octagonal Styrofoam pieces, each 2 inches high. Place a little Royal Icing in between each so that they will stay together. After they have dried, measure the octagon. Using these measurements, make the template (fig. 14-10) for the French doors on each side of the octagon. The type of lattice design used in the middle of the doors is based on individual preference. Frost the octagonal Styrofoam with whatever color Royal Icing the design requires. Place the template on a cookie sheet; then put a piece of waxed paper over it. With white Royal Icing in the bag, outline all the lines of your pattern with tip no. 4. Using white run sugar (see Chapter 11), fill in all areas with a no. 2 tip except the lattice work. Make 9 or 10 panels.

Make the bows (see Chapter 11) for the lower section by using tip no. 101S. You will need 16 of these 1-inch-wide bows for this cake. I suggest you make 30 as they break very easily.

Two sugar mold bells are used to form each of the covered urns shown on the fences. These bells should be made and dried slightly before scooping out some of the sugar in the center. When the small bells have dried, place a ring of Royal Icing using tip no. 13 and glue 2 bells together. Take two 1-teaspoon sugar cubes and glue the largest parts together. Make 8 sets.

Cut an octagonal piece of Styrofoam 12 inches wide and 1 inch high for the platform on which the gazebo will rest. Cut a piece of lightweight

FIG. 14-10

foil about 3 inches larger than the platform. Place a little Royal Icing around the edge of the foil, and center the platform on the foil. Smooth the excess foil up over the sides of the platform. The side completely covered with foil is the bottom. Frost the uncovered sides with a smooth layer of white Royal Icing.

Go around the sides of the platform with 2 horizontal lines using tip no. 48. Place a grape cluster at each corner of the octagonal platform. Place 3 other grape clusters evenly spaced between the corners (see photograph).

The dome must be completely dry before it is placed on a paper to outline the bottom. Cut out the circle ½ inch larger all around. Fold the cut-out paper in half, then in quarters, then in eighths. Be very accurate and notch the creases. Place this paper pattern on a cookie sheet with a piece of waxed paper over it. Center the dome on this pattern.

Because the dome is completely covered with Royal Icing, a pencil may be used to outline a design. If the dome were made of cake, it would be covered with Basic Frosting and toothpicks would be used for marking.

Take a fine pointed pencil and mark the notches at the base, dividing your dome into 8 equal parts. Measure across the dome to find the center on the top (fig. 14-11a). Make a circle about 1 inch in diameter around the center point (fig. 14-11x).

Place a tape measure at a dot on the base, measure up 3 inches, and mark it (fig. 14-11b). Then draw the line up to the circle. Do this all around at every mark on the base. You should have 8 lines. Now go in between each dot (fig. 14-11c) at the base and measure up 2¼ inches (fig. 14-11d). Make these measurements all around. With a pencil, join dots b and d to make the outline for a garland (fig. 14-12y). Use Royal Icing and place the no. 4 tip on the top circle (fig. 14-12x). Apply pressure holding your bag up, and let the icing follow the line e to f (fig. 14-11) all the way down to the base. Push in tip to break icing. Complete the 8 lines.

Starting at the top circle at the center of these lines, make another string using the no. 4 tip. Divide each section in half again and make another line. Keep doing this until the dome looks like fig. 14-13. This is ⅛ of the dome.

The frosting lines at the top of the dome are fairly close together. Placing the no. 4 tip at the garland line (fig. 14-13y), apply a line of Royal Icing going down to the base of the dome between each string of icing (fig. 14-13a).

To make the garland on the dome, see Chapter 11. Using tip nos. 13 and 14, form the garland over the pencil line (fig. 14-13y) on the dome. Where each garland meets, place a small cupped flower. With tip no. 19 go over the circle on the top of the dome (fig. 14-11x).

There are 8 lengths of fencing to go on the 12-inch octagonal Styrofoam base. Each section of fencing is connected by a sugar cube pedestal that

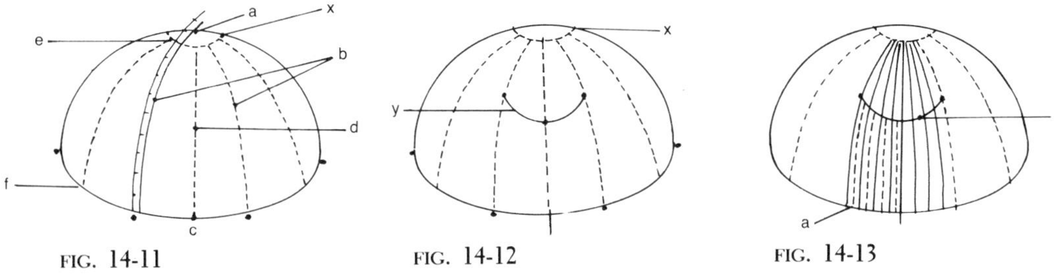

FIG. 14-11 FIG. 14-12 FIG. 14-13

supports the covered urn (2 bells attached together). Allowing for the sugar cube (which is ¾ inch), the fencing should be approximately 11¼ inches long. See Chapter 11 for further details on fencing.

To make the lattices that go on the 8-inch French doors, the run sugar must be completely dry. Make the lattices and immediately place run-sugar door frames on them. Complete all the panels. Make the lattices for the 8-inch frames on the lower tier of the cake in the same way as the French doors.

Attach the bells to the double sugar cubes by making a ring of Royal Icing with a no. 13 tip. Place them against a large book or a high pan for support until they dry.

On the French doors with a no. 4 tip and Royal Icing, make the string work to mark the center of the doors and also the line beneath the lattice above the bows. Attach the bows.

The decorative ornament on the top of the dome is made with a medium-size bell. This bell is divided into 4 sections for a garland. To make the garland use tip no. 13 (see Chapter 11). Go over the garland a second time to give it dimension. When this has dried, make an arrangement of daisies and leaves on the bell.

Attach the French doors to the 8-inch octagonal base of the dome by using tip no. 20 (see Chapter 11). Do one panel at a time by placing the icing on the angle corners of the base plus the upper and lower edge. Carefully remove waxed paper and place panel against icing. Push in evenly all around.

The urns on the sugar cubes may be completed by making a beading design at the joining of the 2 bells using tip no. 13. Using a little dab of icing attach a tiny five-petal flower made with a 59° tip to the top of the bell. Allow to dry completely before attaching them to the 12-inch Styrofoam platform.

The dome of the gazebo must sit on a cardboard disk approximately ½-inch larger than the dome itself. This creates an overhang that allows space on which to attach the flowers that outline the edge of the dome (see photograph).

On the 12-inch frosted platform, put Royal Icing in the center and place the 8-inch octagonal Styrofoam section with the French doors. Measure all sides to make sure that it is centered.

At the joining space between the French doors, using Royal Icing and a no. 67 tip, work upward from the base with a left-and-right leaf motif. Insert 3 or 4 grape clusters in between a few of the leaves. On a piece of waxed paper, place the corrugated cardboard disk, and with a no. 18 tip make a zigzag design about 1½ inches deep around the edge of the cardboard, letting the design go just to the edge. Do not let it touch the waxed paper. With the frosted side facing down, attach the cardboard to the top of the 8-inch octagonal Styrofoam. Center it and press down lightly on all the edges.

While this is setting, make a beading design on the 8-inch octagon to finish the area where it joins the 12-inch base.

With a little bit of Royal Icing on the cardboard disk, center the dome and push down gently. With Royal Icing and tip no. 22 do a zigzag of icing in the area between the edge of the dome and the edge of the cardboard disk. Make sure that the frosting extends a little over the edge of the disk so that none of the cardboard is showing. Now arrange the flowers and leaves that surround the dome.

Place a ring of icing with the no. 22 tip on the small circle at the top of the dome and place an arrangement of stephanotis with the base of the flowers pointing inwards. This circle of stephanotis makes a base for the sugar urn (inverted bell) that crowns the top of the pavilion. When the ring of stephanotis is dry, put icing in the cavity formed by the flowers and gently insert the urn. Make sure it is perfectly straight and do not touch it until it is thoroughly dry.

Now do a small and delicate leaf design on the top of the fences. Let dry.

Before you attach each small urn and fencing, place a beading using a no. 19 tip along the top edge, doing one side at a time of the 12-inch octagon.

To attach the sugar cube urn, center the urn on the corner of the 12-inch octagonal. Repeat this for the next corner, and then place a length of fencing into the beading. Attach the fence to the sugar cube urn with the same delicate leaf design used on top of the fence. Continue first beading the edge, then placing the urn and fencing all around the base. The gazebo section is now completed.

The assembling of the lower layer of the cake is done as shown in fig. 14-14. In order to make the octagonal shape, part of the 8-inch cake has

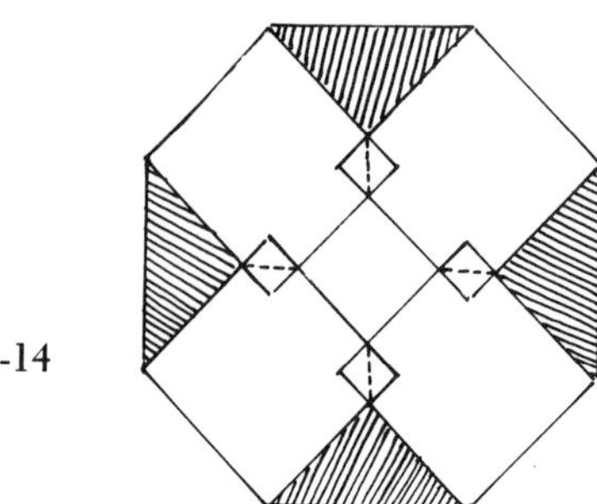

FIG. 14-14

to be trimmed. To determine how much, the 6-inch cakes are cut diagonally to fit in between the 8-inch cakes. Arrange these on your cake board or Plexiglas. Place a layer of frosting in between the joining of the cakes. Place a double layer of frosting on the inside and top of the cakes as this will be covered by the plywood support table (see Chapter 11). Place the 14-inch octagonal cake on the foil-covered plywood and crumb it.

After the icing has set on both layers, glaze them. If a showing of color under the lattice is desired, frost it now. When the frosting has set, apply the lattice frames on the lower cake using Royal Icing (see Chapter 11 on lattice).

Mark the placement of the garlands (see Chapter 11) on the 14-inch layer and apply them using Basic Frosting and tip nos. 22, 20, and 17. Make a double cascade in between the garlands inserting grape clusters at the top and at the bottom.

To join the lattice frames, use Royal Icing and a left-and-right leaf motif inserting a few grape clusters. Do the same leaf motif around the base of the cake.

Apply Basic Frosting on the top edge of both layers to complete the flower arrangements. Do not allow the Basic Frosting to touch the frames. If there is a space between the cake and the lattice frames, make a leaf motif to join them using Royal Icing and having some of the leaves extend over the lattice and frames.

After cake is delivered and arranged on the cake table, put the gazebo in place.

Wedgwood Cake

SUPPLIES (serves 200)

Cakes:
- 16-inch round
- 12-inch round
- 10-inch round
- 8-inch round

8 sugar mold pillars

Flowers:
- 250 stephanotis, blue and white
- 200 daisies, blue and white

Leaves:
- 200 white

Grape Clusters:
- 300, ⅜ to ¾ inches long

Lattice

Top Ornament:
- 5-inch Styrofoam ball

This cake was designed for the daughter of my husband's cousin who loved the color blue. A word of caution about the color blue in frosting. Be very careful that the blues you use are of a delicate pastel tone and that a lot of white decoration and detail is used with it. Otherwise, it can easily become too harsh.

Bake the 16-inch round cake, and, while it is cooling, make the sugar mold pillars for the divider (see Chapter 12 on assembling wedding cakes). The pillars will be placed between the 8- and 10-inch round cakes. This particular design has lattice on the outside of the pillars but only on every other section. (Finish the edging as though the lattice were all around.) In the center is a cluster of blue and white flowers.

Trace the 16-inch cake on a piece of paper and cut it out. The cake shrinks as it bakes so using the pan would not be as accurate. Fold the paper dividing it into 8 equal parts (fig. 14-15). Bear in mind that all the following measurements are given only as an example to explain the measuring procedure; each cake will differ.

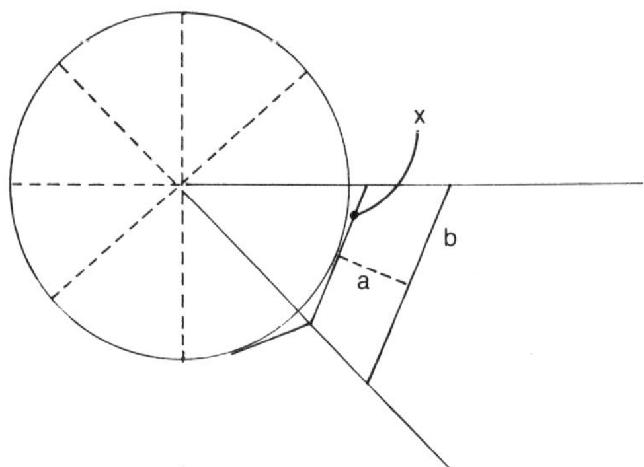

FIG. 14-15

To measure for the leaning lattice pattern, draw line x as shown in fig. 14-15. Line x will be about 6⅞ inches long and is the width of the top of the lattice. Find the center of line x and at that point add line a at a right angle measuring 1½ inches long. At the end of line a make another line parallel to line x to form line b. This line b will measure approximately 8½ inches long depending on the size of your cake, and will be the width of the base of the lattice pattern.

The height of the lattice will be about 4⅛ inches. This measurement is determined by placing a ruler 1½ inches away from the base of the 16-inch layer of cake (fig. 14-16a). Tilt the ruler to rest at the top of the cake (fig. 14-16b). The lattices will be placed at this angle.

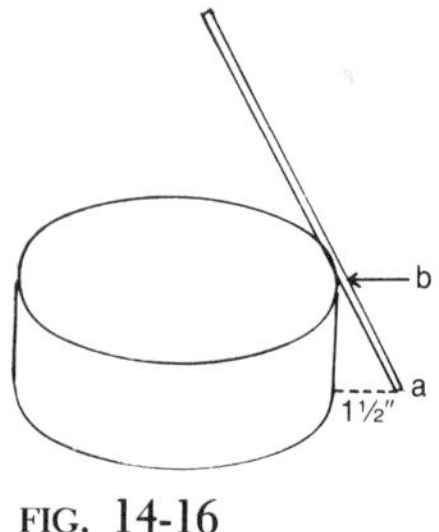

FIG. 14-16

Now that you have the measurements for the lattice pattern, make an outline on a piece of paper. Draw a line the length of line x (6⅞ inches long), which forms the top of the lattice. Find the center of this line and place a mark (fig. 14-17a). At this mark (a) make a right angle and measure 4⅛ inches (fig. 14-17b), which is the height of the lattice. At the base of line b, measure on each side of it 4¼ inches (fig. 14-17c), which is equivalent to line b in fig. 14-15 (8½ inches) and is the base of the lattice. Connect the ends of line (14-17x) and line (14-17c).

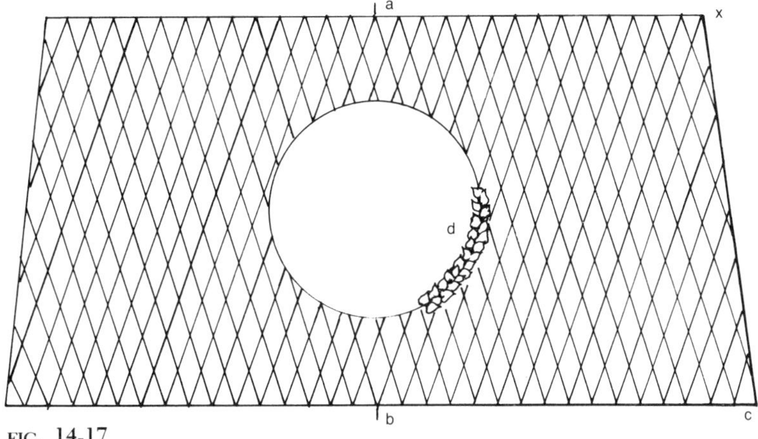

FIG. 14-17

In the center of your pattern draw a circle (fig. 14-17d). I used a glass that measured 2⅛ inches in diameter. Around this circle I planned an elongated diamond-shape lattice (check lattice in Chapter 11). Using a no. 4 tip, make the lines ¼ inch apart. When the lattice is completed, go around all of it with the no. 4 tip to reinforce the edge.

By the time you have completed all the lattice, the first one should be dry enough to outline the inner circle with the left-and-right leaf motif using Royal Icing and tip no. 65 (fig. 14-17d). Any icing that touches this lattice must be Royal.

With Royal Icing make the grape clusters using tip nos. 3, 4, and 5. Do not make any grape clusters larger than ¾ inch.

Make an assortment of blue and white stephanotis and daisies. Check the color blue. You will find that a small amount of Chefmaster royal blue paste color gives a very soft baby blue. The sky blue is more of a turquoise.

The white leaves may be made with nos. 67 and 68 tips. The top ornament is made with a 5-inch Styrofoam ball. See instructions on the Christmas Strawberry Wedding Cake (see Index) for detailed information. The container is done with basket weave instead of wicker. The flowers are attached in the same manner (see cake tops in Chapter 13).

To assemble the cake, read Chapter 12 and see fig. 12-17 for assembling a cake with sugar pillars.

Crumb your cakes all in white. Put the pillar dividers in place but do not attach the top layer until after the cake has been transported.

This top layer is treated almost as if a separate cake. When you measure the corrugated disk (use heavy cardboard), make it ¼ inch larger at the edge so that you may decorate the top cake completely. Place it on a cookie sheet with sides in order to transport it. When the time comes to place it on top of the cake, pick up the edges of the strong cardboard and center it on the cardboard that is on top of the pillars.

Glaze the cakes with blue icing. Avoid mixing the color too strong as a garish blue is not a good food color, and a strong color is difficult to glaze as it often streaks.

Start with the 8-inch top layer and using white Basic Frosting and tip no. 30, make a zigzag of frosting about ½ inch wide around the top edge of the cake and place your flowers. Push tip no. 3 under the flowers and have some stems coming down on the sides of the cake (fig. 14-18).

FIG. 14-18

They may end with either a no. 66 leaf, grape cluster, or small flower.

Decorate the top edges of the 10- and 12-inch cakes in the same way, being careful not to allow the Basic Frosting to touch the lattice.

The lattice on the lower layer is not difficult to do, but you must be careful. Take the paper pattern that was prepared earlier and cut out the center hole. Place the pattern on an angle at the base of the cake. Make sure that you are in line with the pillars (check the photograph). With a cake tester reach through the hole and mark the center on the cake. This is where you will put a small cluster of flowers; 2 stephanotis and a few leaves should fit just right. Remove the pattern and arrange the flowers. Hold the lattice panel in position to check the effect. Do the remaining arrangements and then set the lattices in place.

Before placing the real lattice it might be advisable to cut 8 of the lattice patterns out of light cardboard, tape them together, and place them around the cake. In this way you can check the size.

To apply the lattices, measure out 1½ inches with a ruler (fig. 14-16a). Make a line 1 inch long with a no. 16 tip and Royal Icing on the Plexiglas. Make a ¼-inch-wide zigzag on the top side edge of the cake with Royal Icing and no. 16 tip. Apply the lattice using the 1-inch line as support, and let the top center edge touch the cake. The cake is round so the two ends of the lattice will not touch the cake (fig. 14-15c). Make a small zigzag with the no. 16 tip just to join the lattice to the cake. Apply the lattice all around the cake having the lattices just touching one another. Make a very light elongated zigzag to join one lattice to another using tip no. 13 or 14.

If your measurements have been correct all should go well. Make sure each section of lattice is opposite the sugar pillars.

After the last piece of lattice has been put in place, the first one should be set. With tip no. 68 make a left-and-right leaf motif on the top and sides of the lattices, inserting grape clusters as you move along (see photograph). At the base of the lattices continue the left-and-right leaf motif all around the cake. Then, add a small arrangement of flowers at each of the 8 corners.

Once the cake has reached its destination, place the top layer on and center it over the pillars. With Royal Icing and tip no. 68, fill in with a leaf motif and grapes, starting from the cake and drawing the design over the edge of the cardboard.

Les Belles Fleurs

SUPPLIES

(serves 335)

Cakes:
- seven 8-inch round
- one 16-inch round
- one 12-inch round

Flowers:
- 500 to 600 assorted flowers in mauve, lavender, and white

Grape Clusters:
- 40, ¾ inch, using tip no. 5
- 25, ⅝ inch, using tip no. 4

Bows:
- 20 bows about 2½ inches wide, using tip no. 104

Sugar Molds:
- 1 large urn or candy dish for top
- 6 small round or oval sugar urns

For this cake, make all your decorations first and then bake the cakes.

When your cakes are baked and cooled, place 6 of the 8-inch cakes side by side on the Plexiglas to form a circle. Frost the tops and the insides of the cakes with a double thickness of frosting and crumb the outside circles.

Place your foil-covered plywood table in the center (see Chapter 12). Invert the 16-inch round cake and center it on the support table. Place a double layer of frosting on the top of this cake and crumb around the outside. Insert supports on this layer.

Center a 12-inch foil circle on the 16-inch frosted cake and place a foil-covered cardboard over it. Invert the 12-inch cake and place a double layer of frosting on the top and crumb the sides.

Follow the same process for the top layer except crumb the top and sides.

While the frosting is drying, make the garlands on the small sugar urns. Most of the time they do not show, but I still feel that it gives them a finished look. Before you apply any icing, trace the base of the mold on a piece of foil or parchment paper and cut out 6 to be used later. The small oval urn I use is about 4 × 2 inches and made of glass; I found it at a flea market. Whatever small containers you use, divide them up, depending on the size, and make a garland with a no. 13 tip. The oval one that I use is divided into 6 equal parts.

While your small urns are drying, get the large urn ready for its floral arrangement. Measure the base of the urn and make the Royal-Icing-covered cardboard disk that will be needed when the urn is placed on the top of the cake.

You may divide this large urn into 4 or 6 sections and make a garland on it to complement the cakes on the base. See Chapter 13 on cake tops. If you wish, small grapes may be placed between each swag. Let it dry thoroughly before you go on to the next step.

It is now time for the cake to be glazed and combed. In a small saucepan boil some water. I use the Ateco 3-sided comb, which I find to be the most successful for combing.

Starting at the top of the cake, place a layer of Basic Frosting a little heavier than you would use for a glaze around the outside. Using the comb, dip the finest ridge in boiling water in order to heat it. Wipe it quickly. At the lower edge of each tier and moving up, run the comb against the icing to make vertical ridges. Wipe after each stroke and heat again. Go all around the cake. Chapter 12 on assembling wedding cakes also discusses the decorating comb.

After you finish each layer, take your spatula and smooth out the top edges.

Glaze the tops of all the 8-inch cakes, including the 8-inch top tier.

You need not wait for the top glazing to dry on this cake before you divide it for the garlands. To divide the large cake, use the junctions between the 8-inch cakes at the base as your guide. Place a toothpick on the top edge of the 16-inch cake directly above the joining of two 8-inch cakes. Mark the 12- and 8-inch cakes directly above the toothpick in the 16-inch cake. Complete marking all tiers on the plywood table. See Chapter 11 on making garlands.

For garlands on the 8-inch cakes, measure around the cake that is extending out; then divide the amount in thirds in order to have evenly spaced garlands. Make the garlands on these 8-inch cakes.

After the garlands are completed, place a small amount of icing at each joining of the swags and attach a grape cluster, having the larger grapes at the lower edge.

If the top sugar urn is large and heavy, use cake supports under it.

Center a foil circle on the top layer and place the frosted disks over it. Make the border around this disk using tip no. 17 and Basic Frosting. Holding your bag at a 45-degree angle, make a mound of frosting about ⅝ inch long, release pressure, and pull away. Make other mounds completely around the disk. Insert tip no. 66 sideways in between each mound of icing and make a leaf to the left and another to the right. Repeat the same design between all mounds.

With tips nos. 19 and 67, make the same design around the top edge of all the 8-inch cakes on the Plexiglas and the lower edges of the 8- and 12-inch tiers.

On the lower edge of the 16-inch cake and at the bases of the 8-inch cakes on the Plexiglas, use tip no. 22 and make the same mound of frosting but larger. At the top and bottom edges of this mound, make the same mounds, having these mounds match in placement so that each indentation is the same. Make another mound with the biggest part in between each mound (fig. 14-19). Complete the design by making left and right leaves using a no. 68 tip.

FIG. 14-19

Place a zigzag of Basic Frosting on the top edge of the 12-inch cake and apply the flowers and leaves, leaving flat spaces to apply the bows. Also, do the same on the 16-inch cake and apply the flowers and leaves, keeping space for the bows.

At the top edge of the top tier, place a small cluster of flowers where the swags join. Place small clusters of flowers where the 8-inch cakes join at the base. Do not place too many so that they will not detract from your urns.

When the cake is all decorated, squeeze a small amount of Royal Icing in between the garlands on the 12- and 16-inch layers and attach the bows.

Now complete the urns. Because this is a large cake with a large base, I would put the corrugated cardboard disk over the sugar mold and place the Styrofoam half-ball on it. See Chapter 13 on cake tops for further details.

On your small urns, take a piece of lightweight foil about 12 × 6 inches, ball it up, and attach it to the sugar urn with a little Royal Icing. By the time you have completed the sixth urn the first is ready for a floral arrangement. Complete all of them.

Now take the small pieces of foil or parchment that were cut out earlier and place under the small urns. With a dab of icing, place it a little forward so that the flowers will not touch the back of the cake.

After you have done the top floral arrangement, your cake is completely decorated.

When the cake reaches its final destination, apply the sugar-mold urns.

The Victorian Wedding Cake

SUPPLIES (serves 240)

Cakes:
- one 14-inch octagonal
- two 12-inch octagonal, 7 inches high together
- two 8-inch octagonal, 6½ inches high together
- two 6-inch octagonal, 6 inches high together

Top Ornament:
- 6-inch Styrofoam ball, cut in half

Sugar Molds:
- 8 cherubs
- 8 small bells to be used as urns
- 2 medium bells, cut in half

24 sugar cubes for urn pedestals

4 monograms

4 bows with rounded streamers (make extras)

50 small birds (perched on fences)

Flowers:
- 200 to 300 small white flowers
- 50 lilies
- 50 stephanotis

Grape Clusters:
- 350 assorted, ½ to 1 inch long

Leaves:
- 100 white leaves

Bake all the cakes. Each tier may be baked in 2 or 3 layers. When you have a tier of cake that is more than 4 inches high, I suggest placing foil-covered cardboard in between the layers. It helps support the cake and makes it easier to cut. The cardboard disks are made exactly the same as the ones used in between each tier except that they are cut ¼-inch smaller than the cake. I would suggest using cake supports throughout the cake except the top 6-inch layer. Assemble each tier also on a cardboard disk with a double thickness of frosting in between the layers, but none on the sides. Measure the height and width of the octagonal side so you may make the pattern for the lattice. Place each tier in a separate plastic freezing bag and freeze until you are ready to assemble the complete cake.

To make a template for the lower layer, see detailed instructions on the Wedgwood Cake. Everything is done the same way except that this is run sugar instead of lattice (see photograph). Once the measurements have been taken, make the template. Outline the pattern plus the inner rectangle using a no. 4 tip. Use tip no. 8 for the run sugar. When it has completely dried, use tip no. 2 to do the lines and the polka dots and design it as shown in fig. 14-20 to fit the space.

Make all of your flowers, leaves, grape clusters, and birds (see Chapter 11). Monograms shown for the cake are an optional feature. If they are to be part of your design, they should be made now.

All lattice and string work is done with Royal Icing and a no. 4 tip. When you do the lattice work, make the lines going from left to right first, and then do the opposite direction to complete each piece. As each

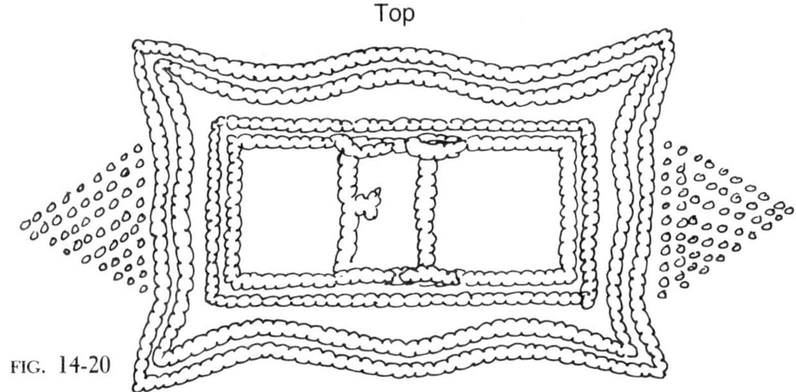

FIG. 14-20

panel is finished, outline it with a string border using tip no. 4 to reinforce each piece. Be sure to make extra lattices.

Mark each piece as you make it. It is difficult to tell them apart and marking them will save time.

Mark the plaques on the base of the 14-inch cake (fig. 14-20), lattices on the 12-inch tier (fig. 14-21), lattices on the 8-inch tier (fig. 14-22), lattices on the 6-inch tier (fig. 14-23), and the fencing (fig. 14-24) just above the plaques. Number each piece with Royal Icing as you make it.

FIG. 14-21 FIG. 14-22

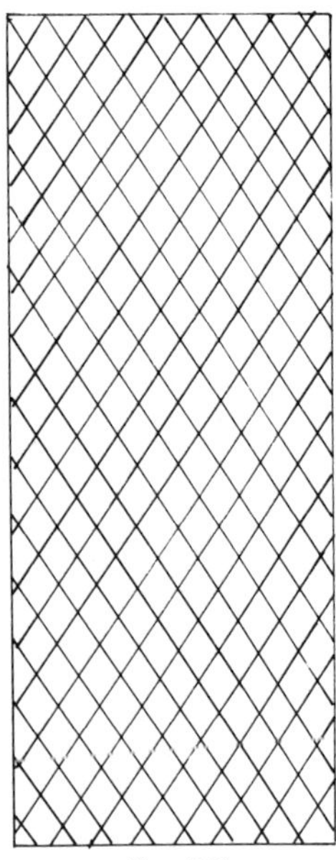

FIG. 14-23

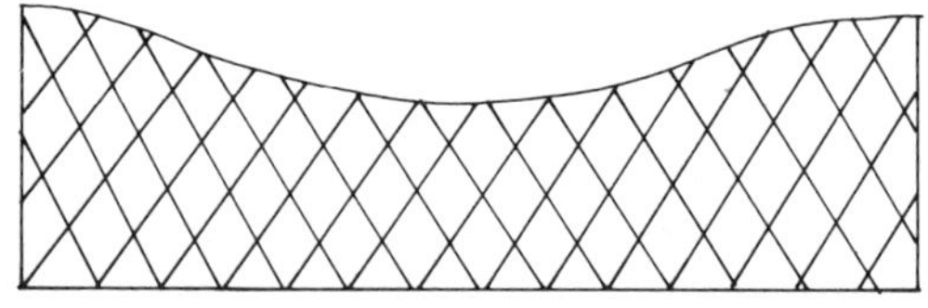

FIG. 14-24

When all the lattices are complete, start making the sugar molds (see Chapter 11).

Make 8 cherubs; molds are available from Maid of Scandinavia or your cake-decorating supply store. Make 10 small sugar-mold bells to be used as urns; when they have dried on the outside and are still soft on the inside, scoop some of the sugar out. This will lighten them for better balance. Once they have dried make the design (fig. 14-25) around the edge with a no. 2 tip.

Take 16 of the 1-teaspoon sugar cubes and place a small amount of Royal Icing on the larger side and attach 2 together, making 8. They will be the pedestals for the small urns between the fencing.

Make 2 medium-size bells out of sugar. With a fine piece of wire about 10 inches long and holding the ends tightly in each hand, cut the bells lengthwise in half. You will need 4 perfect halves. After they have dried, scoop a little sugar out to lighten them; then make the decorations around the top edge (fig. 14-26) using tip no. 2 and Royal Icing.

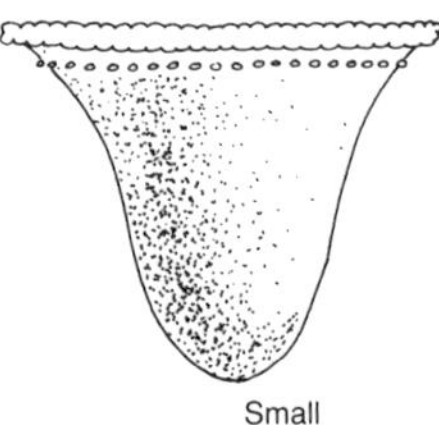

FIG. 14-25

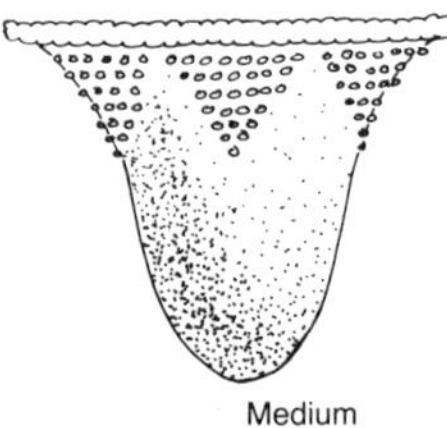

FIG. 14-26

For the wreath of flowers on the 12-inch octagonal that surrounds the monogram, make a circle about 3 inches in diameter. Measure up about 1½ inches from the base, and use a glass to mark a circle as a guide. The wreath is made with leaves, grape clusters, and small flowers.

For the pattern of the bow with curving streamers to go over the wreath, see Chapter 11. 4 bows are needed; make extras.

After the flowers have dried, place a small ball of aluminum foil in each of the small sugar urns. Cover it with frosting, and then fill it with an arrangement of flowers and leaves. When they are completely dried, attach the urns to the sugar cube pedestals with a ring of Royal Icing.

Use a 6-inch Styrofoam ball cut in half for the dome. Trace this dome on a piece of corrugated cardboard and cut it out ¼-inch larger all around. Glaze the dome with a small amount of Royal Icing mixed with a little bit of water. If the icing is too soft, it will just roll off. When the dome is completely dry, divide the dome into 8 equal sections: Place the dome over a 6-inch octagonal pan. Put the tape measure at one of the angles of the pan and go up over the top center of the dome down to the opposite side (fig. 14-27). With a sharp pencil mark along the tape measure with a dotted line. Complete marking the 8 sections of the dome. It is very important that the sections be all the same size. On each of these lines, measure down ½ inch from the center point and place a dot. Join the dots to form a circle (fig. 14-28). Make the lattice on each section; always start the lattice going from left to right. You do not need a pattern for this as it is done directly on the dome.

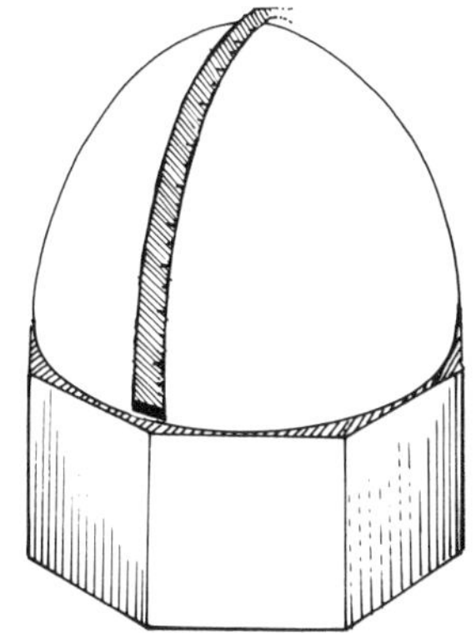

FIG. 14-27

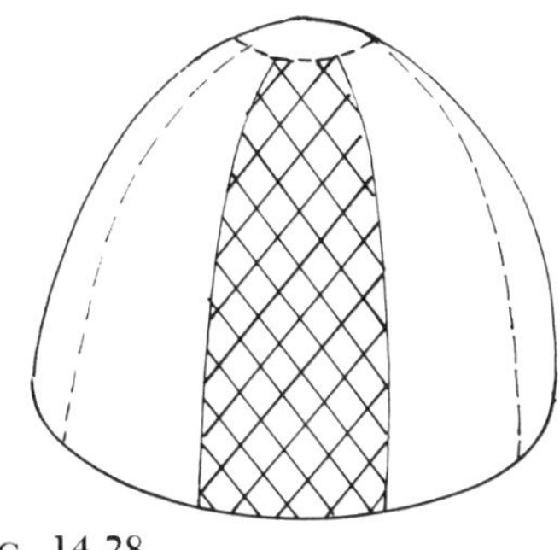

FIG. 14-28

Using Royal Icing and a no. 13 tip, pipe a C design on the inside arches and the tops of all fences (fig. 14-29). When all the decorative pieces have been done, remove the cakes from the freezer and assemble them (see Chapter 12). Crumb and glaze the cake with white Basic Frosting. Allow this to dry before applying the decorations.

FIG. 14-29

Read Chapter 11 on lattice and fencing before you begin to apply the lattice. See fig. 14-30 as a guide.

Start applying the lattice panels to the area under the dome first. With Royal Icing and a no. 19 tip, put a row of icing around each area attaching the lattice panels as you go along.

Attach the lattice arches on the 8-inch octagonal cake in the same way. When it has set, put the cherubs in place. To do this first attach one of the 1-teaspoon sugar cubes on end against the side of the cake with a bit of Royal Icing. Then, with another bit of icing, glue the cherub in place as if it were standing on the little sugar pedestal. You may place a few tiny flowers on the cherubs' heads as wreaths and place another in their hands.

Now attach the lattice sections on the 12-inch layer. These lattice arches go on every other panel. With a little Royal Icing, apply all the half urns under the lattice arches. After they have set, make a mound of Royal Icing and put a flower arrangement in each one.

On the alternating sides of the 12-inch tier, measure from the base about 1½ inches and place a round object (glass or cookie cutter) to mark the circle for a wreath of flowers under a bow with rounded streamers. Using a no. 14 tip make a circle of icing on which to arrange the flowers, grape clusters, and leaves. In the center, place a monogram if you wish. Over the top of the wreath place a Royal Icing bow with streamers.

On the bottom 14-inch tier apply the ornamental panels. The method of doing and applying these panels is similar to those at the base of the Wedgwood Cake.

At the bases of the 6-, 8-, and 12-inch tiers, make a beading design with tip no. 19 and Royal Icing.

Place the 6½-inch cardboard disk and foil on top of the cake. On this, center the dome making sure that the dividing lines on the dome match those dividing the panels on the cake.

The joining of the lattice on the dome and the 6-inch octagon must be covered. With Royal Icing and a no. 14 tip, start at the base of the 6-inch layer and make a C design (fig. 14-29) up to the top of the dome. At the area where the cardboard shows between dome and cake make a zigzag line of Royal Icing. Arrange small flowers, grape clusters, and leaves on both the C design and the zigzag line of frosting, thus framing in the domed pavilion, with a garland of flowers. Crown the dome with an arrangement of lilies in a ring facing outward (see photograph).

Pipe a row of Royal Icing using a no. 19 tip over the tops of the lattices on the 8-inch cake. Carefully attach the fencing to this icing and join each piece with a left-and-right leaf motif.

In order to set the row of fencing on the 12-inch octagon, the areas over the wreath and bow sections must be built out to match the area over the arched lattice. Using tip no. 19 make 2 rows of Royal Icing, one in front of the other. These 2 rows should fill in the space so that the fencing can run evenly from 1 arched lattice to the next. After the 2 rows are placed, come down the 2 sides about 1½ inches. Insert the triangular pieces of lattice. Now set the fencing in position on top of the double row of icing. Pipe a row of icing across the top of the arched lattice and set in the next piece of fencing. Place an upright sugar cube behind each fence joining to support the fencing as well as serve as the pedestal for the sugar urn. You must work carefully and quickly during this operation so that your rows of Royal Icing do not have a chance to set. See fig. 14-30.

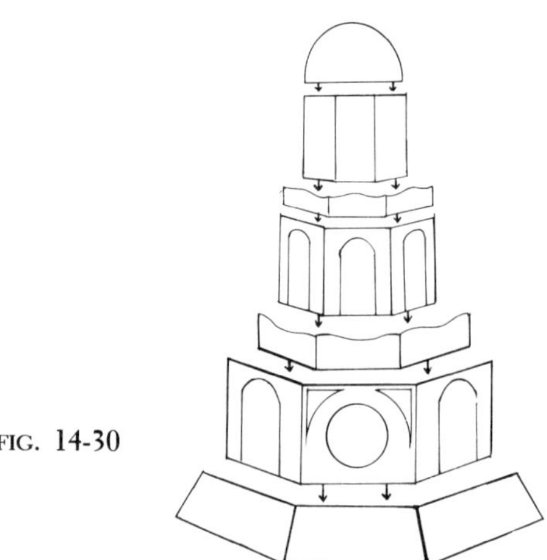

FIG. 14-30

Next apply the fencing pieces that stand in front of the half urns. Pipe a row of icing across the top of the sugar plaques and attach the fencing, which will almost touch the urn.

When the icing has set in the area over the bow, finish it with tiny C scrolls creating an arched effect. Complete the joining of the lattice by doing a zigzag of icing. On this zigzag place a cascade of flowers, leaves, and grape clusters. Pipe another zigzag of frosting across the top of the plaques below the wreath-bow motif and down the sides to the base. Make other lush arrangements of flowers, grape clusters, and leaves here, ending each with a lily.

For the final touch place dabs of icing on the fencing and perch little sugar birds here and there.

This cake was made as an exhibition piece for a special display of period bridal gowns at the Essex Institute in Salem, Massachusetts (the monogram is EI for the Institute). The cake was set next to a beautiful satin gown worn in 1885.

In order to create the Victorian mood, I did a great deal of research on the style and design of the period. During this research I came across a photograph of a wedding cake designed for the wedding of one of Queen Victoria's many children. Some of the features of that cake were incorporated into the design of this one—therefore, the title, Victorian Wedding Cake.

Octagonal Wedding Cake

SUPPLIES (Serves 400)

Cakes:
- eight 6-inch squares
- one 16-inch round
- one 12-inch octagon
- one 10-inch round
- one 8-inch round

Flowers:
- 450 assorted types and colors
- 80 to 100 toothpick flowers

Leaves:
- 60 to 70 toothpick leaves
- 200 leaves

Sugar Molds:
- 8 small round urns

Bows:
- 8 bows 1½ inches
- 4 bows 1¼ inches

Run sugar frames with lattice
8 frames without lattice

Grape Clusters:
- 400 to 500 all sizes

Top Ornament:
- octagonal Cachepot

Bake the 6-inch square and the 12-inch octagonal cakes first. The other cakes may be baked at the same time and frozen, or baked just before you start assembling the cake.

Measure the sides of the 12-inch octagon for the run-sugar panels; then place the cake in a well-sealed plastic bag and freeze.

Arrange the eight 6-inch square cakes on a 27-inch-square Plexiglas base, keeping the cakes at least 1 inch away from the edge. In order for them to fit it will be necessary to cut off a corner of each cake (fig. 14-31). It is important to place the cakes evenly in order to make the framing even. Measure for the 8 panels that are to be placed on the outer sides (fig. 14-31b) of these cakes. Then measure for the panels that will be placed on the 16 sides that join (fig. 14–31a). Bear in mind that these inner side panels must fit into the rather sharp groove formed by the placement of the cakes. These panels will therefore be narrower than the ones on the front. Having completed all your measurements, wrap and freeze the cakes.

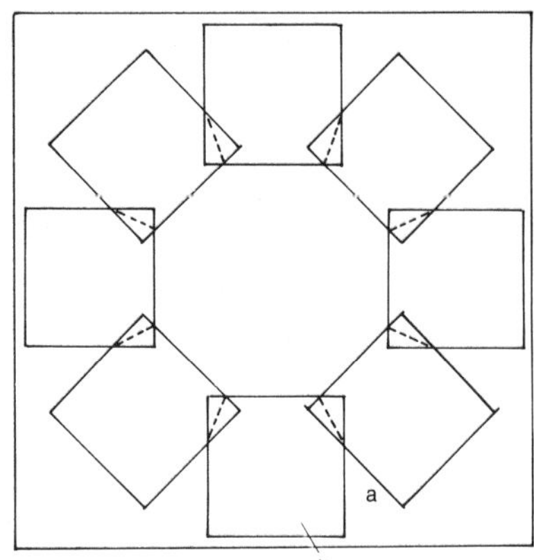

FIG. 14-31

To make the octagonal cachepot, I made each section 3¼ × 2 inches with framing ½ inch wide instead of ⅝ inch. Four of the sides are done with lattice, while the other 4 are plain run-sugar panels with appliqued bows. (See Chapter 11 on run sugar and Chapter 13 on the cachepot for further instruction. Complete the cachepot. Also, check the photograph for guidance.) Complete run-sugar framing.

Make the 1½-inch bows with Royal Icing using tip no. 103 and the 1¼-inch bows using tip no. 102. Be sure to make extras, especially of the smaller ones, as they break easily (see bows in Chapter 11).

On this cake there are 8 small sugar molds, 2⅜ inches in diameter and 1¼ inches high. However, any shape suitable for the area on top of the 6-inch cakes will do. To apply the garlands on these small urns, see Chapter 11 on garlands and Chapter 13 on cake tops.

Make an assortment of flowers and leaves referring to Chapters 3, 8, 9, and 10 for instructions. This cake shows 5-petal flowers along with lily and stephanotis shapes in an assortment of pastel colors, but naturally you may decorate to your own taste.

Make the lattice for the run-sugar frames on the base of the cake and for the cachepot.

While everything is drying, complete the baking of the cakes. By now everything is ready, and you can start building the cake.

On your board or Plexiglas base, place the 8 small square cakes (fig.

14-31). Put a small amount of frosting in between the joinings of the cakes. Frost the insides and about 2 inches over the top of the cakes with a double layer of frosting. Then crumb the remainder of the cakes. Two layers of frosting are always applied to a surface that will be covered by another cake. It is not necessary to glaze but make it as smooth as possible.

Center your support table inside the ring of cakes and invert the 16-inch round cake onto the table. Crumb the sides and place a double layer of frosting on the top. Center a 12-inch round piece of foil on it and then a foil-covered cardboard disk. Invert the 12-inch octagonal cake onto the cardboard. Crumb and continue building the cake with the 10-inch and 8-inch layers. This tall and heavy cake should have supports in every layer. In consideration of the distance that you may have to transport it, you might consider bringing the 2 top layers separately and joining them at your destination (see Chapter 12 on wedding cakes).

When the crumbing layer has set, start glazing from the top down. By the time you reach the lower layer, the top should be dry enough to start the garlands.

To measure for the garlands on cakes 8, 10, and 16 inches, use the octagonal cake as your guide. Mark them with toothpicks (see Chapter 11). Use Basic Frosting and tips nos. 16, 19, and 20 to make the swags and 19 and 20 for the drops in between. Insert a grape cluster into the base of each drop and also place a few grapes in each garland (see photograph).

While the garlands are setting, place a row of bamboo around the inside edge of the frames. To make the bamboo edging, place a no. 4 tip directly over the icing that was used to outline the run sugar. Holding your bag at a 45-degree angle and starting at the corner, apply pressure and pull away for about ⅜ inch so that the icing is smooth. Continue the same pressure and push the tip into the icing and pull out. Two short jerky motions will create the ridge you see in bamboo (fig. 14-32).

FIG. 14-32

Pull the icing so that it will be smooth and do the same motion again until you have gone completely around the inside of the framing. Do all the framing for the lower cakes and the 12-inch layer. Also, do the same detail on the pieces for the cachepot using tip no. 3.

By the time you have completed all the frames, the first one should be dry enough for you to start placing the frames on the cakes (see Chapter 11 for complete instructions). Apply all the framing on the 12-inch octagonal cake, and, when these are in place, attach the bows in the center with a spot of Royal Icing.

To complete these panels, do a leaf motif at the joining between the frames.

To attach the frames on the bottom cakes, set the front frames in place first. Using Royal Icing and tip no. 30, make a rectangular line of icing on the edge of the cake and attach the frame. These frames are placed first so that, should there be a fitting problem, an adjustment can be made by pushing the side frames further into the joining space. Next apply a line of Royal Icing on the side areas where the frames will be attached and the joining spot. When putting the side frames in place, if you can carefully push the 2 frames that meet in at the same time in a sort of wedge formation, the icing will stay on the back where it belongs. Should any icing ooze out, clean it up at once with a small dry paintbrush. Complete the placement of all frames.

By the time the last one is completed, the first frame should have set enough to do the left-and-right leaf motif with grape detail on all the corners. Do the same border around the top edge. If it is too difficult to do the leaf motif in the sharp narrow joining of the frames, omit it.

On the lower edge next to the Plexiglas, repeat the bamboo design using Royal Icing and tip no. 7. Do this around all the 6-inch cakes. Start in the sharp narrow joining and work out to the front of the cake. Then do the areas across the front of each frame.

Make a heavy left-and-right leaf border with Basic Frosting to completely cover the edge of the plywood support table.

Now arrange the flowers and leaves in the areas requiring them.

Now there remains only the placement of the large octagonal cachepot and the 8 small urns (do not forget the small foil disks for these). I would not suggest placing these until the cake has been set up on its table.

You have now scaled the heights of cake decorating. Congratulations!

Gift Box Cake

SUPPLIES (serves 350)

Cakes:
- two 16-inch round, about 8 inches high together
- two 12-inch octagonal, about 7½ inches high together
- two 8-inch octagonal, about 7 inches high together

Bow:
- large cluster

Ribbon:
- 10 flat (includes 2 extras)

Flowers:
- 220 tiny flat flowers, using tip no. 59°

All the cakes must be baked before you can determine the length of the ribbons. Make each tier in 2 or 3 layers with a cardboard and foil between each layer (see Victorian Wedding Cake). When you have cardboard disks dividing each layer, make them ¼ inch smaller than the cake, filling in the space between with Basic Frosting if necessary to make a smooth finish.

Assemble all 3 tiers, placing them one on top of the other with the frosting just under the foil so that they can be separated for freezing once the ribbon measurements have been determined.

To do this, measure the height of the top 2 tiers and add 1 inch (fig. 14-33). Freeze your cakes until you have the ribbons and bow completed and dried.

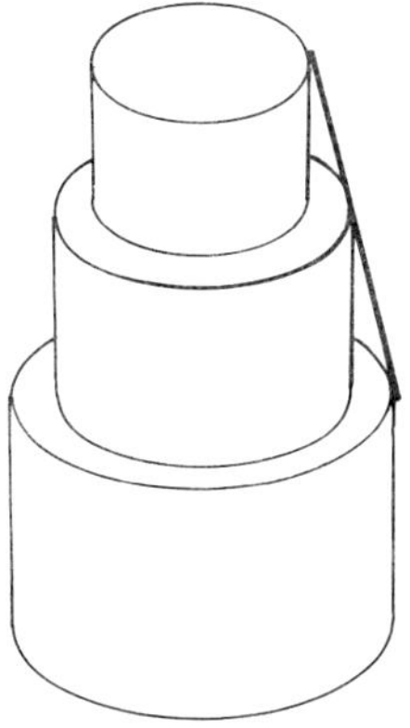

FIG. 14-33

To make the ribbons, draw a pattern the length of your measurement and 1⅜ inches wide. Take a bag of Royal Icing and tip no. 127. This tip is too large to use with a coupling so just insert it in a canvas bag.

Cut 10 pieces of waxed paper about 1 inch larger at each edge than the pattern, and place it on your pattern. These ribbons should be made on something that has an edge, such as a table, counter, or a cookie sheet with a lip. Before the ribbon is set to dry, pull the waxed paper over the edge of whatever surface you are working on to make a hook of about ½ inch (fig. 14-34). The hooks will be at the top of the cake. To make the ribbon, hold the bag at a 45-degree angle with the largest part of the tip against the pattern line to give it a heavy edge. Start at one end and pipe completely to the other end of the pattern in a continuous stroke. Reverse your pattern and do the same thing on the other line. The icing should overlap in the center. With a hot dry spatula, go over this seam to make it look like one smooth ribbon.

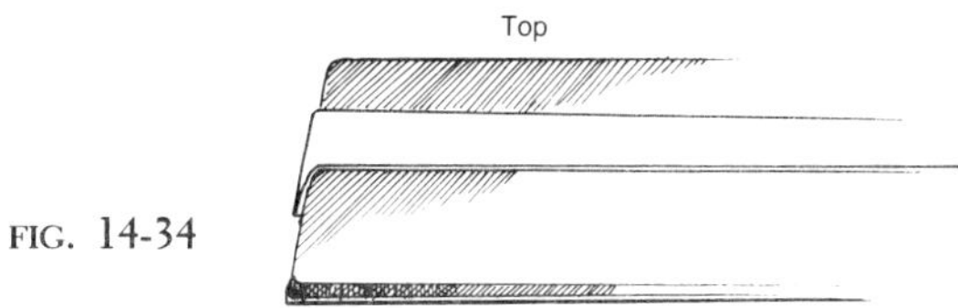

FIG. 14-34

While the ribbons are drying, make about 40 loops in the same color using tip no. 127 (see Chapter 11 on bow clusters for complete instructions). This bow may be completely assembled and dried before it is placed on the cake.

By this time the ribbons should be completely dried. Using tip no. 4 and the same color, make French dots on each side of the ribbon every ½ inch (fig. 14-35a).

Make the tiny 4- or 5-petal flowers using tip no. 59° or 101 (see Chapter 9 for further details) on waxed paper.

To do the embroidery on the ribbon, use soft green Royal Icing with tip nos. 2 and 65 for the stem and leaves (fig. 14-35b). While the icing is still soft, place the flowers. Stop the decorations about 1 inch from each of the ends; it will be continued after the ribbons have been attached to the cake.

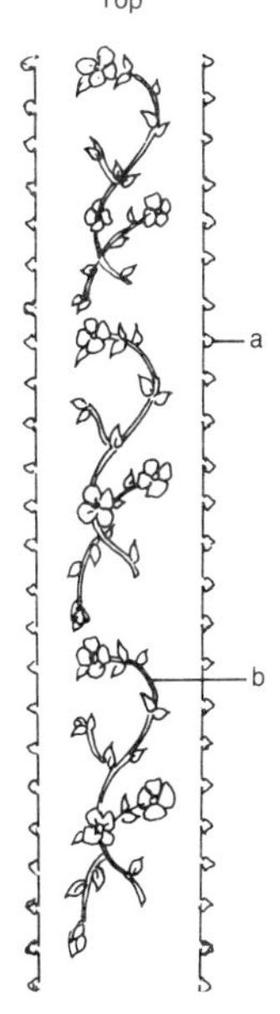

FIG. 14-35

Take the cakes out of the freezer and assemble them; crumb and glaze in white. Let the frosting set a little before starting the polka-dot design.

When making a dot of any type, do not let it come to a point but keep it rounded. The dots will take longer but the results are well worth the effort. The polka-dots, ribbons, and bows should all be the same color.

With the same color and with Royal Icing in the bag, place the no. 5 tip against the cake and squeeze lightly. Try it on something else first until you master the technique. You may place the dots in a haphazard arrangement or follow a pattern (fig. 14-36). Do this all over the cake.

Top

FIG. 14-36

Your cake is now ready for the ribbons. Carefully remove the waxed paper and place a little dab of icing on the top edge in the center of one of the octagon sides. Place another dab on the middle layer where the ribbon will touch and another dab where it touches the bottom layer. Carefully, very carefully, attach the ribbon.

By the time you have attached the last ribbon, the first has set enough for you to extend the ribbon. With the no. 127 tip and the same color Royal Icing as the ribbon, continue the ribbon in the same manner as before down to the base of the cake. When you complete one, smooth off the overlap in the icing with a hot spatula. It should look like one long ribbon.

Having completed the ribbons at the base, extend the ribbons across the top of the cake to meet in the center, keeping the center area flat.

Once these ribbons have set, apply the French-dot edging and complete the embroidery.

When all this is done, put a dab of frosting on top and attach the bow. Now your cake is all tied up in a neat package waiting to be delivered.

Swan Cake

SUPPLIES

(serves 300)

Cakes:
- two 14-inch square
- one 12-inch round
- one 8-inch round
- four 6-inch round
- three 6½ cup ring molds

Sugar Molds:
- 1 large from a cereal bowl
- 1 ring base for bowl
- 2 swans
- 4 small sugar urns

Grape Clusters:
- 40, ⅝ inch long
- 20, ¾ inch long

Flowers:
- 600 to 700

Leaves:
- 400 to 500

Lattice fencing:
- 12 to 16 pieces, 1⅛ inches high

Bake the 14-inch square cakes and place on a cooling rack. Whenever you have 2 cakes that will be joined together like these will be, cut off about ¼ inch, the brown part, on the sides that will be joined.

Place the cakes side by side and measure the length and width of the top of the cake. Divide the length by 4 or 5 to make your pattern for the fencing (see photograph). The width may be divided into 2 or 3 sections. Long pieces are harder to handle making it more likely that they will break. Make the lattice fencing using tip no. 4 (see Chapter 11 on lattice and fencing for further instructions).

To make the top ornament use a large cereal bowl and an individual ring mold (see Chapter 13 on cake tops). Make the swan arrangement on an 8-inch piece of corrugated cardboard, following the same instructions for sugar swans in Chapter 13. Starting from the outer edge, cover the surface with a leaf design using Royal Icing.

You will also need 2 sugar swans and 4 small sugar urns that will be placed on the 4 extended round cakes. The urns should measure about 2¼ inches wide and 1¼ inches high and will be filled with a floral arrangement. Do not forget to cut a small foil disk to place under each urn.

Make all the decorative pieces. For the ⅝-inch grape clusters, use tip no. 4 and for the larger ones, tip no. 5. Make the leaves using tips nos. 67 and 68.

The breathtaking look of this cake depends largely on the lavish use of flowers in a mass arrangement. Make plenty of flowers; if you have any left over, store them in a cardboard box in a cool place and use them on another cake.

On the top edge of the fencing pieces, make a mock roping using Royal Icing (fig. 14-37). Hold your bag at a 45-degree angle, place tip no. 4 at the top left side corner of the fence, and make a rotary motion. Complete all pieces.

FIG. 14-37

Bake and cool all the cakes; invert the two 14-inch-square cakes in the center of the Plexiglas or very strong board base. Place the 2 trimmed sections together. Frost the top of the cakes with a double layer of frosting and crumb the sides. Be sure to use cardboard dividers and supports (see Chapter 12 on assembling wedding cakes).

Place the 12-inch and 8-inch tiers on top and crumb. When dry, glaze the entire cake.

Put the 6-inch round corner cakes in place. For the best effect, these should be about 1 inch lower than the 14-inch-square cakes so cut the tops off evenly. In order for these cakes to fit into the main cake, cut out a quarter wedge (fig. 14-38). Fold a waxed-paper pattern as shown in Chapter 4 to get a precise cut. Crumb the inside of the wedge and push it into the corner of the main cake. Do this with all of your 6-inch round cakes.

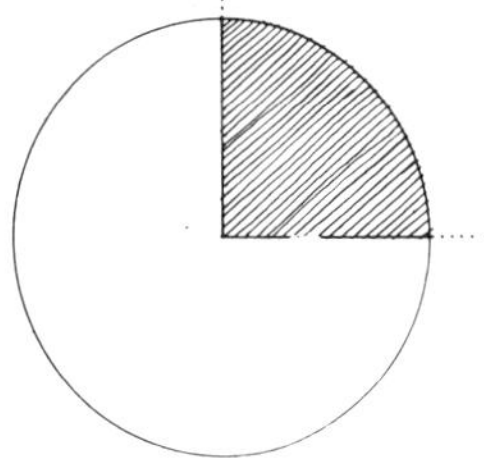
FIG. 14-38

Take the ring-mold cakes (if they are frozen they are sometimes easier to handle) and cut them in half (fig. 14-39). Crumb one completely and place it in position against the base of the cake. Place 2 half-ring molds next to each other on the long sides of the base, between the round cakes.

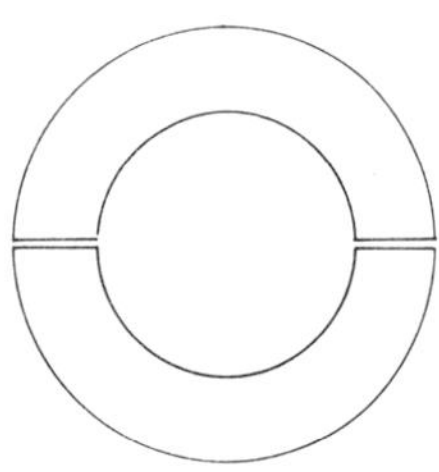

FIG. 14-39

One will be placed at each short end. Quickly crumb the next one and put in place. As these pieces thaw out they become difficult to handle so you should work as fast as possible. Keep all rings of cakes frozen until you are ready to crumb. Continue to work around the cake.

Make the garlands on the 2 top layers using tips nos. 19, 21, and 22 (see Chapter 11 and check the photograph). Make the drops one over the other, in between the swags with tip nos. 19 and 22. Then push a grape cluster in at the end.

On the ring molds at the base around the cake divide each into 3 sections and make the garlands with tips nos. 18 and 19. Use tip no. 19 for the drop in between the swags.

To make the lattice on the sides of the 6-inch round cakes, take the waxed-paper pattern with the quarter wedge cut out and fold it in half so that the cut section is together (fig. 14-40). Fold it twice more, dividing it into 8 equal parts (fig. 14-41). Place the paper on a 6-inch cake and put a toothpick at each crease. Put another toothpick directly below at the bottom of the cake next to the Plexiglas. Place the tip of your spatula at one lower toothpick and bring the blade at an angle to touch one upper toothpick that is to the left of the toothpick directly above the lower one. Do this at every toothpick and then reverse the line of the spatula going to the toothpicks to the right. This will make crosses for you to use as guidelines.

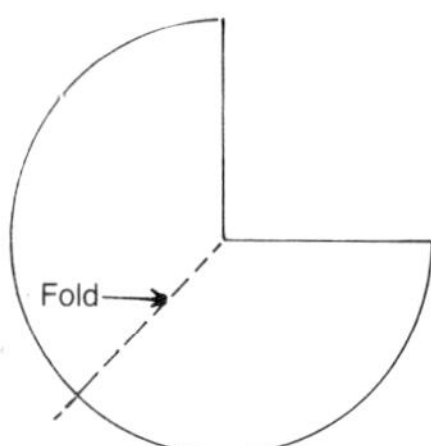

FIG. 14-40

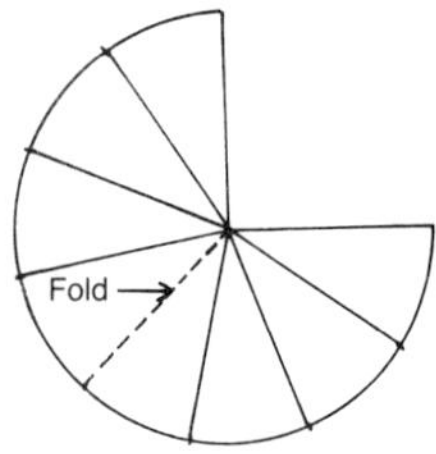

FIG. 14-41

Hold the bag of white Basic Frosting on an angle and place a no. 48 tip on a line at the Plexiglas; apply pressure and work up to the top of the cake. Do all of the lines going at this angle and then the lines going in the opposite direction. Do all 4 cakes.

On the top surface of the two 14-inch square cakes not covered by cake, make a sunburst design using tip no. 48. You can make guidelines with your spatula or a long knife. Each of the sections may be divided in half by marking the center of each line (fig. 14-42a), then in thirds (fig. 14-42b), or even in quarters, depending on the space available. On each one of these lines starting at the base of the round cake, pipe the frosting to cover it. The lines may touch one another at the base of the round cake but not at the outer edge.

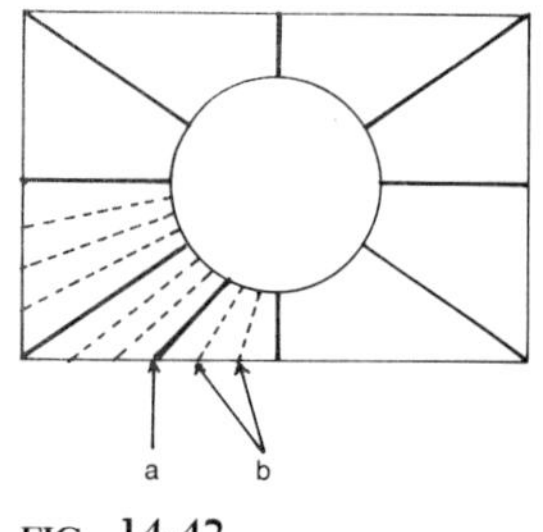

FIG. 14-42

With a no. 9 tip make a zigzag design of frosting on the top edge of the 12-inch round cake and arrange your flowers and leaves.

At the base of the 12-inch round cake do the same thing as well as on the top edges of the half-ring cakes.

At the top edge of the rectangular cake make a border for your fencing with Royal Icing. Hold the bag at a 25-degree angle, place tip no. 20 at a corner edge, and apply pressure to make a mound (fig. 14-43). Stop squeezing, pull about ½ inch, and make another mound. Keep doing

FIG. 14-43 

this until you reach the next corner. Take a section of fencing and place it in the center of the mound. Apply the fencing as quickly as possible because the Royal Icing sets very quickly. (For more information, read Chapter 11 on lattice and fencing.)

Continue placing the fencing on the other 3 sides of the cake. Pipe mock roping to join each section of the fencing. Using tip no. 66 and Royal Icing insert the tip sideways in between each mound and pull a leaf to the left and another to the right (fig. 14-43).

Make the same border with Basic Frosting on the top edge of the 6-inch round cakes, inserting a grape cluster where the cross design meets. Complete the border with the no. 67 tip.

Following the same design, make the final border on the lower base of the cake using tip nos. 21 and 68.

Apply the floral arrangement and the swans on a piece of foil on the top cake. With the arrangement in place surround it with a zigzag of frosting on which a ring of flowers and leaves may be placed.

Place a small urn on each of the 6-inch round cakes. Place a disk of parchment or foil under each.

Manchester Wedding Cake

SUPPLIES (serves 165)

Cakes:
- one 14-inch octagonal
- two 10-inch octagonal
- one 8-inch octagonal

Flowers:
- 450 four-petal flat daisies, using tip no. 59°
- 300 lilies, stephanotis, and daisies
- 50 to 60 cupped daisies, using tip no. 60

Leaves:
- 250, using tip nos. 67 and 68

Sugar Molds:
- bell-shaped urn
- ring mold for base

Scrolls:
- 10 pair (left and right) C-shaped scrolls

Lattice:
- 16 pieces, plus extra for breakage

This cake was designed as the centerpiece for an exhibit of historical wedding gowns at the Historical Society of Manchester, Massachusetts. It was based on design elements found in a cake-decorating book published at the turn of the century.

Bake all your cakes. Measure the height and width of the sides of your 14-inch cake for lattice. Assemble the 10-inch cakes by putting a double layer of frosting on top of the lower layer; then add foil and cardboard. Measure the height and width of the sides for the lattice. While these cakes are together, plan the size for the C-shaped scrolls that will be placed vertically at the 8 sides of the 10-inch cake. Make a pattern for this scroll (see the scrolls in Chapter 11 for guidance). Check the pattern next to the cake and judge its size and shape by eye. You will need 8, so make 10 for insurance. Separate the cakes and freeze them. Before the lattice panels are made, you must have the 450 flat petal daisies. Place a daisy at every other crossing of the wet lattice (see photograph) or create your own design.

Check Chapter 11 for lattice and fencing. These lattices are made in the same way except that you will be using a wider tip, no. 47. Make pieces of lattice to fit the sides of the 10- and 14-inch cakes with Royal Icing leaving a space between each line the width of the tip. This type of lattice is faster and easier to handle. Make all the panels and let them dry on a flat surface. Make all the lilies, stephanotis, and daisies. Also, make about 50 cupped daisies ⅛ inch smaller than the no. 7 nail using tip no. 60.

The sugar ornament for the top is made with a bell-like candy dish and an individual salad ring mold. See cake tops in Chapter 13 for complete instructions.

When all the decorative pieces are completed, start assembling the cake.

Place your cake on Plexiglas and assemble with cardboard and foil separators. Crumb and glaze with white Basic Frosting. Once it has set, make the garlands on the 8-inch octagonal cake using tip no. 20 and going over them twice. On the top edge of the octagon, make a rippling design using tip no. 67. To do this, hold the tip at a right angle to the cake, apply a great deal of pressure letting it ripple, and then pull. Make one leaf next to another on the ripple border (fig. 14-44).

FIG. 14-44 

Place a foil circle and a foil-covered cardboard disk that has been frosted with Royal Icing on top of the cake to support the sugar urn and flowers. Arrange a row of flowers on the edge of the cardboard. Place stephanotis where the garlands meet.

Place all the lattices on the cakes as explained in Chapter 11 on lattice and fencing.

Make a beading or bulblike design (fig. 14-45) around the base of the 8-inch cake using Basic Frosting and tip no. 9.

FIG. 14-45 

After the lattices have set, make an up-and-down leaf design (fig. 14-46) on the top edge of the 10-inch octagon in Royal Icing.

FIG. 14-46 

The border motif as shown in fig. 14-47 is applied to the base of the 10-inch octagon and the top and bottom of the 14-inch octagon. At the base of the 10-inch cake, using tip no. 18, and with a continuous rotary motion, make the little circular "doughnut." Make each one with two layers of frosting to give them a built-up appearance. Holding tip no. 66 sideways, pipe a leaf design, one facing left and one facing right, at the center of each circle (fig. 14-47). Make the same border on the lower

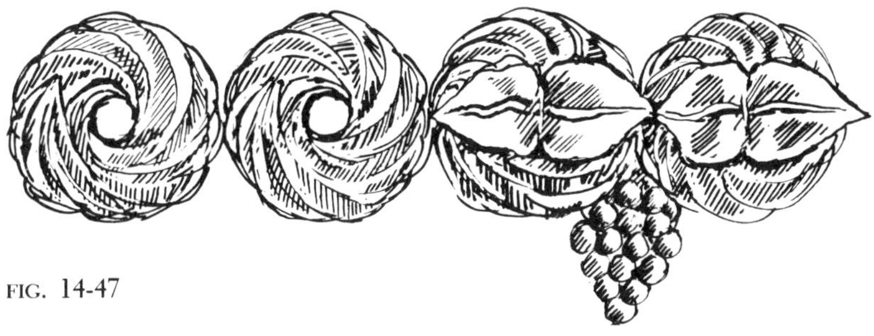

FIG. 14-47

edge of the lattice connecting the cake to the Plexiglas using tips nos. 20 and 68.

On the upper edge of the lowest tier at the angle of the sides, start a left-and-right leaf motif going to the base of the 10-inch octagon and continuing up to the top. This motif joins the lattices as well as helps to hold the C scrolls in place. As soon as you have one of these motifs done, apply the scroll as shown in the photograph. Finish all 8 edges making sure that the scrolls are straight.

At the top edge of the 10-inch octagon where the curl of the scroll is away from the lattice, place 3 stephanotis and a few leaves.

On the top edge of the lowest tier, make the same ring design but with a no. 20 tip. Insert one of the cupped daisies in each of these circles. Place a few stephanotis at the base of the C scroll as shown in the photograph.

To join the lattice on the lowest tier, make a left-and-right leaf motif starting at the base and moving up to the scroll. Tuck 2 or 3 stephanotis in the leaves at each edge. At the base on these angles make a cluster of 3 lilies.

On the Plexiglas, tuck grape clusters between all the circles (fig. 14-47). Place a little dab of frosting under each cluster to make it stick.

When the urn is placed on top, you will have a cake with the elegant traditional air of Edwardian charm.

Bride's Magazine Cake (February, 1983)

SUPPLIES (serves 325 to 350 people)

Cakes:
- eight 8-inch round, each 4 inches high
- one 16-inch round, 3¾ inches high, to be cut into an octagon
- one 10-inch octagonal, 3½ inches high

Sugar Molds:
- top bell-shaped urn (large candy dish)
- 8 oval urns, each about 3½ inches long (round may be used)

Scrolls:
- 10 pairs (left and right), includes 2 extra sets

Bows:
- 10 bows, 3½ inches wide with streamers, using tip no. 104, includes 2 extras
- 6 bows, 1½ inches wide with streamers, using tip no. 101, includes 2 extras

Grapes: variety; 200

Leaves:
- 60 to 70 toothpick leaves
- 150 assorted sizes and colors

Lattice:
- 10 each for the 16- and 10-inch octagons, includes 2 extra

Flowers: (all colors to taste)
- 180 toothpick flowers for cake top
- 250 assorted flowers for small urns
- 40 stephanotis
- 8 large lilies
- 24 small daisies
- 60 small 1-inch daisies
- 30 small ½- to ⅝-inch cupped daisies

Start by making all your flowers. Make the sugar molds (see Chapter 11). The length of the scrolls for this cake is 4½ inches but measure to make sure that it is the proper size for yours. Make 10 complete scrolls (see Chapter 11). Make the bows and grapes as shown in Chapter 11.

The 8-inch round cakes may be baked, cooled, and measured for height before being placed in a plastic bag to be frozen.

Before the lattice pieces can be made, the 10- and 16-inch cakes must be baked and measured. Before you use the 16-inch pan, trace it on a piece of newspaper and cut out the circle. Carefully fold the circle in half, then in quarters. Keeping the wedge shape, fold again so that you have 8 equal parts. Cut the paper on line A - B (fig. 14-48). The length of this line is the width of the bottom piece of lattice. Check this measurement against the cake as the cake shrinks when baked.

After the cake is baked and cooled, place this newspaper pattern over the 16-inch cake and cut off the excess cake to make an octagonal shape. Place your cake on a flat surface and measure the height. The lower cake lattice is about 6¼ × 3¾ inches. Note these are approximate measurements; yours should be determined by the size of your cake.

The 10-inch octagonal cake is baked, cooled, measured, and frozen in an airtight plastic bag. The lattice pieces for this cake measure about 4¼ × 3½ inches. Check Chapter 11 on lattice and fencing and make 10 lattice panels for each cake.

FIG. 14-48

Now that you have all the pieces completed, start preparing everything that can be done before you remove the cakes from the freezer.

Place garlands on the small urns and using tip no. 65 make a left-and-right leaf motif forming the swags. For more detailed information see Chapter 11. Complete garlands on all small sugar molds (fig. 14-49). Let dry.

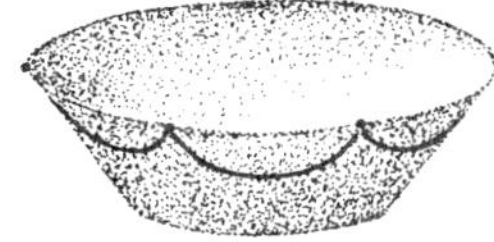

FIG. 14-49

Before you do anything on the top ornament, trace the ring base to make the corrugated disk for it to set on. See Chapter 12. Divide the top urn in 4 equal parts and make 4 low swags using tip no. 15. For more details see Chapter 11 on garlands. Make the garland, using tip no. 66. Place leaves, flowers, and small grapes on the garland. When all of this is dry, make the toothpick top floral arrangement (see Chapter 13). Make sure that you let it dry after each step. When your top is completed, place the small bows at the lower edges of the swags on the garland. Let it set in a dry place until you are ready to place it on the cake.

The garlands on the small urn should be dry, but before you decorate the top trace the base on a piece of paper. Using this pattern cut out 8 pieces of foil or parchment paper (grease-resistant paper) for the small urns to rest on the 8-inch round cakes.

To complete the tops on the small urns, choose the 8 most perfect molds. Take a piece of lightweight foil about 12 × 6 inches and crush it in your hands to form a mound. Place a little frosting on the sugar to hold the foil in place. By the time you have completed the eighth mold, the first has set enough to start the floral arrangement. Each urn takes approximately 25 flowers. Remove the waxed paper from all 25 flowers. At the same time peel the leaves from the waxed paper; place these in a small bowl so that they will be easier to handle.

With a no. 22 tip and Royal Icing, cover the foil completely. Start arranging the flowers around the base. The flowers at the base support the others. Insert leaves wherever you feel necessary.

Before you remove the 8-inch cakes from the freezer, trace the 8-inch pan on a piece of newspaper and cut out 8 circles.

Place a 27-inch-square Plexiglas on your working table and arrange the 8 newspaper circles evenly in a round staying at least 1 inch away from the edge of the glass (fig. 14-50). Where the paper overlaps, fold each of the patterns the same amount so that the cakes will be cut evenly.

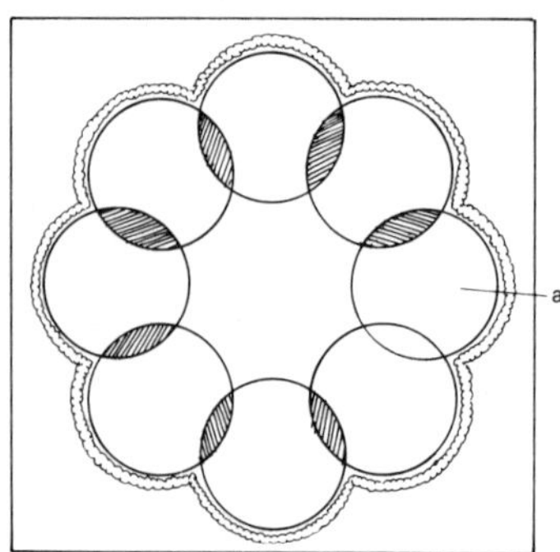

FIG. 14-50

With a no. 3 tip and any type of frosting outline the outside edge of the patterns (fig. 14-50a).

If you use a larger piece of Plexiglas, the cakes may be placed side by side evenly in a circle, but first measure the door opening through which you will be carrying the finished cake before purchasing the Plexiglas. Allow at least 1 inch of clearance.

Remove the newspapers from the glass and take the 8-inch cakes from the freezer. Use the 8-inch paper patterns to cut the cakes so that they will all fit just inside the guideline. The cakes will not fit directly on the guideline you made because the cakes bake smaller than the pan.

Crumb all these cakes with a thin layer of Basic Frosting on the outside edge of the cake and a double layer on the top and inside the cake ring.

Center a foil-covered plywood support table in the middle of the cakes (see Chapter 12).

Invert the 16-inch octagonal cake on the foil-covered plywood table. Frost the top with a double thickness of frosting; crumb the sides. This layer does not need supports.

Center a 10-inch round piece of foil on the 16-inch cake; place a foil-covered cardboard on top of it. Invert the 10-inch octagonal cake on the cardboard and crumb the top layer.

All cakes are now sealed to ensure freshness. Always crumb the cake with white Basic Frosting.

As soon as the frosting has set, frost the top of the 10-inch cake with white frosting; then glaze it with a hot spatula. When you are glazing a cake, always work from the top down.

Mix pink frosting, and glaze the sides of the 10- and 16-inch cakes. Place a very thin layer of white frosting on the tops of the 8-inch cakes that extend beyond the support table. Inasmuch as the frosting on these cakes will have dried, another thin layer should be applied in order to give them a good final glaze. Then glaze the sides.

While the frosting is drying, draw the outline for garlands on the 8-inch cakes. Measure to find the centers (fig. 14-51). If the glazing is not completely dry, do not allow ruler to touch. The tape measure may also be used, but then the cakes would have to completely dry (fig. 14-

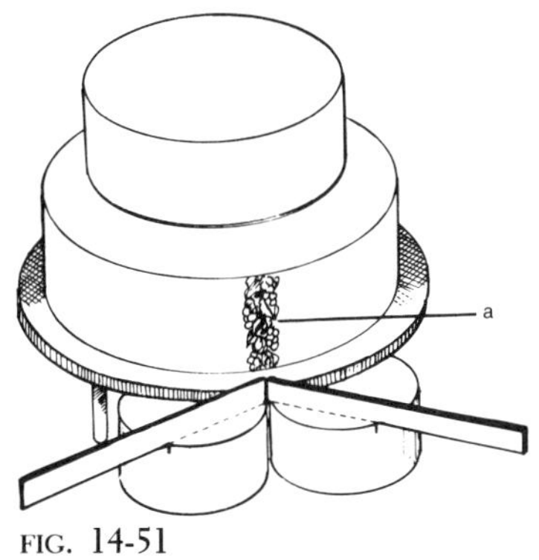

FIG. 14-51

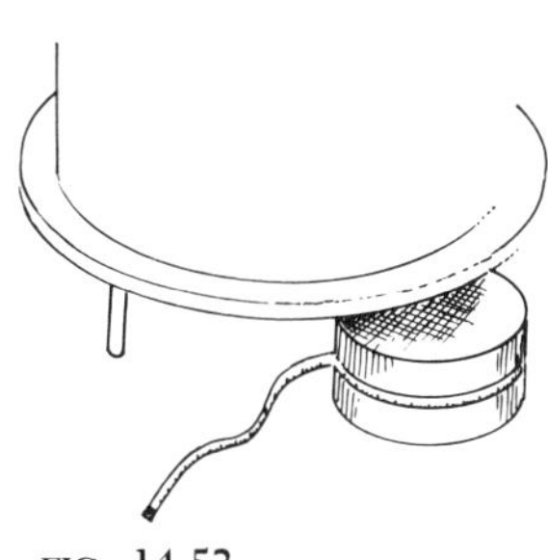

FIG. 14-52

52). The swag goes down about 2 inches; draw a guideline (fig. 14-53). See Chapter 11 on garlands. Using tip no. 22 and white Basic Frosting, make a swag one thickness of frosting. Cover swag with leaf tip no. 68; then insert a few flowers and grapes. Continue swags all around the 8-inch cakes.

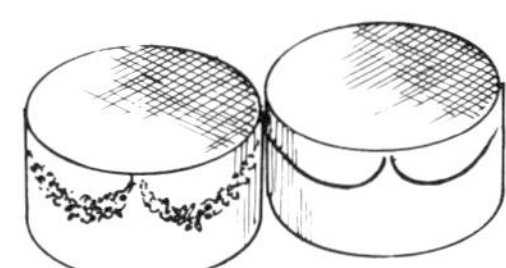

FIG. 14-53

To apply your lattice, see Chapter 11 on lattice and fencing. This must be done with Royal Icing. Complete the lattice on the 10- and 16-inch cakes and allow to dry. By the time you complete the second layer, the first is ready for the next step.

Using tip no. 19 and white Royal Icing, make the top and bottom edge borders on the 10-inch cake. Hold your bag at a 45-degree angle and squeeze to make a mound; pull away and make another mound. After you have completed one border, change to tip no. 67. Insert the tip sideways in between each mound, apply pressure, and pull one leaf to the right; then do one to the left (fig. 14-54).

FIG. 14-54

Now is the time to place the Royal Icing cardboard for the urn (see Chapter 13). If you have a soft-textured cake, put in cake supports so that the urn will not sink into the cake; then place the piece of cut foil and finally the cardboard glazed with Royal Icing. Make sure it is centered. Around the cardboard make the same border that you used around the cake, using tips nos. 19 and 67 with either Basic Frosting or Royal Icing.

Start at the top edge of the 16-inch octagon and, with a no. 67 tip and Royal Icing, make a left-and-right leaf design going to the bottom edge of the 10-inch octagon, then up to the top edge of the 10-inch octagon. Place the C scroll directly on top of this leaf design. Make the leaf design on the next edge and place the next scroll. If the scrolls have an up and down design, make sure they all match. Continue picking out the best scrolls to complete this design of your cake. On the top of the scroll where it joins the top layer of cake, place a small amount of Royal Icing and place 2 small daisies back to back. You may add a couple of small green leaves as well.

With tips nos. 19 and 67 and white Royal Icing, go around the top and bottom edges of the 16-inch octagon doing the same border as is on the 10-inch octagon (fig. 14-54).

Pipe a left-and-right leaf border starting at the base of the 16-inch octagon and using Royal Icing and a no. 67 tip. Complete it by inserting a few clusters of grapes over each joining (fig. 14-51a).

Using tips nos. 19 and 67 with Basic Frosting in your bag, make the same border as the mound design on the top edge of the 8-inch cakes. If using doilies they should be placed before you make the bottom border. See Chapter 12 on assembling wedding cakes for further details.

Do the same type border but heavier on the base of the 8-inch cakes with Basic Frosting and tips nos. 32 and 68.

Where the 8-inch cakes meet, place 2 pink stephanotis in the lower corners, one on each side. Do not add leaves here; you do not want any color to detract from your urns.

On each top of an extended 8-inch cake, place a little dab of frosting more forward than center so that your floral urns will not touch the lattice. Secure the piece of foil or parchment paper that will protect the sugar urn on the frosting. Place the urns on the cakes when you reach your destination. For a final touch attach a 3½-inch bow with a dab of Royal Icing to the joining of swags on each 8-inch cake.

French Terrace Cake

SUPPLIES

(serves 200)

Cakes:
- one 14-inch square
- one 12-inch round
- one 10-inch square
- two 8-inch round

Bows: 20 bows, 1¼ inches wide, includes extras

Flowers:
- 175 to 200 small flowers
- approximately 100 daisies
- 50 stephanotis
- 60 to 80 toothpick flowers

Leaves:
- 50 toothpick leaves

Top Ornament:
- sugar mold from large cereal bowl
- sugar ring base

Lattice Fencing

First bake your 10- and 8-inch cakes. While waiting for them to cool, make all of your flowers and leaves.

Follow the complete instructions for making the top ornament in Chapter 13. For the garland design on the bowl, use tip no. 67. With Royal Icing, pipe a leaf and then another one starting a little ahead of the first one and ending a little shorter (fig. 14-55). Continue until you have completed the garland. Tuck a few small flowers in between the leaves and a stephanotis where the garland reaches the rim of the bowl. The garlands on the cake will be done the same way using Basic Frosting.

FIG. 14-55

When your cakes have cooled, cut one of the 8-inch round cakes in half and place the halves against the sides of the 10-inch square (fig. 14-56). Place your tape measure against the top ridge of the half-round cake (the dotted line, fig. 14-56a) where the fence will be. Let us say that it measures 12½ inches. (Do not take these measurements as fact for each cake varies.) Divide the measurement by 4 for 4 sections of fencing. If the measurement is 12½ inches, then each section of fencing will be 3⅛ inches long. Measure both half circles for they may not be the same.

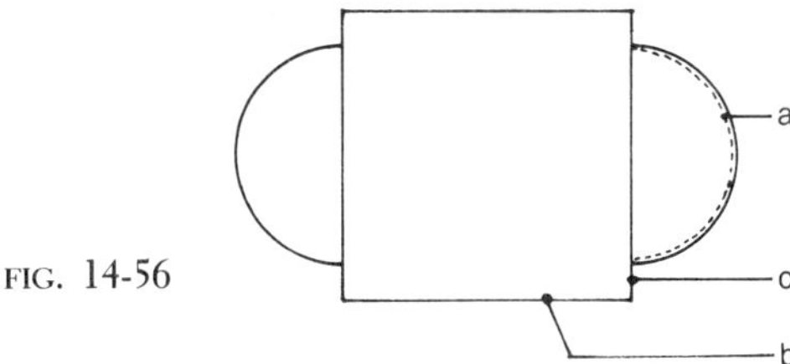

FIG. 14-56

Now measure the length of the 10-inch square cake (fig. 14-56b). Divide this measurement by 3 for 3 sections of fencing. Also, measure for the small piece of lattice that will connect the curved fencing to the straight piece (fig. 14-56c).

Freeze your cakes until you are ready to assemble them. Check Chapter 11 for instructions in the making of lattice and fencing. When you make the individual fencing for the half-round cake, cut a piece of waxed paper the size of the fencing sections plus ½ inch at each edge. As soon as you complete a section, place it on the side of the 8-inch round pan (fig. 14-57). These pieces may be placed on the pan at one time. Place a small amount of royal icing under the two ends of the waxed paper to secure it to the pan while drying. If you allow any icing to go under the lattice, it will break when you remove it.

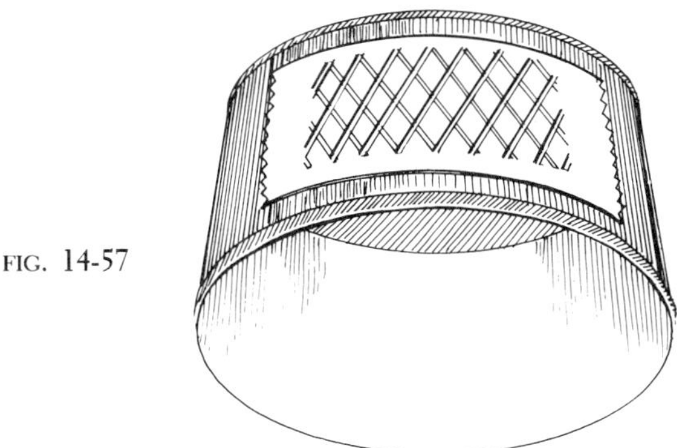

FIG. 14-57

As soon as each lattice piece has dried, use tip no. 8 and make a beading on the top edge. Hold a Royal Icing bag at a 25-degree angle and apply pressure until it forms a ball. Release pressure, pull away ¼ inch, and make another ball. Continue in the same way until you complete the piece of fencing.

The lattice will dry fairly quickly; if you have only one 8-inch pan, remove the lattice as soon as it is dry and make more. Be sure to wedge your round pan while the lattice is on it so that it doesn't suddenly roll away. Complete all the fencing.

Make 20 bows out of Royal Icing using tip no. 101 and making each 1¼ inches wide.

Finish baking the cakes. You can start assembling them (see Chapter 12) when they have cooled.

Invert the 14-inch square cake in the center of your Plexiglas. Crumb it and place a double layer of frosting on the top. Cut the 12-inch cake in half. If you have a problem finding the center, fold a pattern of the cake in half to give you an exact center. Place a half cake at each end of the 14-inch square; then frost the top with a double layer of frosting and crumb the sides.

Make cardboard dividers as explained in Chapter 12 in the shapes of the 10-inch square and the two 8-inch half-rounds.

Center the 10-inch square of foil on the cake and place the 8-inch foil half-circles at each end. Place the covered cardboards on the foil and invert your cakes on the cardboards.

Frost the top layer of this section with a double layer of frosting and crumb the sides.

The final 8-inch round cake is inverted on its foil-covered cardboard centered on the 10-inch square cake. Crumb this cake.

To divide the top round cake, trace the bottom of the pan on waxed paper. Cut it out and fold it into 8 equal parts. Notch the creases, place this pattern on the dried top, and mark the notches with toothpicks.

Using tip no. 67 and Basic Frosting, start at the top right of a garland and apply a leaf. Pull away and make another leaf, starting ¼ inch ahead and making this leaf a little shorter (fig. 14-55). Continue this way until you complete the garland. Immediately insert the tiny flowers and go on to the next until you have completed all the garlands.

Place a stephanotis at the top of each garland on the 8-inch round cake. A pair of stephanotis are placed at the top of each garland on the bottom layer.

On the top edge of the 8-inch cake make a border with tip no. 20 using white Basic Frosting. Hold the bag at an angle and apply pressure until the frosting mounds. Do not make them too large. Pull away and squeeze on another mound all around. Then place 2 leaves made with tip no. 67 in between each mound, one to the left and one to the right. These leaves should end close together so that they will slightly overlap

FIG. 14-58 

(fig. 14-58). Repeat this border at the bases of this layer and the middle layer.

The base of the cake is done in the same manner but using tips nos. 22 and 68 for larger mounds and a much heavier border.

Now apply the fencing. At the top edge of the 10-inch square, holding your Royal Icing bag with tip no. 7 at a 45-degree angle, apply pressure to form a bead. Pull away and form another bead. Complete this design along one side of your 10-inch cake (the space of 3 pieces of fencing). Carefully remove a piece of fencing from the waxed paper and insert it into the beading. Insert the next one, joining the two together with a thin line of Royal Icing. Continue until all your fencing is in place. (Check Chapter 11 on lattice and fencing if you need further instructions.) After the fencing has set, apply the bows with Royal Icing.

Where each section of the fencing joins, have the garlands begin and end (see Chapter 11). Apply small flowers to complete the design.

Using Basic Frosting and tip no. 19, make a zigzag row of frosting about ¾ inch wide on the upper edge of the bottom layer and arrange your flowers and leaves on the zigzag.

Complete the cake by arranging your cake top.

CHAPTER 15

Smaller Cakes

Rose Noel

SUPPLIES

Cakes:
- 8-inch round
- 10-inch round
- 12-inch round

Sugar Molds:
- sugar mold from a cereal bowl
- sugar ring mold for base (individual salad ring)

Flowers:
- 175 roses, stephanotis, and daisies
- 50 to 60 Basic Frosting roses

Leaves:
- approximately 100 soft green leaves
- approximately 100 holly leaves

Marzipan Red Berries: 80 to 100

Start by making all of your white flowers, roses, stephanotis, and daisies. When I use roses on a cake, I generally make them out of Basic Frosting unless they are to go on a top ornament for which I use Royal Icing.

Make the soft green and holly leaves as explained in Chapter 10. To make the red berries use the recipe in Chapter 12 for marzipan. Take some mixed almond paste about the size of a golf ball, apply red food coloring, and mix it thoroughly with your hands. Roll out a small amount of the red almond paste on waxed paper until it is the thickness of a pencil. With a knife cut it into ¼-inch pieces. Roll each little piece between the palms of your hands into a ball. Keep the almond paste covered with a damp cloth so that it doesn't dry out before you are finished. When completed let the berries dry on a plate at room temperature.

Make the sugar molds for the top ornament and allow to dry. Make a wicker design on the sides of the mold (see Chapter 7). Complete the top ornament (see Chapter 13).

Assemble the cake following the instructions for assembling a wedding cake in Chapter 12, placing the foil and corrugated disks between each tier.

Crumb and glaze the cake with white Basic Frosting. As soon as the frosting has set a little, plan your garlands (see Chapter 11). The cake is divided into 6 equal parts with the garlands alternating on the middle layer. Use tips nos. 20, 19, and 16 for the swags and no. 20 for the large drops in between. Place a rose on each drop just slightly above the end.

Make a roping around the top of the 8-inch cake using tip no. 30.

With Basic Frosting and tip no. 30, do a zigzag of frosting on the top edge of the 10- and 12-inch layers. Arrange flowers, leaves, and berries on the zigzag.

Using tip no. 22 make a heavy roping around the base. Insert a rose with a few leaves and berries in the roping under each drop in the garland.

Instead of singing Christmas carols, they will sing your praises!

Cachepot Cake

SUPPLIES

Cakes:
- 12-inch square
- 10-inch round, cut in half
- 9-inch octagonal, 2 inches high

Cachepot

Flowers:
- 50 small white roses, using tip no. 101,
- 50 small daisies, using tips nos. 59° and 101
- 12 white stephanotis
- 12 cupped daisies
- 75 assorted toothpick flowers
- 125 assorted flowers

Leaves:
- 50 toothpick leaves
- 100 assorted leaves

Grape Clusters:
- 200, ½ to ⅝ inches long

Lattice

The cachepot is a small square container usually made of porcelain, popular in the 18th century. This delicate and charming box has always been one of my favorite devices for decorating a cake top (Chapter 13), especially when filled with an assortment of spring flowers. This particular cake was designed to appear in the Fifth Avenue windows of Tiffany's in New York City.

The Tiffany cake was made over Styrofoam shapes for display purposes, but the following instructions are for a real cake.

Bake the cakes. If you cannot find a 9-inch octagonal pan 2 inches high, use a 10-inch square or a 9-inch round pan and cut the cake to the desired shape. When you cut off the sides of any cake to shape it, you weaken it; anything placed on top will require supports.

Before you place the 9-inch octagonal cake in the freezer, trace around it on foil and cardboard. Wrap, bag, and freeze the cake.

Measure the length of the 12-inch square cake. Divide the measurement by 4 for 4 sections of lattice on each side. For detailed instructions read Chapter 11 on lattice and fencing.

When working on Styrofoam, in many respects it is easy to do lattice as you can place the cake at any angle, which is what I was able to do in this case. However, when working with a real cake this would be impossible.

Cut the 10-inch cake in half and place the halves against the 12-inch square cake. Measure the top edges of the sides of both half-round cakes (fig. 15-1). Divide the measurement of each half by 6 for 6 equal lattices (see Chapter 11 on lattice and fencing).

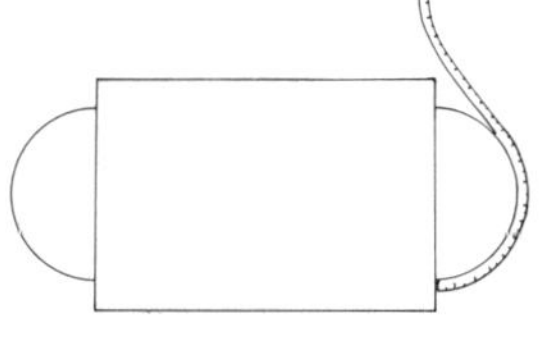

FIG. 15-1

Do not forget to measure for the small corner pieces of lattice that will connect the round and square lattices on the cakes.

Make all of your lattice pieces and a few extra. It is better to have them and not use them than to be short.

This cake has a variety of colored flowers. I used lilies, daisies, roses, jonquils, narcissus, and pansies. Make about 75 toothpick flowers for the cachepot.

Make all the leaves in assorted green shades using tips nos. 67 and 68.

Many grape clusters are needed to cover the joining of the lattice. With white Royal Icing and tips nos. 3, 4, and 5, make the grapes ½ to ⅝ inches long. Make about 50 white roses in Basic Frosting or Royal Icing using tip no. 101. With white Royal Icing make 50 small flat or cupped daisies using tips nos. 101 and 59° and about a dozen cupped daisies ¾ inch in diameter with tip no. 60. Make a dozen white stephanotis.

Remove the cakes from the freezer. Invert the 12-inch square in the center of the Plexiglas. Place a double layer of white Basic Frosting on the top and crumb the sides. Attach the two 10-inch halves on either side of the cake and crumb them in white. Place the 9-inch octagonal piece of foil on the center of the 12-inch square, and put the foil-covered cardboard over it. Now invert the 9-inch cake over it and crumb. When all have dried, glaze the small cake and the top surface of the large one with white Basic Frosting.

Glaze the sides of the large cakes in yellow, the same color as the background of the cachepot.

Before doing the lattice, complete the 9-inch octagonal by putting in supports for the cachepot. Over the cake place the foil and cardboard to support the cachepot (see Chapter 13 on cake tops for detailed instructions).

Frost the cardboard with white Royal Icing and glaze it. Place it on the cake. It will be dry before the cachepot is ready to be placed on it.

The decorations on the 9-inch octagonal cake are done very delicately and all in white as you do not want to detract from the beauty of the cachepot and the lattice sides of the cake. For the garlands on the 9-inch cake (see Chapter 11), make a leaf design using tip no. 65 and insert small white flowers and grape clusters. Around the upper and lower edge, use Basic Frosting with tip no. 27 at a 25-degree angle, apply pressure and make a puff or mound (fig. 15-2). Keep them small! Stop squeezing, pull away, make another puff, and continue all around the cake. In between each of these puffs insert leaves, using tip no. 66 sideways, pulling one to the left and the next to the right. Complete the 2 borders. On the top at the corner angles place a ¾-inch daisy, and, just below it at the base, place a stephanotis.

FIG. 15-2

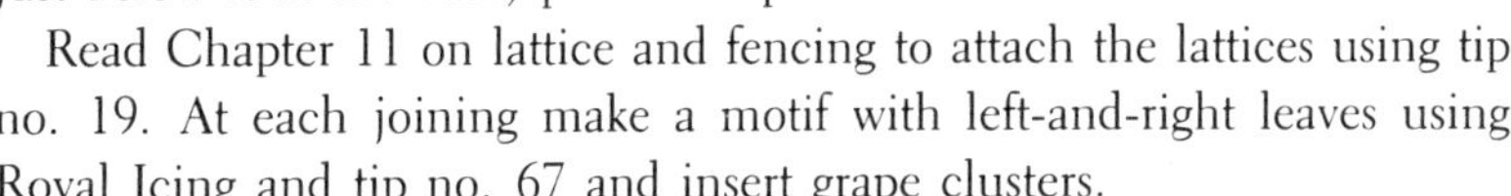

Read Chapter 11 on lattice and fencing to attach the lattices using tip no. 19. At each joining make a motif with left-and-right leaves using Royal Icing and tip no. 67 and insert grape clusters.

Around the base of the cake make the same design as you did around the 9-inch octagon. Use Royal Icing and tips nos. 22 and 67. Insert a grape at every other leaf.

On the top edge of the lattice make a left-and-right leaf motif to cover the lattice. Do not allow Basic Frosting to touch the lattice as it will weaken it. Once you have placed a leaf over the lattice, you may make a narrow zigzag with the no. 9 tip and Basic Frosting to apply the flowers and leaves.

At the point where the square cake meets the round cake, place a little cluster of flowers on the Plexiglas.

Terra-cotta Tier Cake

SUPPLIES: (serves 140)

Cakes:
- 14-inch round
- 10-inch round
- 8-inch round
- 6-inch round

Flowers:
- 300 assorted flowers
- 24 lilies of the valley

Leaves:
- 150 leaves in assorted lengths
- 50 longer leaves for the top

Grape Clusters:
- 20, about ½ inch long, tip no. 3
- 24, about ⅝ inch long, tip no. 4
- 60, about ¾ inch long, tip no. 5
- 35, about 1 inch long, tip no. 7

Sugar molds:
- sugar mold from cereal bowl, 5 × 2 inches
- sugar ring base from individual salad ring, ¾ × ⅝ inch

If you have not read Chapter 12 on assembling wedding cakes, I suggest you do so. You will find it of great help before you start.

To start assembling, invert the 14-inch round cake on a 20- to 24-inch Plexiglas or heavy wood board (round or square). As you are going to have a cake directly over this, place a double layer of icing on the top of the cake and crumb the sides.

Put cake supports in this layer.

Center a 10-inch foil circle on the 14-inch cake; place a 10-inch cardboard covered with foil and then the 10-inch cake inverted over it. Place a double layer of frosting on the top and crumb the sides. Put in 4 supports.

Now do the same thing with the 8-inch and 6-inch layers. These layers do not require supports.

Once this crumbing layer of frosting has dried, you will need a small saucepan of boiling water to comb the cake. I prefer the Ateco triangular comb. Use the middle size on this comb, and, starting on the top layer, put a heavy layer of frosting around the cake. Dip the comb in boiling water and wipe it quickly. Starting at the base of the 6-inch cake pull upward to top edge. Clean the comb on the edge of your frosting bowl and dip it in boiling water on every stroke. The hot blade is the secret to having nice clean ridges. If you are not happy with the results, frost the cake and try again. As soon as you complete the top layer, glaze the top surface smoothing the edges.

As soon as you complete each layer smooth out the top edges around the cake. Comb all 4 layers.

While waiting for the top layer to dry, divide the sugar urn in quarters, make garlands on the urn, and then fasten it to the sugar ring base. Let dry before going any further (Chapter 13).

Trace around the 6-inch pan on a piece of waxed paper to make a pattern for the placing of the garlands. Fold the pattern into 8 equal parts for 8 swags and notch the ends. Place the pattern on the top of your cake and mark all 4 layers (Fig. 15-3a) as shown in Chapter 12. On the 6- and 10-inch layers, place toothpicks to mark the cake in sixteenths. Fig. 15-3 shows a quarter section of the cake.

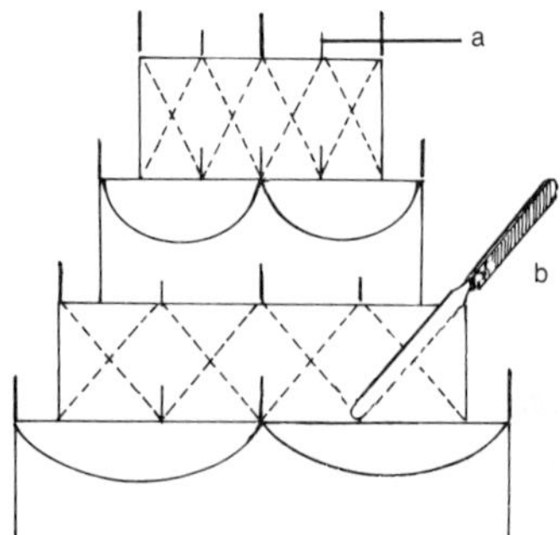

FIG. 15-3

You now have 16 toothpicks around the top edges of the 10-inch and 6-inch cakes. Place toothpicks directly below the top toothpicks on the bottom edge of the same cake. Make a line with your spatula by placing the tip of the blade on the lower toothpick and pulling it against the cake to the toothpick on the upper right (fig. 15-3b). Complete all the marks in this direction. Now reverse it and make the lines going in the opposite direction making X marks. Do the same on the 6-inch cake.

Following the directions in Chapter 11 for garlands, make the swags on the cake (as shown in fig. 15-3) making one row with tip no. 19 and going over it with tip no. 16.

Make the drops in between the swags with tip no. 19 on the 8-inch cake with white Basic Frosting. Hold your bag at a right angle to the cake and place it where you want the drop to end (see sketch in Chapter 11). Apply pressure until you get the size needed. Slowly pull up tip and bag at the same angle and release pressure slowly until you reach the top of the cake. Push a medium-size grape cluster into the base of the drop. Make all the drops on both layers. As you do the 14-inch layer, add more pressure to make a larger drop or use a no. 20 to 22 tip. Use the smaller grapes on the top and larger ones at the base cake.

To make the lattice use tip no. 47 with Basic Frosting and keep the serrated edge towards the outside. Hold the bag in an upward position on an angle and start at the base of the line. Keep an even pressure and slowly pull up, covering the line. When you reach the top, stop squeezing and push the tip into the frosting to break the line. Make all the lines going in one direction; then do the cross lines.

At the top edge of the lattice cross lines on the 6-inch cake, make a sideways C design with tip no. 16 and Basic Frosting (fig. 15-4). Holding the bag at a right angle to the cake, squeeze and form the sideways C all around the cake; go over the C the second time using the same tip. Apply a cluster of grapes where the Cs meet. Make the same design at the top of the 10-inch cake using tip no. 19 and applying a little larger grape cluster. The cardboard disk to support the cake top should be placed on the 6-inch cake (see Chapter 13). Using tip no. 15 repeat this same design using the ½-inch grape cluster. On this one, a grape may be placed at every other C.

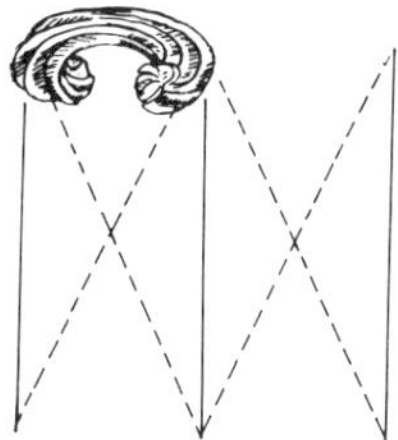

FIG. 15-4

Around the outer edge of the 6-inch round, make Cs back to back with tip no. 16 and place a few leaves where they join together (fig. 15-5).

FIG. 15-5

Place the flowers around layers 8, 10, and 14 as shown in the photograph.

If doilies are going to be placed on the lower edge, now is the time to do so. Place a toothpick at the bottom edge under each grape in between each garland and divide this section in thirds using 2 toothpicks and form a C as shown in photo. Following the same C motif, use tip no. 22 with the Basic Frosting bag. Go around the C motif a second time to give it a thick look, but this time use tip no. 19 for the final touch. When this is completed, insert a large grape cluster where the Cs join.

The cake is now complete—all but the top ornament. For this size cake it is not necessary to use a cardboard before placing the half Styrofoam ball on top of the urn. It is a matter of choice. After the Styrofoam ball is attached, cover it using tip no. 22 with Royal Icing. Place the flowers on the urn and insert leaves. When completed, very carefully insert lilies of the valley to complete your floral arrangement.

Daisy Cake

SUPPLIES (serves 230)

Cakes:
- 16-inch round
- 14-inch round
- 10-inch round
- 8-inch round

Flowers:
- 250 to 300 daisies all sizes (40 to 50 wired on different lengths)

Leaves:
- 100 white leaves, using tip no. 68

This cake is very elegant for a garden wedding or for any occasion.

Invert the 16-inch cake onto a board or Plexiglas 22 to 26 inches in diameter. Frost the top with a double layer of frosting and crumb the sides. Center a 14-inch foil circle on the 16-inch cake and place a 14-inch foil-covered cardboard disk on it. Invert the 14-inch cake onto the cardboard; place a double layer of frosting on the top and crumb the sides. Continue this procedure until all 4 layers are completed.

Smooth the top layer of frosting. Because this cake will be completely covered with basket weave, you need not glaze it. The results will be far superior if the frosting on the cake is not lumpy and does not have any air bubbles, but glazing will make the frosting too smooth to hold the basket weave on it.

Fill 2 bags with white Basic Frosting for basket weave and place tip no. 8 on one and tip no. 48 on the other. See Chapter 7 for details on how to do basket weave.

Start at the top layer and work down until the 4 layers are completed.

Using tip no. 4 or 5 and a bag of bright yellow Royal Icing, fill in the center of each daisy to a nice rounded mound and then place granulated sugar on the centers. Invert flowers and tap lightly so that the sugar adheres only to the yellow.

To make your hovering daisy top, see Chapter 13 for complete details.

The decorative roping should be applied on the outer edges of each cake using tip no. 22 and white Basic Frosting. With the same tip, do a zigzag design that will fill in the space between the decorative roping and the cake layers. To these rows of frosting apply the daisies and leaves that encircle each layer of cake. Allow some of the flowers and leaves to overhang the roping for a more realistic effect.

Place the wired arrangement on the 6-inch cake and join with the same roping. For a heavier border, the roping on the base of the cake may be done with white Basic Frosting using tip no. 32.

This "Daisy Cake" was designed for the opening of a Priscilla of Boston Bridal Shop some 15 years ago and has been one of my most successful efforts.

Christmas Strawberry Cake

SUPPLIES

Cakes:
- 16-inch round
- 12-inch round
- 10-inch round

Flowers:
- approximately 175 daisies

Leaves:
- approximately 200

Strawberries:
- approximately 75 made of marzipan

Bows:
- 2 large drooping bows with flying streamers

Top Ornament:
- 5-inch Styrofoam ball
- sugar ring mold

Make all your daisies and, after they have dried, insert the yellow centers (see Chapter 9). The green leaves are made with tips nos. 67 and 68 and should be a soft green.

See Chapter 11 on how to make a drooping bow with detachable streamers. Use tip no. 125 and white Royal Icing and make extras.

For the strawberries make the recipe for marzipan in Chapter 12. Take some mixed almond paste about the size of a tennis ball in your hands and mix in red food coloring until it is a bright red color.

Take about a quarter of the red almond paste and cover the rest with a damp cloth so that it does not dry up. Roll the almond paste in the palms of your hands until it is a smooth ball.

Roll out the almond paste on a piece of waxed paper until it is the thickness of your index finger and then cut it into ¾-inch pieces. Take each piece and roll it around in the palms of your hands until it is a smooth ball. Shape one end into a rounded point to resemble a strawberry. Fold a damp cloth in half and place the strawberries in between until you are ready to complete them.

Roll each strawberry in coarse red sugar to give it the strawberry look.

If the sugar does not stick, leave them under the damp towel a little longer. Set aside to dry. When completely dry, using tip no. 65 or 66 depending on the size of the strawberry, make the green calyx on the top.

The top ornament is done in a different manner than the usual sugar urns. For this I use a 5-inch Styrofoam ball only. Mark around the center of the ball with a pencil line. On the lower half you will make wicker work, and the upper half will be the base for leaves, berries, and flowers.

Make the sugar-mold ring first so that when the wicker is done you will be able to invert the ball onto the dried ring.

Now cover half of the ball with wicker (see Chapter 7) using tip no. 8. When it is dry, make a roping around the center.

Apply a coating of Royal Icing to the rest of the ball and apply flowers, strawberries, and leaves. Allow to set while you complete the cake.

Assemble the 3 cakes on a Plexiglas base following instructions in Chapter 12 on assembling wedding cakes. Crumb the cakes with a fairly smooth surface on which to put the wicker.

With tip no. 9 and Basic Frosting, start the wicker work on the top layer of the cake and continue down until all layers are covered (see Chapter 7).

Make a row of roping around the top edge of the upper layer with tip no. 10. Also make a row of roping on the top edge and at the base of the bottom layer with tip no. 12.

Place an arrangement of flowers, leaves, and strawberries around each layer.

Lastly, attach one bow on the bottom layer and one on the middle layer as shown in the photograph. Put a little Royal Icing just below the roping and attach the two streamers; with another dab of icing attach the bows.

Although this cake is presented as a Christmas wedding cake, it is as changeable as the New England weather. Without the strawberries and instead a full assortment of daisies, it is a perfect summer cake for a garden wedding.

Flower Swag Cake

SUPPLIES: (serves 85)

Cakes:
- 5-inch round cake
- 8-inch round cake
- 12-inch round cake

Flowers:
- 175 to 200 roses, lilies, stephanotis, and daisies

Sugar Molds:
- sugar mold from cereal bowl
- sugar ring mold for base

Make all the flowers before you start baking the cakes. When the daisies are dry, make the yellow centers with granulated sugar on top of each one.

The sugar-mold top ornament is made in a cereal bowl. When it is dry, decorate it with wicker using tip no. 8. The base is made in the individual salad ring mold.

I bake the top layer of this cake (5 inches in diameter) in an old-fashioned 1 pound coffee can. I line the bottom with waxed paper and grease the sides. Candy often comes in this size can also. Bake all layers of cake.

Read Chapter 12 on assembling a wedding cake. For a small cake, I like to use a silver tray instead of a board or Plexiglas for it gives a small cake a look of importance. If you do use a silver tray, place a foil-covered disk under the cake to prevent scratching the tray.

Let the cakes cool then assemble, crumb, and glaze with white Basic Frosting.

This cake is divided into 6 equal parts for the garlands (see Chapter 11). Mark the lines of the garlands with toothpicks.

Using tips nos. 19 and 67 and Basic Frosting, make the border around the top edge of the 5-inch cake. Apply pressure to make a mound with the star tip. Stop squeezing and pull away about ½ inch; continue all around the cake (fig. 15-6). Using the same tip, do the same design on the lower edges of the 5- and 8-inch cakes.

FIG. 15-6 

With tips nos. 20 and 68, do the top edge of the 8- and 12-inch tiers plus the base of the cake.

Using tip no. 19 make the garlands with a slight zigzag motion and attach the flowers and leaves as shown in the photograph.

Shown in pale blue and yellow, this cake works beautifully in any color combination you wish.

Pink and Blue Basket Cake

SUPPLIES

(serves 100)

Cake:
 Large oval, (14¾ × 10¼ inches)
Flowers:
 200 assorted pink and blue flowers
Leaves:
 150 leaves

Sugar Molds:
 sugar mold from large bowl
 sugar ring mold for base

This cake was made for a wedding but could be used for a bridal shower or a special birthday.

Detailed instruction for making the flowers are in Chapters 8 and 9. Make the sugar molds following instructions in Chapter 11 and then put basket weave on the mold as discussed in Chapter 7. As soon as you complete the basket weave on your sugar mold and while it is still upside down, place the sugar-mold ring on top and press down onto the basket weave. Check on all sides to make sure that it is even. Use a level if you find it necessary.

To bake this cake, I use a disposable heavy-aluminum oval roasting pan and I bake it in 2 layers.

After the cakes have cooled and it is time to assemble them, put a little frosting in between each layer. These layers should be inverted when put together (fig. 15-7); trim a little off the sides before crumbing it.

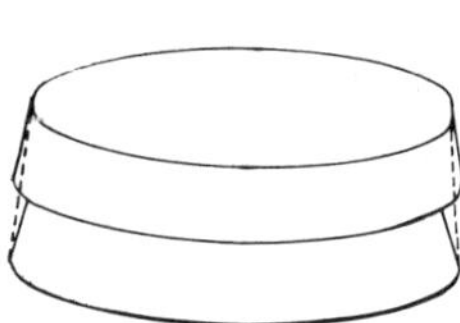

FIG. 15-7

It is not necessary to glaze the sides of the cake because it will be covered with the basket weave, but the frosting should be without lumps or air bubbles for a smooth finish. Glazing the cake makes it too smooth for the basket weave to adhere well.

After the basket weave is completed, take tip no. 30 and do a zigzag motion about 1 inch wide around the top edge of the cake; then place your flowers on the zigzag. Have some flowers falling down the sides in an irregular fashion.

Make a heavy roping around the base of the cake with tip no. 32 and insert 6 clusters of flowers, evenly spaced, to bring some color to the lower edge of the cake.

See Chapter 13 on cake tops for instructions on completing the sugar mold.

Victorian Fan

SUPPLIES (serves 100)

Cakes:
- three 14-inch square
- 14 ribs for fan (includes 3 extras)

Bow:
- 4-inch bow (make extras)

Flowers:
- 20 to 25 stephanotis
- 75 to 100 small cupped daisies, white, pink, and mauve

Leaves:
- 70 to 80 leaves, 1 to 1¼ inches long, using tip no. 67

You may make these cakes 2 to 4 inches high depending on how many people you wish to serve. To serve 100 people bake 3 cakes each 2 inches high, making sure that each has the exact amount of batter so that they are all the same thickness when put together.

Cut the cakes as shown in fig. 15-8. Make a pattern on a large piece of paper following the dimensions given. Place the pattern on the baked cake. On line x where the cakes will be joined, cut off the edges of the adjoining cakes so that the cakes have the same soft texture throughout. Use 1 cake to get 2 adjoining pieces, one for each layer (fig. 15-9).

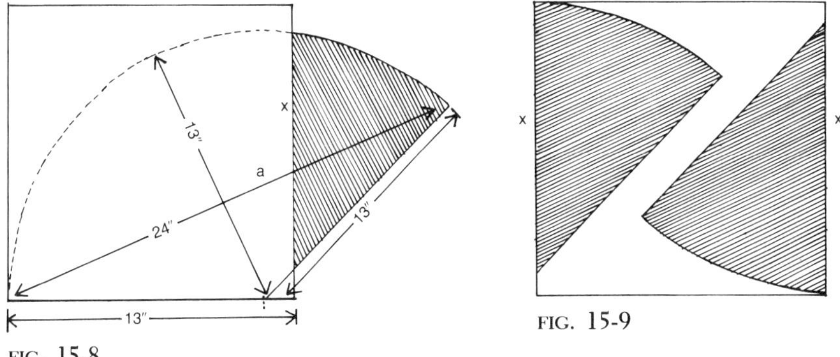

FIG. 15-8

FIG. 15-9

If you bake the cake first, you will have to freeze it. The ribs are a combination of run sugar and lattice. Read Chapter 11 for further instruction.

Tear a piece of waxed paper about 3 inches wide and place over pattern (fig. 15-10). Outline the narrower section with the no. 4 tip and a bag of white Royal Icing. Use run sugar for the inner section. With the no. 4 tip, make the lattice. Join the run-sugar section so that it is one piece. There are 12 ribs on this cake; make 2 extra. When they are dry, make a line and leaf design on each using tips nos. 2 and 65S as shown in fig. 15-11.

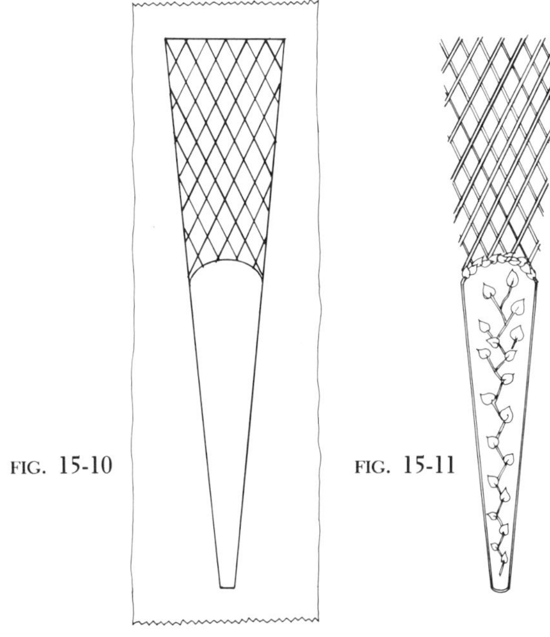

FIG. 15-10

FIG. 15-11

Make 4-inch bows with the no. 104 tip; you will need one (but make extras) for the front of the fan. Check bows in Chapter 11.

Using tip no. 59, 60, 101, or 102 make a variety of small cupped daisies. To get the color mauve, add a little violet or pink or use light burgundy paste color. When the flowers are dry, fill in the centers with yellow or white icing and give them the sugar treatment to coat the centers.

If you make a carrot cake, put cream-cheese frosting in between each layer (not too much for the cakes will slide). Also crumb it with the cream-cheese frosting. It is a little more difficult and it does take more time, but it is delicious and well worth it.

Center the cake on a rectangular piece of Plexiglas. It is very important to have the cake flat on top because of the ribs. Crumb it in white Basic or cream-cheese frosting. Let it dry thoroughly. When you glaze the top of the cake, pick up one of the colors used in the flowers. The cake in the photograph was glazed in a very soft shade of mauve. Glaze the sides with white frosting. If you have a high cake, put garlands on the sides as shown in the photograph.

Make roping around the top edge with tip no. 20 and at the base of the cake with tip no. 22.

The most successful way of placing the ribs on the cake is to measure the longest distance on the cake (fig. 15-8a), divide it in half and mark the line with your spatula. This is the center of the cake. Turn a rib over on a paper towel and carefully remove the waxed paper. With tip no. 16 dab Royal Icing in the center of the lower run-sugar section and place the edge against the center line on the cake leaving about 1½ inches for the top roping. Place the next rib very close to the first. If the 12 ribs do not fit, use 11. Keep them all flat. At this point, you can see how important it is to have a flat surface on this cake. Place all ribs.

The joinings of the ribs are done with tip no. 5 in a bamboo design along the run sugar and with tip no. 7 where the lattices join. Try it on a piece of waxed paper before you start on the cake. Holding the bag at a 45-degree angle, squeeze the bag so that the icing comes out smooth. Keeping the pressure the same, do a push-back-push motion twice close together, and then pull straight back again (fig. 15-12). This makes little ridges, giving it a bamboo look.

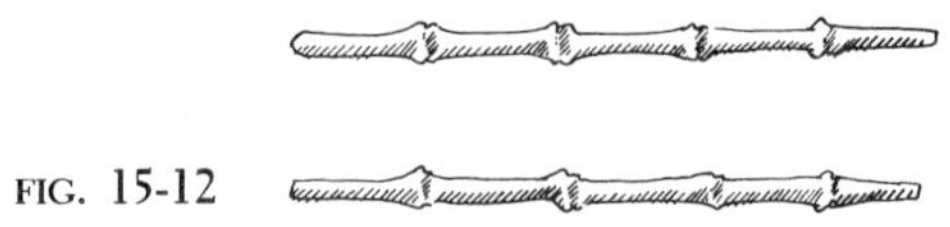

FIG. 15-12

Do this design between each of the ribs. With tip no. 7, do the side edges of the fan (fig. 15-13a). Continue the bamboo with tip no. 5 between the ribs to a point at the lower center of the fan (fig. 15-13b).

Using tip no. 5, this same bamboo design may be made where the run sugar meets the lattice on the ribs (fig. 15-14), or make tiny leaves

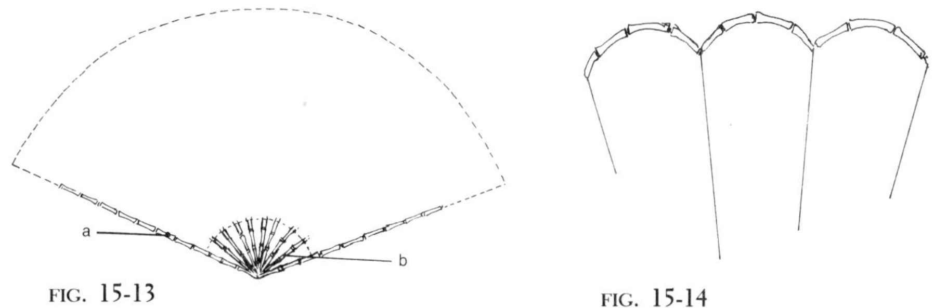

FIG. 15-13

FIG. 15-14

using tip no. 65 (fig. 15-15). Try it on a piece of waxed paper to see which design you prefer.

FIG. 15-15

With tip no. 16 and Royal Icing arrange your flowers by placing a stephanotis slightly down on each rib and mixing in the cupped daisies to form the arch of each rib. Insert the leaves (see photograph).

At the point of the fan where all the ribs meet, put a little mound of frosting and place 4 or 5 flowers back to back. Insert a few leaves.

With Royal Icing, place the bow on the front.

Long-stem Flower Cake

SUPPLIES

Cake:
- 14¾- × 10¼-inch oval cake

Leaves:
- 3 dozen ferns on wires
- 60 Royal Icing leaves

Flowers:
- 75 to 100 wired flowers in a variety of shapes and colors
- 70 flowers for the base of the cake

Sugar Molds:
- oval sugar mold with a base

This is a small cake but a showpiece. When I was first married, we had a sink put in our bathroom. When I saw the carpenter cut out the oval board, my first thought was "What an ideal shape for a cake." I used a roasting pan and cut the cake to make an oval (see Chapter 6), until I found a heavy-aluminum oval roasting pan at the supermarket. This pan is excellent for baking but be very careful when you remove it from the oven as the pan tends to bend and crack the cake. The pan may be used over again quite a few times before disposing of it. I use a vegetable brush to clean it.

Make all the decorations ahead of time. Once you start working on the cake, the top arrangement should be completed.

Cut the millinery or floral wire to the lengths desired. Keep the wires long; then, when you make the arrangement, cut the wire to the length desired just as you would cut the stem of a flower when making a floral arrangement.

Read Chapters 8, 9, 10, 12, and 13 for guidance on making the wired arrangement.

I have an oval Italian pottery urn that I use to make my sugar mold. I line it with heavy foil for the urn has many cutouts and will not hold the sugar. Make sure the foil is flat or the sugar mold will not come out. Pack the mold with sugar (see sugar molds in Chapter 11) and invert it to dry. For the base, I could not find a mold to use so I started with a square jewelry box and made a sugar mold; then I made a bell mold directly on top. While the sugar was still wet, I shaped the mold with a paring knife. Make sure the top of this piece is wide enough to hold the oval urn. Do the best you can with the sugar and let it dry. When it is completely dry, use Royal Icing to perfect the shape.

My urn was not quite high enough; so I cut out a piece of Styrofoam 1 inch thick and glued it to the top of the sugar urn with Royal Icing. The Styrofoam is the base for the floral arrangement.

Both sugar molds will not be perfectly smooth but as long as they have graceful lines and are not lumpy they will do nicely. Put a thin layer of Royal Icing on both molds before you start the wicker. Use tip no. 7 and see Chapter 7 for weaving instructions.

When you do the oval basket, make sure you allow enough space without wicker on the bottom so the pedestal can be fastened later. After both pieces are thoroughly dry, turn the large urn over onto a piece of waxed paper and make a roping on what will eventually be the top edge using tip no. 9.

Measure the base of the pedestal and cut a cardboard exactly the same size. Prepare the cardboard as suggested in Chapter 13.

At each corner of the cardboard place a cake support to act as a little table for the top urn.

With Royal Icing attach the pedestal to the base of the urn. Use a level to make sure that it is even. Allow to dry thoroughly. If possible, make something like this a week or more in advance in order to let it dry thoroughly before you invert it to make the floral arrangement.

Turn the urn right side up and frost the top surface with green Royal Icing. Start the wired floral arrangement at the center and work out. If the edges need a little covering up, add another row of Royal Icing roping and tuck in a few flowers.

Place the cake top to set in a dry area until you are ready to place it on your cake.

Prepare the cake board; then invert your cooled cake on it. Crumb the top with green Basic Frosting and the sides with white Basic Frosting.

The reason you crumb the cake before you apply wicker or basket weave is that, if the design is not perfect, you cannot tell because the frosting underneath is the same color. Besides, the frosting seals your cake for freshness and acts as a base for the weaving.

Using tip no. 9 and white Basic Frosting make the wicker design around the cake.

Place the supports for the urn in the cake; then place the cardboard covered with Royal Icing before you go on to the next step. To create the grassy look on the surface of the cake, I used tip no. 3 because I wanted each blade to be perfect. Hold your bag straight up, apply pressure for a base, and then pull up. Tip no. 133 will also give a grassy look. Make the grass directly up to the cardboard.

Make a heavy roping around the top edge of the cake using tip no. 10. Place a ring of flowers at the base and insert the leaves. When you place the top ornament, your cake is completed.

Gâteau Chinois

SUPPLIES

Cake:
- 14-inch octagonal, 4 inches high

Flowers:
- 30 to 40 assorted flowers
- 16 assorted pink and white lilies for the base

Leaves:
- 40 to 50 leaves

Run Sugar:
- 10 small Chinese characters
- 3 large Chinese characters

This cake was made for a bridal shower for a person who loved the Oriental style. The large Chinese character represents a charm to bring 10,000 ounces of gold (fig. 15-16), and the small character is a charm to bring wealth (fig. 15-17).

To make the Chinese characters, place the pattern on a cookie sheet with waxed paper over it. Make the Royal Icing a little softer, not flowing, as it has to stay in one place when squeezed out. Test it first to see if the icing will do what you want it to do. If not, empty the bag and change the consistency and try again. Holding the royal icing bag at a 45-degree angle, place tip no. 3 so that the icing will roll out and form the rounded edges around the outside part of the design. Fill in all areas until the designs are completed. Make at least 2 extras of each design.

FIG. 15-16

FIG. 15-17

Bake the cake in an octagonal pan. After the cake has cooled, crumb with white Basic Frosting. When completely dry, glaze in pink.

With tip no. 8 and a bag of Basic Frosting, start at the base of a corner. Holding your frosting bag straight up, apply pressure for about ½ inch and then make the push-back-push motion twice. Pull straight for ½ inch and make another push-back-push motion twice, always keeping the same pressure. Make 3 bamboo sticks on each corner (fig. 15-18).

FIG. 15-18 

It might be a good idea to first attach the small characters on each side of the cake with Royal Icing; then you will know how much space you have to work with. If more bamboo sticks are needed add them now. Do the bamboo at the base of the cake, using tip no. 12 so it will act as a support for the characters.

Using tip no. 12 make the same bamboo design around the upper edge of the cake. Change your tip to no. 8 and continue doing the bamboo design on top of the cake starting on the outside edge of the cake and going around for a few inches.

Invert your character (fig. 15-16), put a little Royal Icing on it, and place it in the center of the cake.

If you think you need to apply more bamboo circles before you make the ring of flowers, do so. Allow enough space around your center design.

Place your ring of flowers around the last row of bamboo. Insert the leaves. At each corner on the base, apply 2 lilies with a few leaves.

The Name Cake

SUPPLIES

Cake:
  large oval cake,
    14¾ × 10¼ inches
Run Sugar:
  name of your choice (Paul)
Grape Clusters:
  30, ⅝ to ¾ inches long
Flowers:
  50 white daisies with yellow centers
Leaves:
  50 leaves

This was a confirmation cake for Paul. It could be used for a bridal shower with the bride's name in the center and small sugar-mold bells on the garlands. It could also be used for a baby shower with a large pair of booties in the center and tiny pairs of booties scattered all over the cake or along the garlands.

Make the white daisies complete with yellow centers sprinkled with sugar (see Chapter 9).

Make the name out of run sugar (see Chapter 11). Make sure it will fit on the cake.

Make the grape clusters using tip no. 5 (Chapter 11). Make the leaves (see Chapter 10).

To bake the oval cake, use a heavy-aluminum roasting pan that you find in supermarkets. This cake may be baked in layers. When you remove the pan from the oven, support the bottom of the pan as it tends to bend.

When the cake is cool, invert it on a round, oval, or rectangular board and crumb it with white Basic Frosting.

When it is dry, glaze it with yellow frosting or the color of your choice.

Measure around the cake with a tape measure, and divide it into 8 equal parts. One toothpick should be at each end of the cake and the sides divided into 4 equal parts. Mark each part with a toothpick.

Before you make the garlands (Chapter 11), measure in 2½ inches from the edge and mark a line with a toothpick or spatula. Using tip no. 20, make a roping on this line all around the cake.

Make the garland on the side of the cake and add a few grape clusters. Make the roping around the top edge using tip no. 20.

To do the top design in between the roping draw a light line with a toothpick to mark the center. With Basic Frosting and tip no. 19, start at the center line and go up, around, and down towards the center. Do the same design on the opposite side of the center line (fig. 15-19). With the same tip, make a design down the center of the hearts (fig. 15-20).

The pair of booties for the center of a shower cake are made with 4 marshmallows, 2 for each bootie. Take 1 marshmallow and with your kitchen shears cut off a piece about ⅜ to ½ inch thick (fig. 15-21). This piece will form the toe. Take the other marshmallow and trim about ½ inch off the side, using the larger piece to form the cuff and heel of the bootie (fig. 15-22).

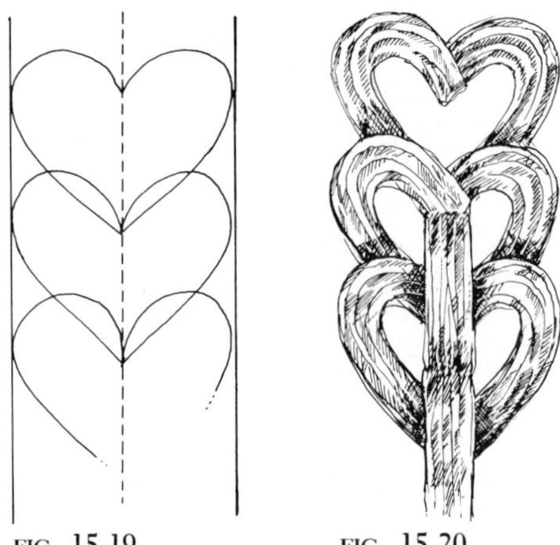

FIG. 15-19

FIG. 15-20

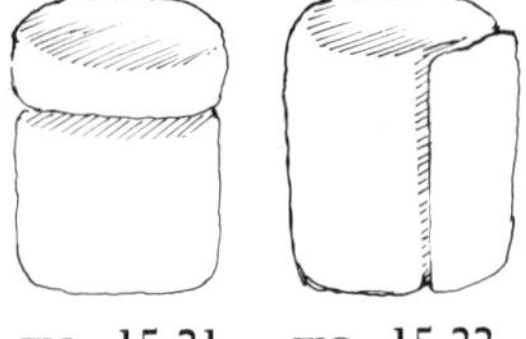

FIG. 15-21 FIG. 15-22

To decorate the bootie, place the marshmallow on a piece of waxed paper (fig. 15-23). With Basic Frosting and the no. 13 tip you may apply little tiny stars over the entire bootie for a dainty texture. For a knitted look use the same tip, make a narrow zigzag starting at the base (fig. 15-24), and go all around the bootie. Over the toe section go from side to side, allowing enough space for the raised stitching to look like a moccasin (fig. 15-25). At the top where the foot would go in, place a dab of frosting and smooth it with your spatula or make a circular design with the same

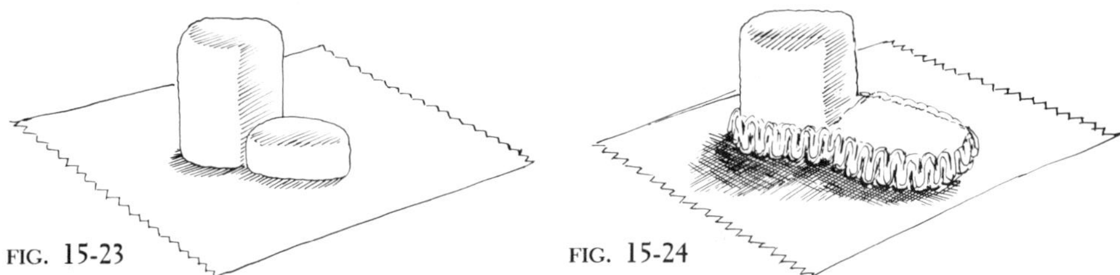

FIG. 15-23

FIG. 15-24

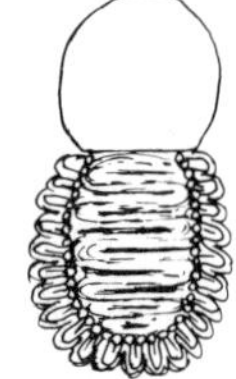

FIG. 15-25

tip by starting in the center and going around until you get to the edge and the area is completely covered (15-26).

Cover the remainder of the marshmallow with the zigzag motion. On the top edge you can make a ruffle using tip no. 102 and a contrasting color (fig. 15-27). Place the heaviest part of the tip against the edge and thin part going up. With a slight vibrating motion apply pressure and go

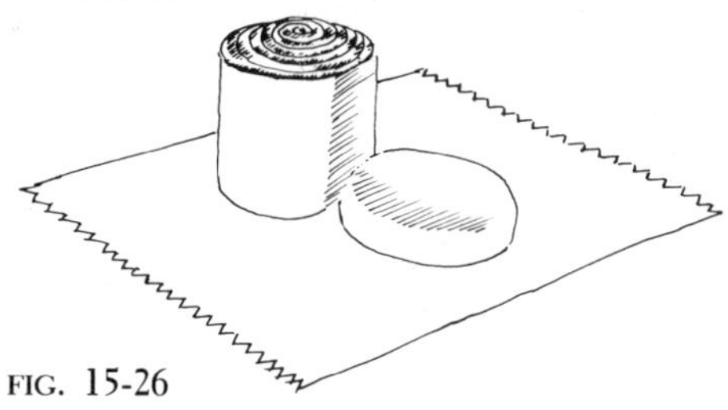

FIG. 15-26

FIG. 15-27

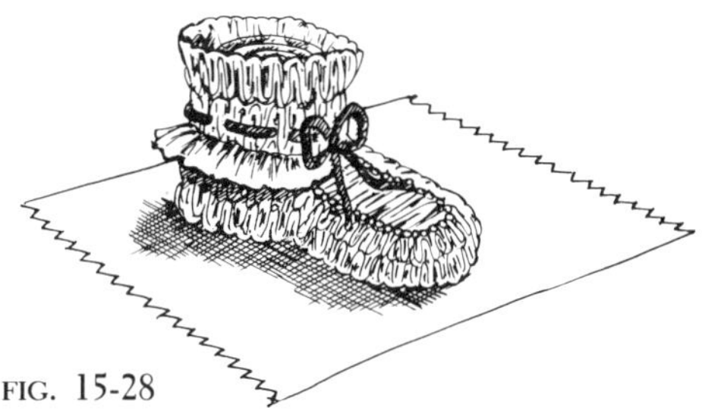
FIG. 15-28

all around. A ruffle can also be placed lower down on the bootie by starting at the center front with the thick part of the no. 102 tip pushing slightly into the frosting so that it will not fall off. Apply pressure with a slight up-and-down motion for the frosting to ripple (fig. 15-28). If you place the ruffle down on the bootie, the top edge may be finished by making a zigzag using tip no. 13 a little higher than the marshmallow.

To make the ribbon tie, insert a no. 2 tip about ½ inch away from the center front, apply pressure, pull out tip and continue pressure; then push into frosting about ½ inch away. Stop squeezing. Continue all around the ankle every ½ inch. In the center front tie a bow.

Decorate both booties the same way. After they have dried, put a little icing under the soles and place them on the cake.

The piped booties are not as complicated. The size of the booties will determine the tip you will use. Hold the bag at a 45-degree angle and with the tip against waxed paper, apply pressure for the frosting to mound to make a pleasing foot. Without pulling the tip away, hold the bag straight up and make a small circle to form the heel. Continue going up the angle in a spiral motion. Stop squeezing as you continue to go around the spiral so that the end of the icing will just blend in. Use Royal Icing for these booties.

To make the final touches, use a contrasting color and make a tiny bow (fig. 15-29).

FIG. 15-29

CHAPTER 16
One-tier Cakes

The Heart

SUPPLIES

Cakes:
- two 10-inch heart shapes
- one 7-inch heart shape

Flowers:
- 150 pink and white lilies and stephanotis (see Chapter 8)

Bows:
- 3 bows, 3 inches wide

Leaves:
- 150 leaves in all shades of green

Make the flowers in a variety of shapes and shades of pink.

Using tip no. 125 and Royal Icing, make the bows 3 inches wide and make extras. Make the leaves (Chapter 10) using tips nos. 67 and 68 out of green Royal Icing.

After your cakes are baked and cooled, place them on a Plexiglas base as arranged in the photograph and crumb them with white Basic Frosting. Before you join the cakes, glaze in pink those sections that will be difficult to reach once they are touching one another.

Now mark your garlands with toothpicks (Chapter 11). The top and lower edge of the cakes are both done using tips nos. 21 and 67. The garland is done with the same design but using tip nos. 18 and 66. Make a mound of frosting with the star tip by holding your bag at a 45-degree angle. When the mound is the desired length, stop the pressure and pull away. Make another mound and do the same thing. Using your leaf tip, pipe leaves, one going to the left and one going to the right (fig. 16-1).

FIG. 16-1 

Complete the garlands in the hard-to-reach places at the center before pushing the cakes together. Once they are joined complete glazing the cakes in pink.

The lattice may be done with Basic Frosting or Royal Icing using tip no. 4. I prefer Royal Icing as it makes a more delicate lattice. Be sure to avoid air bubbles in the icing as they will break the strings. See Chapter 11 for more information. Complete the lattice on all 3 cakes.

Complete the garlands and the top edge of the cakes with Basic Frosting. When completed, attach the bows with Basic'Frosting. However, if you were to have the bows hanging to one side of the cake, they should be attached with Royal Icing.

The border on the base of the cake should now be completed and the flowers arranged as in the photograph.

Mom's Birthday Cake

SUPPLIES

Cake:
  sheet cake, 13 × 9 inches
    or other size

40 to 50 assorted flowers
30 to 40 leaves
Bow with detached streamers

This cake was baked and decorated for my mother's birthday but may be used for any occasion.

Make assorted flowers (see Chapters 3, 7, and 9) and leaves (see Chapter 10). Make the bow with tip no. 104 and Royal Icing. Follow instructions in Chapter 11. When you make the streamers, place the waxed paper over the edge of a book to make the ribbons bend.

Crumb and glaze the baked cake with white frosting. At the top edge of the cake using tip no. 32 and a bag of white Basic Frosting held at a 45-degree angle, start at a corner and squeeze until the frosting mounds. Stop squeezing and pull away (fig. 16-2a). Make the mound quite large. Make another mound of frosting next to the first and continue until you have gone all around the top edge of the cake. Then do the same around the base of the cake; make the same mounds going down on each corner.

Change the tip to no. 3 and make a tiny zigzag motion around the top edge and in between each mound (fig. 16-2b). Change the tip to no. 102 and with the thickest edge against each of the lower mounds of icing make a ruffle (fig. 16-2c).

To make the floral spray, add a little mound of white Basic Frosting in the center where the flowers will be placed just to give height to the

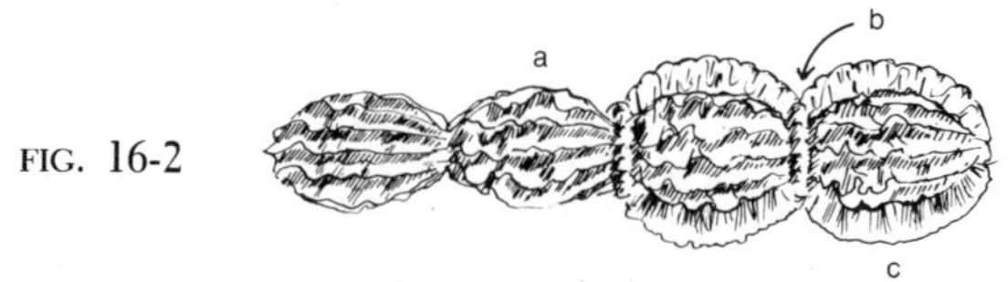

FIG. 16-2

arrangement. Attach the flowers by adding a little frosting under each; place on an angle to give a more realistic look. Insert the leaves.

The final touch is the bow. For this bow, which will be flat on the cake, Basic Frosting may be used. Place the streamers first and then the bow over them.

Fondant Cake

SUPPLIES:

Cake:
- 14-inch octagonal cake

75 to 100 flowers, shades of yellow, lavender, and white

30 to 40 grape clusters, ⅝ to ¾ inch, using tip no. 4 or 5

60 to 75 leaves

Lattice, 18 halves (2 extras)

The flowers, grapes, and leaves should be completely dry before starting to decorate. The cake has to be baked, cooled, and, just before freezing it, measured for the width and height of the side panels.

When you have to make a pattern with the right and left side exactly the same, complete one side and reverse the pattern to get the exact opposite.

Make a pattern the height of your cake and half the width as shown in fig. 16-3. Mark it top side and bottom. Make the vertical and horizontal lines ¼ inch apart.

With tip no. 3 and a bag of white Royal Icing, make the lattice with extra left and right pieces. By the time you finish the lattice on the last design, the icing has dried enough on the first piece for you to make the beading or whatever design you choose to go on the curved top edge. See lattice and fencing in Chapter 11 for a variety of designs.

These left and right pieces may be done as one but the lower area has such a small area where it is joined that it breaks very easily.

Crumb your cake and let it set. Glaze the cake rounding the top edges to give a poured fondant look.

Place a mound of frosting in the center of the cake. The higher you want your flowers to be, the higher you make the mound. Apply the flowers and leaves with the grapes tucked in around the edges.

By this time, the glaze is dry enough to place the lattices. Follow the directions on lattice in Chapter 11. All joinings and any icing touching the lattice must be Royal Icing.

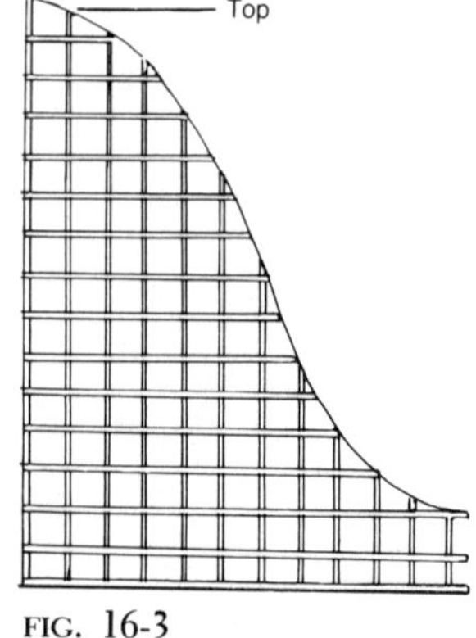

FIG. 16-3

Place all 8 sides of lattice. When you reach the last joining, the first has set enough for you to make the left-and-right leaf design or whatever design you wish on side edges and the joining at the lower edge of the lattice.

The lower border of the cake is also done with leaf tip no. 68 with a left-to-right motion starting near the lattice and pulling out.

Garnish the base with a grape cluster at the corners and where the lower lattice joins.

On each corner at the top edge make a small mound of icing and fit in 4 flowers close together with a few leaves. Do not make these too large as you do not want to detract from your lattice work and the center arrangement.

The Briana Cake

A silver tray lends a touch of elegance to any cake. This cake (fig. 16-4) may be made in any size with or without a candle. No instructions are necessary.

This cake was designed for the first birthday of my hairdresser's granddaughter who was christened Briana.

FIG. 16-4

The Bow Cake

This cake (fig. 16-5) may be made in any size; the size of the looped bow would vary accordingly.

Comb the sides of the cake. If it is a high cake, add a garland (Chapter 11). Place a heavy ring of flowers around the top edge of the cake.

At the base of the cake use a heavy C-scroll motif. Without the looped bows, this cake with its heavy scroll work and rust, yellow, and white flowers would be ideal for a man who loves to garden.

FIG. 16-5

The Mini-Wedding Cake

This cake (fig. 16-6) is excellent for a small home wedding, shower, anniversary, or any occasion that calls for something extra special.

You may also turn this modest effort into a very grand one by adding 2 or 3 layers using the same lattice motif and the same top ornament.

To make the top ornament, read Chapter 13. Make the lattice and tuck in a few grape clusters around the edges. Around the top edge, make an arrangement of flowers and leaves.

FIG. 16-6

Bootie Cake

Wedgwood with booties. This simple yet elegant cake (fig. 16-7) may be used for numerous occasions; a baby shower, christening, or a birthday cake. Eliminate the booties and you have a beautiful design for all occasions.

The flower arrangement on the top of the cake has as its base a mound of frosting. The size of the mound of frosting determines the size of the arrangement.

The frosting must be glazed smooth over the edges of the cake.

To make the garlands, see Chapter 11. Reverse the garland on the cake top. The making of the booties is explained in the directions for The Name Cake in Chapter 14.

For a christening the color can be either pink or blue according to the gender of the guest of honor.

FIG. 16-7

CHAPTER 17
Novelty Cakes

Boot Cake

SUPPLIES

Cakes:
- two 14-inch square cakes, each 4 inches high

Flowers:
- 150 to 200 chrysanthemums and daisies

Leaves:
- 125 leaves

One pair of boots
- 20- × 10-inch sheet of Styrofoam, 1½ inches high

The boots are made up before you start baking the cake. I tried to make these out of cake, but because they had to be life-size, the awkward size and the weight presented a definite problem. Also, the person for whom they were made wanted to keep them as a remembrance of his 50th birthday. Then I went to a maker of mannequins and window-display items. There I found a pair of knee-high legs made of fiberglass used to display stockings. I had them cut down to the height of the boot that I was using as a model.

Royal Icing was applied to this form and built up in layers until it assumed the shape of the boot. Real heels were attached and covered with frosting. Once the Royal Icing foundation was dry, I copied the design of the model boot in icing.

I next stuffed the leg of the boot with tissue paper and stuffed foil at the top on which I placed a mound of Royal Icing. On this mound of Royal Icing a cluster of large yellow and white daisies was arranged.

Once your flowers (Chapters 6, 8, and 9) and leaves (Chapter 10) are made and dried, bake your cakes. This particular cake was a carrot cake.

Invert the cooled cakes on a Plexiglas base. Where the cakes will be joined, cut off about ¼ inch on each cake. Center the cakes and then crumb them.

Because the boots were quite heavy and not too steady, they required some sort of sturdy platform on which they could stand. For this a sheet of Styrofoam covered with foil was used. It was coated with Royal Icing on the top and sides and made very smooth.

Glaze the top and sides of the cake to prepare it for basket weaving (see Chapter 7). Use tips nos. 8 and 48 for the weave. Center a sheet of foil on the top of the cake for the Styrofoam platform to rest on; do lattice work on the top (fig. 17-1) and basket weave on the sides of the cake.

FIG. 17-1

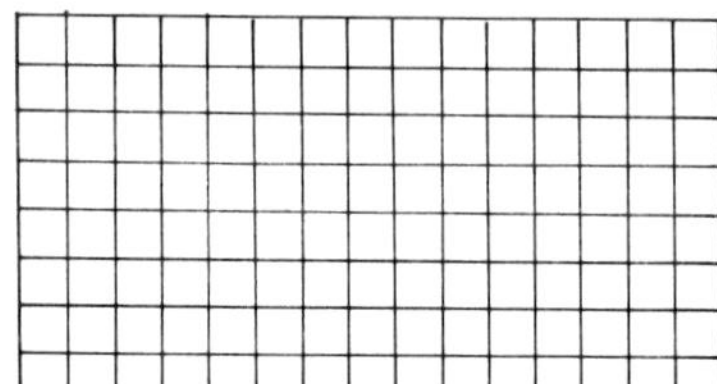

Do the same lattice and basket weave on the Styrofoam platform. When dry, place it on the cake and join it to the cake with a roping design with tip no. 20. This same roping is used on the top edge of the cake. Roping around the base is done with a no. 22 tip.

Place the flowers on the cake as shown in the photograph. Transport the boots separately and place them on the cake when it is set on the table.

Needless to say, the birthday gentleman got a kick out of his boots and keeps them to this day in a glass case.

Telephone Cake

SUPPLIES

Cakes:
- 16-inch round cake
- 9- × 5-inch loaf cake
- 8-inch square cake

Flowers:
- 150 multicolored assorted flowers

Leaves:
- 150 assorted green

Royal Icing push buttons

This cake was made for the birthday of a sixteen-year-old for obvious reasons. On the other hand, it could be appropriate for any age!

Prepare the flowers and leaves first. Next, make the squares for the push buttons: Take Royal Icing and thin it down slightly so that when you put a small amount on a piece of waxed paper, it spreads a little before it sets. (Incidentally, this is a good way to represent balloons on a cake.) When these small disks have dried, use a serrated knife and cut them all into the same-size squares. The smaller the square, the more difficult they are to handle.

Bake all the cakes and freeze the cakes that you will be using for the telephone for they are much easier to cut and carve when frozen.

Place the 16-inch cake on Plexiglas and crumb it. Glaze the cake as soon as the frosting has set.

Mark for the lower scrolls around the base of the cake by either measuring around the cake and dividing it into 8 equal parts or make a waxed-paper pattern and fold it into 8 wedges. Mark each section with a toothpick.

Divide each section in half again for 16 toothpick markers for the border pattern. Place your ruler at one of the toothpicks, measure 2½ inches out on the Plexiglas, and mark with a little dab of frosting (fig. 17-2a). At the next toothpick measure 1 inch out and mark (fig. 17-2b); from the next toothpick measure 2½ inches again. Repeat this all around the cake. Place a no. 16 tip and Basic Frosting in your bag and make the C (fig. 17-2c) for a guideline. After you have gone all around the cake, measure up onto the cake opposite line a 2 inches (fig. 17-3a). Opposite line b measure up 1 inch (fig. 17-3b). Continue these markings all around the cake. With a toothpick join to make a swag line (fig. 17-3c). After the swags are marked, you are ready to apply a line of frosting to which the ruffle will be applied. Pipe this line using Basic Frosting and tip no. 16 directly on the toothpick line all around the cake. Give this a few minutes to set during which time the scrolls on the Plexiglas can be completed. Go over the guidelines for the scrolls on the Plexiglas twice using Basic Frosting and tip no. 20. As you go over this a third time come down sharp at the corners and back again to continue the scroll (fig. 17-3d). Insert tip no. 68 and make a leaf between the scrolls (see figs. 17-2 and 17-3).

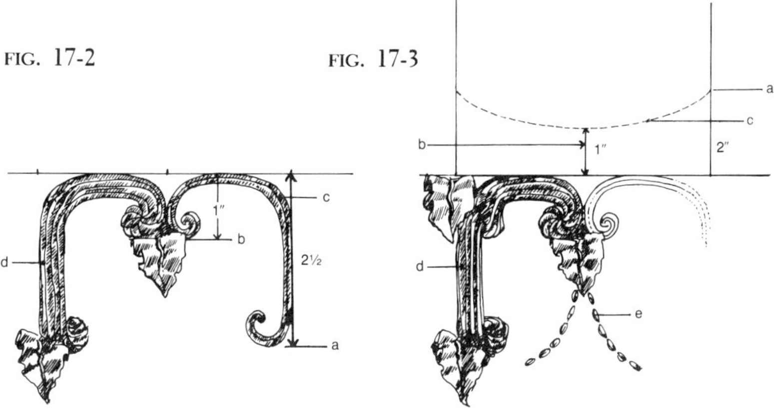

FIG. 17-2 FIG. 17-3

To do the ruffle on the swags, use Basic Frosting and tip no. 104. Hold the heavy part of the tip just over the swag line against the frosting and apply pressure making a slight up-and-down motion to form a ruffle (fig. 17-4a). With tip no. 16 make a beading at the top of the gathered ruffle (fig. 17-4b). Just above this make another beading line (fig. 17-4c) using tip no. 14. Using the same star tip make a dotted design coming out from the leaves on the scrolls (fig. 17-3e).

FIG. 17-4

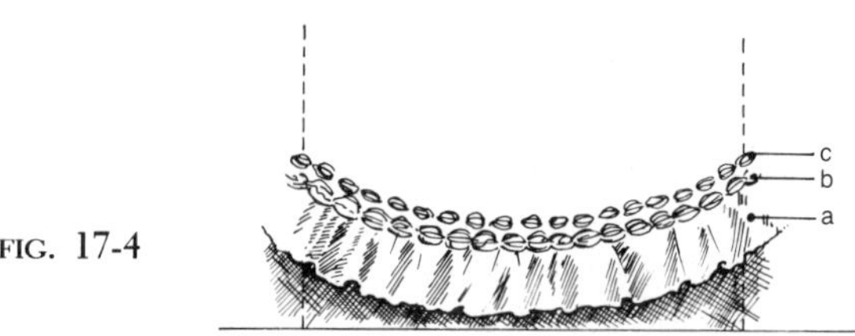

Around the top edge of the cake make a puff border. To do this, hold the no. 20 tip against the frosting and squeeze a mound; stop squeezing and pull away about ½ inch; squeeze again (fig. 17-5). Most of this border will be covered with the floral arrangement.

FIG. 17-5

To make the telephone, remove the 8-inch cake from the freezer. Using your own phone as a guide, cut and carve the cake to look like the base of the phone. When you have finished, cut a piece of cardboard the size of the phone base and wrap it in foil. Cut a piece of foil to match the size of the cardboard and place this on the cake where you intend to place the phone. Put the phone base in place and smooth out your sculpturing efforts.

Place the loaf cake on a piece of waxed paper, carve it the shape of the receiver, and try to crumb it before it thaws. When crumbed, place it in the freezer long enough for the frosting to freeze. When the frosting is frozen, it is much easier to pick up and to remove the waxed paper. Place the receiver in position on the cake.

Apply the push buttons and with a no. 7 tip, make a small beading (fig. 17-6) around the base of the phone and receiver. The telephone cord is made with a no. 10 tip. Finally do the floral arrangement.

FIG. 17-6

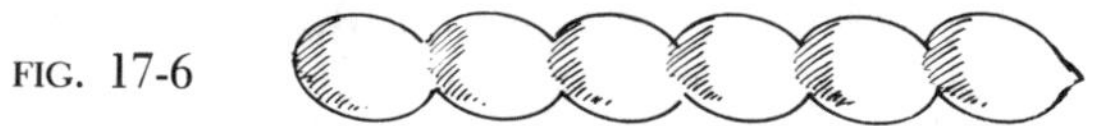

Now you can dial a cake!

The Drum

SUPPLIES

12-inch round cake,
6 to 7 inches high

Royal Icing Emblem

This cake may be made for a child's birthday with drum sticks instead of the eagle. It is ideal for a man who has an interest in history or for an occasion that calls for a patriotic theme. Read the section on run sugar in Chapter 11 before starting the eagle.

The eagle (fig. 17-7) is made in 4 separate pieces, the eagle, the shield, the arrows, and the branch with leaves.

To make the eagle use Royal Icing in varied shades of gray. This is done with a slightly softer Royal Icing but not as soft as run sugar.

With tip no. 16 at the inside lower wing (fig. 17-8a), start by doing a zigzag up and down until you fill in this section. Go on to the next section (fig. 17-8b) and fill in with a slight overlap of icing. Fill in other sections (fig. 17-8c and d) in the same way.

FIG. 17-7

FIG. 17-8

Do the same thing on the opposite side starting at the outside edge and working toward the shield. Change to tip no. 24 and starting at the lower part of the tail feather, proceed in the same manner continuing on to the upper leg.

Start at the lower neck with tip no. 24 and follow in the same manner, but reduce the pressure as you get close to the eye. When this icing has set, with white Royal Icing place the no. 3 tip at the mouth and apply pressure to form the beak. Holding your bag upright, place the same tip where the eye should be and apply pressure to form a nice round ball. Let it set for a minute and flatten it a little with your finger.

Under the shield, make just a flat zigzag to fill in the space as the shield will be placed over it when all is dry.

Outline all the lines on the shield using tip no. 4 with white Royal Icing. Let dry completely before you start doing the run sugar. The run-sugar colors are: gold (golden egg yellow in Chefmaster paste colors), blue (royal blue), and red (holiday or Christmas). Use a no. 2 tip for all the colors. Allow each color to dry before you go on to the next.

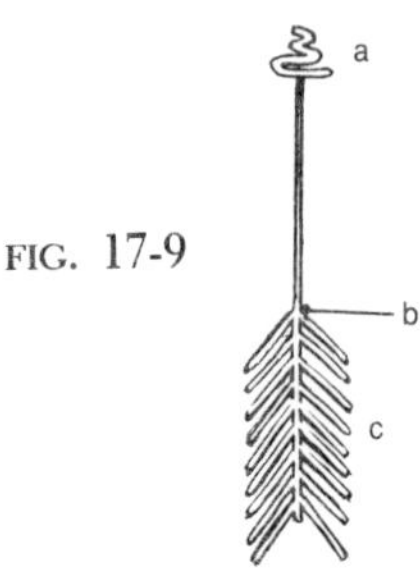

FIG. 17-9

To do the arrows, fill your bag with light brown Royal Icing. Insert a flat wooden toothpick into a tip no. 4 leaving just ⅛ inch for you to hold; pull out very slowly. Place the toothpicks on a piece of waxed paper about 1 inch apart. Cover about 6 toothpicks.

On one end of each toothpick using the same color and tip, form the arrowhead with a zigzag starting just over the toothpick about ¼ inch wide and making each line shorter until you get to a fine point (fig. 17-9a).

For the feathered end, using the same color and tip, place the tip at the end of the toothpick and extend the shaft ¼ inch to make it a little longer.

About 1⅜ inches from the base of the arrowhead, place a no. 2 tip against the toothpick, apply pressure, and pull out (fig. 17-9c). Keeping the lines on an angle, continue these lines in the same way until you reach the end of the frosting. Do the opposite side. With the same tip, go over the toothpick where the feathers begin (fig. 17-9b).

The lower part of the branch in the eagle's other claw may be done directly on the cake or done separately and applied. Whichever way, use green Royal Icing with a brownish tinge and tip no. 6 for the large branch and no. 4 for the small. For the leaf use tip no. 65 with a soft green color.

The cake may be baked in 2 or 3 layers with a small amount of filling in between. Cardboard dividers may be used. Invert the cake on a clear piece of Plexiglas.

Crumb your cake with white frosting. After it is completely dry, glaze the top surface with white frosting. Glaze the sides with blue frosting, being very careful not to get any blue on the top. Let set until it is thoroughly dry so that the red color doesn't run.

With red frosting and tip no. 124 with the thickest part above the ridge of the cake, go all around the cake. Where the red frosting meets, use a hot dry spatula (dip spatula into boiling water and wipe dry) to smooth off the joining. Reverse your tip having the thickest part on the lower edge and overlapping the thin edge on the previous red about ¼ inch. Make another row of red frosting. Where the 2 thin edges overlap use the hot dry spatula to smooth them into one piece.

Make the same band on the lower edge of the cake. Start with the thickest part against the base first; then reverse the tip to do the top edge of the lower band.

Again allow to dry completely so that the red will not run onto the blue or onto the white.

Make a circle of waxed paper the size of the cake; fold it into eight wedges (Chapter 4). The top of your cake should be thoroughly dry by now. Place the pattern on the top and insert toothpicks between the red and white icings to mark the 8 sections. These markings indicate where the side string will begin.

At the lower edge of the cake place a toothpick in between the toothpicks at the top edge.

Using a toothpick to draw the lines and starting at the upper edge at a toothpick, mark (by making small indentations in the icing) a line going down at an angle to the half-way mark, then on with a straight line to the lower toothpick (see photograph). Complete these markings all around the cake.

With tip no. 5 and holding a bag of white Basic Frosting straight up, start just about ½ inch away from the base on the side of the cake, apply pressure, and make a small rotary motion to give the appearance of roping. Continue this technique following the toothpick line until you reach about 1 inch from the top edge. Make all the roping lines around the cake.

When the white has dried completely, add the black frosting. With tip no. 5 hold the black frosting bag down so that when you apply pressure the frosting will cup over the edge and form the hook. Apply pressure so that the frosting will widen; then carefully cover the edge of the white.

On the lower edge, join the 2 ends of the rope to the Plexiglas with a dab of black icing. The center clamp can be accomplished by making a single string of black frosting from one side to the other of the double roping.

To place the eagle plaque on the cake, turn the run sugar over on a piece of paper toweling. Slowly remove waxed paper and quickly place Royal Icing down the head, neck, and around the whole mold, plus a little in the center. Invert and place on cake slightly above the center to allow space for the claws.

Place Royal Icing around the shield and a little in the center. Invert immediately onto eagle. Press down lightly. It should be slightly raised. Whenever you apply a run sugar decoration on a cake, do it quickly because the icing you apply to adhere it can soften the design and make it break when you pick it up.

It is very important on this cake that each color be allowed to dry completely before the next is added. If the colors run, it will ruin the whole effect of your cake.

Place 3 arrows close together. A little Royal Icing may be used to hold them in place. Place the branch on the opposite side.

For the claws to clutch these objects, use tip no. 6 and a bag of golden-egg-yellow frosting. Holding the bag at a 45-degree angle, place tip under the body and above the tail feather, apply pressure, and push in and out to give the ridge line in the legs. Just about ¼ inch before you start the talons, apply more pressure to make it bigger. Change to a no. 4 tip and form 3 talons, one at a time, going around the arrows as though it were clutching them. Do the same thing on the opposite side for the claws that clutch the branch.

Car Cake

SUPPLIES (serves 250)

Cakes:
- two 14-inch squares for bottom layer
- one 17- × 10-inch
- 1 large loaf pan
- 1 6-inch square

Flowers:
- 200 daisies and chrysanthemums

Leaves:
- 150 assorted leaves

Run sugar for car

This cake was designed for the birthday of a collector of antique cars. The cake represents a 1936 Ford roadster with a rumble seat. The same car can be placed on a smaller cake if you have fewer people to serve.

Begin by making all of your flowers in shades of yellow through copper. The large heavy chrysanthemums are made with Basic Frosting. The daisy shapes are made with Royal Icing.

Make an assortment of green leaves from dark to light using tips nos. 67 and 68.

To make the car bake the cakes in a large loaf pan and a 6-inch square pan. A pound cake recipe would be perfect, but any other recipe that bakes a solid cake with a fine texture would do. Freezing the cakes makes it easier to cut and shape them.

Place the loaf cake on a foil-covered cardboard (have a matching piece of foil to be placed on the cake itself). You are now ready to become a sculptor. With a sharp knife start cutting (or carving) your cake into the desired shape. Cut a little at a time watching your overall proportions. The 6-inch cake is used for the roof section and for the spare tire which attaches to the back of the car.

The bumper and headlights are made of Royal Icing and the number plates of run sugar. This run-sugar piece can be made a little larger than necessary and then "sawed" to the desired shape with a serrated knife.

The body of the car was covered with Basic Frosting, and all the trimmings were done in Royal Icing.

Bake the remaining cakes. When they are cooled, remove ¼ inch from one side of each of the 14-inch cakes. Place these cut sides together on a Plexiglas base. Cover the top of this large rectangular cake with a double layer of frosting and crumb the sides.

Trace around the 17- × 10-inch pan on a piece of cardboard. Trace this shape twice on foil making one piece of foil large enough to wrap around the edges of the cardboard. Center the smaller piece of foil on the cake and place the foil-wrapped cardboard on top of this. Now invert your top cake onto the cardboard. Crumb this cake.

When it is dry, glaze the top surface in yellow keeping the sides white.

Place another very thin layer of frosting on the sides and make it smooth for basket weave (Chapter 7).

Do the basket weave using tips nos. 48 and 8 on the sides of the 2 layers using white Basic Frosting.

When this is completed, do a lattice design on the top surface using tip no. 48. Starting at one side, make a line parallel to the edge about ½ inch away. The width of each line determines the spacing. Continue making the lines until you reach the other side of the cake. Turn your cake around and repeat the process keeping the same space between the lines (see photograph).

Make a heavy roping around the top and lower edges of each cake using tip no. 22.

Now take your car and center it on the top of the cake on a piece of foil. Arrange the flowers starting at the base of the cake with larger flowers and graduating to the smaller ones as you reach the upper areas. Scatter the small flowers around the car.

You are now ready to take to the road.

Butterfly Cake

SUPPLIES

Cakes:
  16-inch round
Bows:
  20 each 1½ inches wide, includes extras
Butterflies:
  15 in a variety of sizes and colors
Flowers:
  100 daisies in a variety of sizes, types, and colors
Leaves:
  50 to 75 green leaves

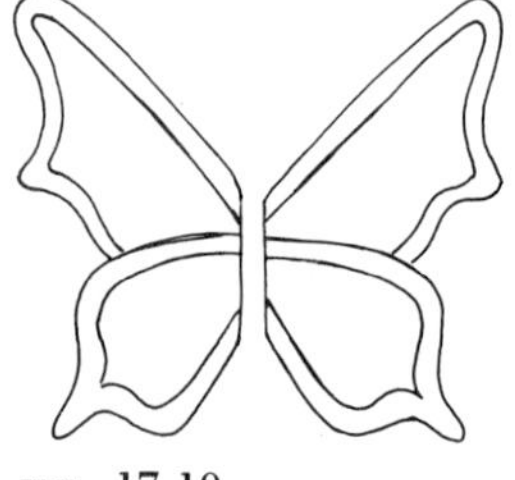

FIG. 17-10

All of the decorations may be made before baking the cake. Make the daisies in whatever colors you wish (see Chapter 9). Make the bows using tip no. 102 with Royal Icing. Follow instructions in Chapter 11. See Chapter 10 for leaves.

Cut 15 squares about 4 × 4 inches, of waxed paper. Place waxed paper over the patterns (figs. 17-10 and 17-11) to make the butterflies. Butterflies are done in run sugar using tip no. 4 for everything. When you do the butterflies, make the wings side by side. The bodies will be added later. When they are completely dry, decorate the tops with Royal Icing (fig. 17-12).

FIG. 17-11

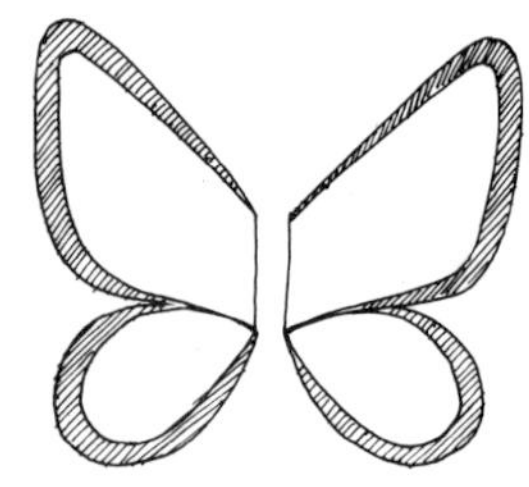

The inside part of the butterfly in fig. 17-13 is filled with run sugar, and the outside ridges are done with a no. 3 tip to create the lace effect.

The butterfly in fig. 17-14 is done with tip no. 2. Do all the lines of the butterfly using the Royal Icing recipe in this book; then outline all of it as shown in the sketch with small zigzag motion.

When the wings are dry, open a large book and, with the wings still on the waxed paper, position the wings so that the center space for the

FIG. 17-12

body will be in the crease of the book. Place the no. 4 tip where the wings begin and pipe a mound of icing for the head, release the pressure to make an indentation, apply pressure for a heavier body, and then taper to nothing (fig. 17-15). Complete all butterflies. Do not remove the waxed paper until you are ready to use them.

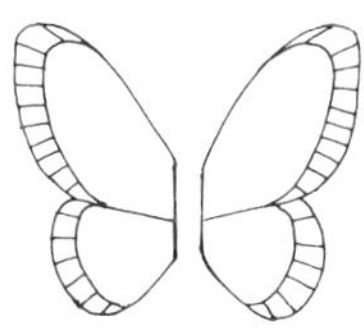

FIG. 17-13

Now is the time to bake the cake. While it is baking and cooling, make Basic Frosting to crumb and glaze the cake.

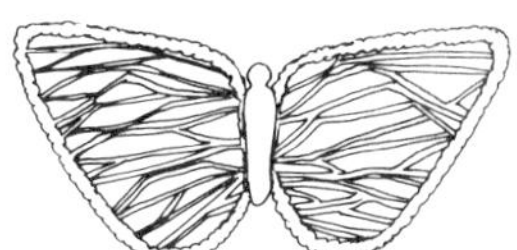

FIG. 17-14

Measure for the lower scrolls around the base of the cake by either measuring around the cake and dividing it into 8 equal parts or fold a waxed-paper pattern into 8 wedges (Chapter 4). Mark each section with a toothpick.

Divide and mark each section in half again making 16 sections for the border pattern. Place a ruler at a toothpick and measure 2½ inches out on the Plexiglas and mark with a little dab of white Basic Frosting (fig. 17-16a). On the next toothpick, measure 1 inch out (fig. 17-16b) and the next, 2½ inches out, and so on all around the cake. Place a no. 16 tip with Basic Frosting in your bag and form the letter C (fig. 17-16e) to make a guideline. After you have gone all around the Plexiglas, measure and do the same thing on the side of the cake. Change to tip no. 20

FIG. 17-15

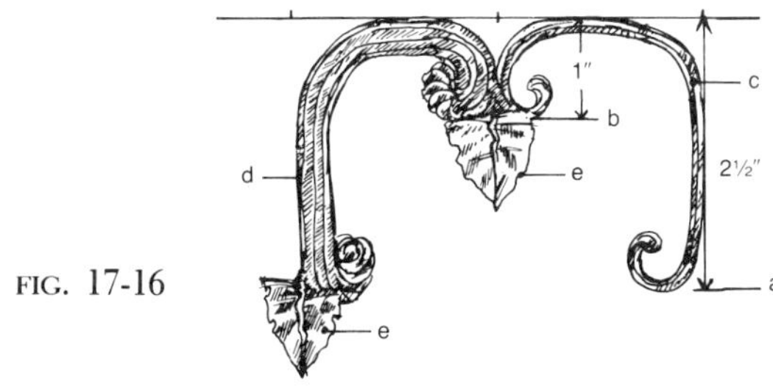

FIG. 17-16

and go over the guidelines twice (fig. 17-16d). At the end of each C section place a leaf made with a no. 68 tip (fig. 17-16e).

Just below the high point of the C on the side of the cake, place a bow made with Royal Icing. See the photograph. Arrange the flowers, leaves, and butterflies.

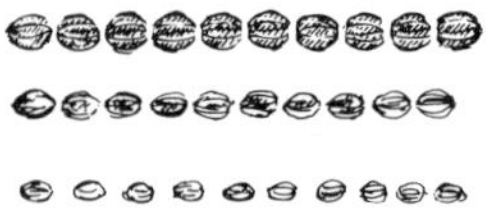

Make a serpentine design around the border using tips nos. 13, 14, and 16 (fig. 17-17). Put little dots of Basic Frosting around the cake; then follow it with dots from the other 2 tips.

FIG. 17-17

To apply the candles, make a large star with Basic Frosting and tip no. 30; then push the candle in the center and place 3 flowers around it. If it does not hold, try again with more frosting.

Jack-in-the-Box

SUPPLIES

Pound cakes:
- 2 cakes, each 6 inches square and 3½ inches high; or 3 cakes, each 6 inches square and 1¾ inches high
- 1 cake baked in a 7-ounce round can
- 2 cakes baked in ½- and ⅓-cup aluminum measuring cups

Animal sugar molds

2 to 3 recipes Basic Frosting (see Index)

5-inch-square cardboard for lid

FIG. 17-18

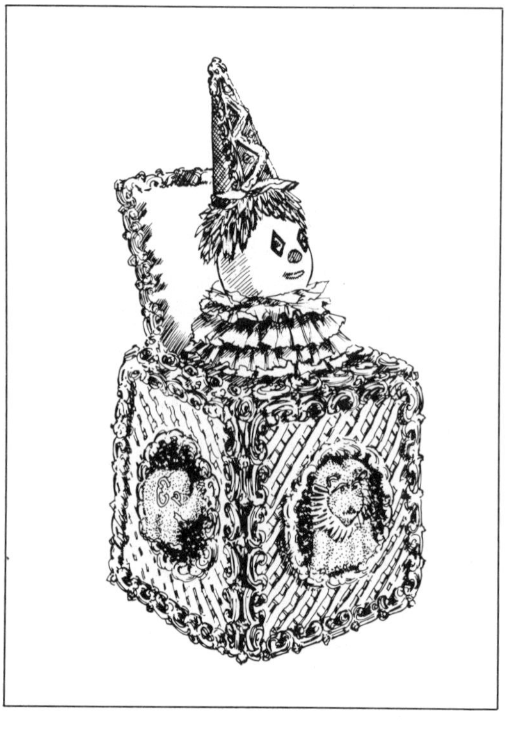

Who is this madcap fellow who has just appeared in a mass of ruffles, his flaming orange hair in need of a barber? He is the irrepressible Jack who lives in a box! And such a box—all gold and green, covered with white lattice work, and inlaid with ferocious green lions and pink elephants.

On this cake you will learn the art of carving with cake in order to build Jack's head. Pound cake should be used to ensure a solid texture. As soon as you are finished, Jack will flip his lid, and how the children will adore him!

Sugar Molds

The first step in this project is to make the sugar molds. Later on in the chapter, I will explain how this cake can be decorated using different designs not requiring molds.

For this cake, you need 4 animal sugar molds (see Chapter 11). These molds are common items in cake supply stores. If you wish to place a mold on the cover, you need 5, but it must be a small mold so that it will not bend the frosted cardboard cover. Before applying the molded figures to the cake, allow them to dry for at least 24 hours but longer if possible.

Cake Construction

The smallest of the square wedding-cake pans is used to bake the cakes. If that is not available, use a 6-inch-square brownie pan and bake as many layers as needed for a cake 7 inches high. See fig. 17-19.

FIG. 17-19

For the ruffled neckline section, bake a cake in a 7-ounce can. Wash it thoroughly and treat the can as you would any other baking container. Grease and line it with waxed paper; then pour in the batter and bake. For Jack's head, grease and flour both the ½- and ⅓-cup aluminum measuring cups. Pour in the batter and bake.

Because of the weight of this cake, place it on a piece of plywood covered with foil and a glassine doily. Place the square cakes on the board and crumb with white frosting, applying only a small amount between the layers to prevent sliding.

If your cake is 6 inches square, cut a firm, but not thick, piece of cardboard 5 × 5 inches.

To make Jack's head, assemble the 2 small cakes baked in the measuring cups. Apply a little frosting to the tops so that they form a ball when attached. Hold this head shape by having the thumb on the bottom and fingers on top. Crumb with white frosting on outer edges. Set aside to dry.

Mixing the Colors

To prepare the colors, you will need to proceed as follows: Take 3 mixing bowls with lids and place about 2 cups Basic Frosting in each. Mix rose pink, mint green, and a light royal blue, 1 color in each bowl. In another bowl, mix 1 full recipe of bright yellow Basic Frosting for the background. Cover all these mixed colors with a lid or a damp cloth to prevent drying.

Fill a canvas bag with white frosting for the features of the animals. Attach a no. 2 tip and put aside. To do the borders, use a no. 19 tip and fill your canvas bag with a small amount (a rounded teaspoon) of green, then blue, then pink, then yellow, then back to green, and so forth until you have enough in your bag to make a border.

Fill a parchment bag with yellow frosting and use a no. 30 tip. Put a no. 16 tip in a parchment bag and fill with pink frosting. With your Ateco tip no. 127 in a canvas bag, fill with frosting of alternating colors (pink, blue, yellow, green).

Frost the 6-inch block of cake and one side of the cardboard lid with yellow icing. Then glaze. With the no. 2 tip on the bag of white frosting, outline the features and toes of the sugar-mold animals (figs. 17-20 and 17-21).

FIG. 17-20

Take the largest sugar mold you will be using and place it on a piece of parchment. Then draw a circle around it using a glass or plate with a suitable circumference and cut it out. Center this paper circle on each side of the cake and outline it with a toothpick. You will insert your animal in this space.

FIG. 17-21

Boxed In

Now for the lattice. If you want to indicate the lines with a long sharp knife, place the end of the blade on one corner and score the frosting diagonally. Using the no. 47 tip, start at the upper left-hand corner, apply pressure to secure icing, and squeeze gently. Then pull slowly to keep the lattice flat until you reach the line of the circle. Do all the lines running in one direction; then reverse to create the cross-hatch effect.

Behind the animal molds is a textured background. To make this, use yellow frosting in a parchment bag with a clean no. 30 tip. Place this tip against the cake and apply pressure until frosting comes from around the sides of the tip. Release pressure and pull away. By repeating this over the area you should create a flat textured effect. With a canvas bag filled with white frosting and a no. 15 tip, outline the yellow circle with a series of capital Cs as shown in figs. 17-20 and 17-21. Squeeze some yellow frosting onto the back of your sugar mold and place your animal inside the yellow circle. Hold it a few seconds, pushing against the cake, until it is securely fastened. Do this on all 4 sides of the cake.

For the box top, turn the frosted piece of cardboard over onto a piece of waxed paper. Frost and add lattice work to match the box. If you made a small sugar mold for the top, prepare the circle and add the mold.

Using your prepared multicolored frosting bag with a no. 19 tip, go around each side of the cake with capital Cs. After doing 4 sides and around the top, repeat the same procedure right on top of each C to achieve a raised look.

Jack Pops Up

Plan the placement of Jack's neck (7-ounce can), leaving enough space behind him for the lid. Place this section on your box.

If your cake is on a lazy susan, it will simplify the application of the ruffle around the neck. Use the multicolored frosting bag and a no. 127 tip. With the thickest part of the tip at the neck base, apply pressure to add the ruffle all around. Join the ruffle at the back because the lid will cover this section. Do the next row of ruffles a little higher. Continue in this manner until the circle of ruffles is small enough for the head to be attached. Holding the head in the same manner as indicated earlier, glaze with white frosting and place in the center of the top ruffle. If you feel you would like to secure the head, take the rose stick (¼-inch dowel) and push it through the head and down into the cake. I often do this in my classes because the cake has to be transported home before the icing has a chance to set.

The hat may be made from a waffle or sugar cone. Before you start decorating, place the cone on the head and press in gently to imprint a circle as a guide for the hairline. Decorate the hat and let stand until Jack's hair has been added. With a small amount of yellow icing in a bowl, add orange or red paste color for hair. Using a parchment bag filled with orange icing and a no. 13 tip, place the tip at the outlined circle on the head and apply pressure. Pull out to give it the untamed hair look. Give Jack as much hair as you like, making it shorter in front. With the no. 127 tip on a bag of multicolored frosting, keep the thick part of the tip on the inner circle and make a circular ruffle around the top of his head. Immediately place the decorated cone on the ruffle.

By this time, the lattice work on the box cover is dry. Turn it onto the yellow underside and make the capital C motif along 3 edges. Place the undecorated edge against the cake and lean the lid against Jack's head. For a more open lid, make a slit in the cake and insert the cardboard about ½ inch. This extra ½ inch has to be allowed for when you cut the cardboard. However, I strongly recommend the lid-against-the-head method for beginners for the other method requires more skill.

Decorate the outer edges of the cover with the same C design used for the box.

For the final touch on the border, take the parchment bag with the no. 16 tip and pink frosting, and space stars between border designs along the box seams. At the corners, make a double circle.

Jack's Face

The colors for Jack's face were not mixed at the beginning because such small quantities would dry before you could use them. Mix a scant tablespoon of black frosting and place in a parchment bag with the no. 2 tip. With this bag, form the diamond-shaped eyes.

With the no. 13 tip in a parchment bag, add a scant tablespoon of blue icing and form stars for his eyes. Mix a tablespoon of red frosting and put it into a parchment bag. With a no. 2 tip, form the mouth as shown in the photograph. Place the same tip in position against the face to make the nose, and apply enough pressure to form a ball.

Variations on a Theme

The sides of the box may be decorated in many different ways. The lattice can be done in the manner discussed but the center circle omitted as shown in fig. 17-22.

Or you can glaze the sides and cover in any color desired. Use any of the rose tips to make vertical, horizontal, or even diagonal stripes. By leaving a space between stripes, the background color will be seen as illustrated in fig. 17-23.

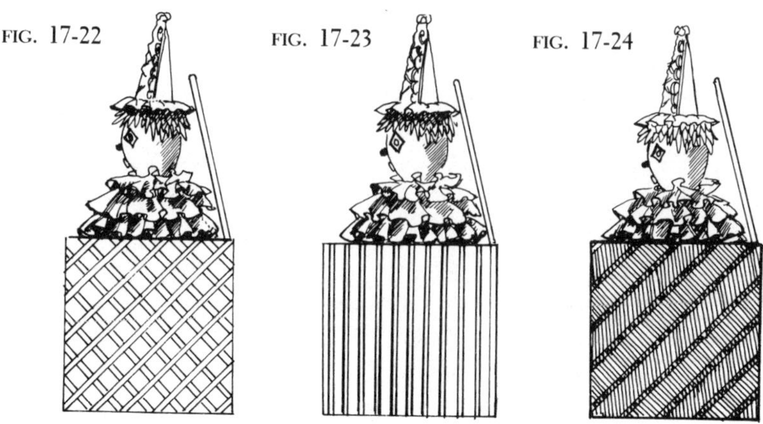

FIG. 17-22 FIG. 17-23 FIG. 17-24

Another method of decorating the box is to use 2 rose tips in 2 different bags with 2 different colors. These stripes may also be done vertically, horizontally, or diagonally. With the thickest part of the tip upward, starting at the side on the top left corner, apply pressure and keep the tip flat against the cake. Release pressure and break the icing at the top. This will just barely cover the corner. The first few stripes are difficult. Take the other rose tip (tips do not have to be the same size) and, following the same diagonal line and overlapping a scant ¼ inch, make another stripe as shown in fig. 17-24. Continue in this fashion until all the sides are completed.

Humpty Dumpty

SUPPLIES

9 × 5-inch loaf cake
Cake baked in 1-cup aluminum measuring cup

Bright-eyed and securely clutching his wall, Humpty Dumpty is a child's delight and a cake decorator's challenge (see fig. 17-25).

This project requires time, but what fun Humpty is to dress in bright and giddy colors not ordinarily used on a cake. On his natty suit you will have a chance to learn ruffling, and his arms and legs require figure

FIG. 17-25

piping. To our flower collection we will add the drop flower, which grows in profusion about his wall, and you will also become an expert in cake "masonry."

Before the Fall

Place the loaf cake on a board with large enough margins to allow you to add flowers around the wall (fig. 17-25). You may frost the loaf with brown-tinted Basic Frosting, but I have my classes use the chocolate butter cream because it is so luscious. The butter cream could be used for decorating, but the results are not as sharp as with the Basic Frosting.

FIG. 17-26

Some years ago when my children were small, I made a large Humpty Dumpty sitting on an angel cake loaf. That, with the butter cream frosting, was their choice. The taste was fabulous but the decorative results were not. Butter cream does not make as sharp and crisp a design as Basic Frosting. The wall sagged, but fortunately the cake was devoured before Humpty fell off. I learned that the wall must be firmer than angel cake to support a heavy decoration and that, delicious as butter cream is, the final product is not as striking to look at.

CHOCOLATE BUTTER CREAM FROSTING

4 ounces (1 stick) butter; (margarine may be used)
1 pound confectioner's sugar
1 medium egg
1 teaspoon vanilla
Unsweetened cocoa to taste

Have butter at room temperature and place in a bowl. Add the egg and about half the box of sugar. Cream by hand or with an electric mixer until well blended. Add the remaining sugar and the vanilla. Blend well. Add cocoa and mix thoroughly. If you want a deep color, add brown food coloring. This recipe may be used without the cocoa for other occasions.

It is not necessary to crumb and glaze this particular cake unless it has a crumbly exterior. Then you have no choice. Apply butter frosting; then smooth it out with your spatula. Another way to smooth it out is to use your fingers as soon as it dries enough to be touched without sticking.

Take about ½ cup Basic Frosting and add a scant ⅛ teaspoon of chocolate butter cream. This is used to crumb the cake that was baked in the measuring cup. If the batter has overflowed or mushroomed, just ignore it; once Humpty Dumpty's coat goes on, it will not be noticeable. After the head has been crumbed and while the frosting sets, start to mix the colors and get the decorating bags ready.

Prepare the Colors

Now is the time to decide what type and color of masonry Humpty will be sitting on. Either gray or white is suggested for mortar. If you decide to use white, the gray bag in the list may be omitted. If you prefer gray, put enough icing in the bowl for the gray and black amounts. Mix it by adding a small amount of black to your icing to achieve a gray shade. Fill your bag half full. Then add more black to the remainder of the icing for the black bag.

The first number on the list is the first tip you will be using in that particular bag. The white and black canvas bags are the only two that require waxed paper on the couplings to prevent the frosting from hardening. If the gray is not used, the no. 3 tip may be placed on the white icing bag.

The red for the mouth will have to wait until the cake is completed. You may use a parchment bag and cut the paper to form a small hole. However, the results will be far better if you use a no. 2 tip.

Tip Numbers	*Color*	*Bag Used*	*Amount of Icing*
3, 193	white	canvas	½ to full bag
3	gray	parchment	½ bag
2, 7	black	canvas	¼ bag
104, 13, 193	pink	canvas	full bag
13, 193, 2	yellow	canvas	scant full bag
68	green	parchment	scant full bag
12, 193	violet	canvas	1½ bags
2	red	parchment	scant tablespoon

Wall to Wall

You have a choice of 3 different types of masonry designs shown in figs. 17-27, 17-28, and 17-29. For the first one (fig. 17-27), use the no. 3 tip with gray or white frosting. Holding your bag at a 45-degree angle and starting at the base on the left-hand corner, apply pressure and squeeze a straight line all the way across to the other corner. Make a parallel line ¾ inch higher, then another ¾ inch higher, and so forth, until you

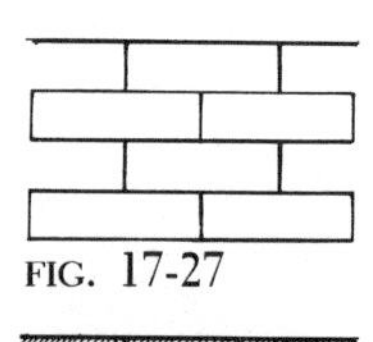
FIG. 17-27

FIG. 17-28

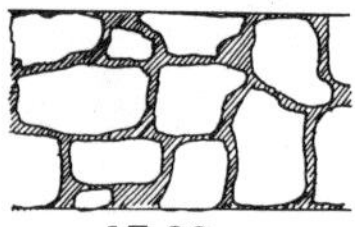
FIG. 17-29

reach the top of the cake. To form the bricks, continue with the same bag. Add a vertical line by putting the tip on the upper line, applying pressure, and bringing the tip to the lower line. Stop squeezing and slightly push the tip in to break the frosting. You should not have any points sticking out. Do this on all sides of the wall as well as the top section.

The next type of brick masonry, shown in fig. 17-28, is a little different. Use the no. 3 tip with gray or white icing. Start at the base of the wall and, with a slight up and down motion, go across the lower section only once. Hold the bag straight up and form 2 straight lines close together and a scant ½ inch long. About an inch away, make 2 more vertical lines. Continue until you have gone all the way across. The next step is to make 2 horizontal lines close together, joining all these ends. When you do the next group of ½-inch vertical lines, center them between the lines on the first row to form your brick design. Continue in this fashion until the whole wall is covered. This pattern may also be done brick by brick using the same method.

The fieldstone wall, shown in fig. 17-29, is also very impressive. Follow the lines shown or create your own design. If you wish, you may fill in mortar between each stone using a no. 3 tip. Fill in by squeezing the tip either from left to right or up and down and holding your tip close to the cake. Your wall will appear very realistic.

Position the crumbed cake baked in the measuring cup directly in the center of the loaf cake (fig. 17-26). Glaze with the off-white icing ½ inch above where Humpty joins the wall.

Putting Humpty Together

Use the no. 12 tip on the bag of violet icing to make the collar, and start at the center front. About 1 inch up on Humpty's head, apply pressure, going from left to right. Continue around the head, raising the collar line slightly on the sides and back, then lowering it again to the joining at the center front. If you have a lazy susan, it is especially useful for this cake.

To do the coat under the collar, use the no. 12 tip. Starting at the front, use an up-and-down motion, keeping lines close together. Continue from the purple collar line to the base next to the loaf cake. Fill the space all around. Then dip a spatula in hot water and use it to smooth out his coat.

To apply the ruffle around the collar section, put your arm around Humpty. With the no. 104 tip on the bag of pink icing, start squeezing with the thickest part of the tip against the frosting at the left center front. As you squeeze, move the tip up and down very slightly to create a ruffle. With a lazy Susan, it can usually be done in one operation without breaking your ruffle. If you stop and start again, make a pleat over the end so that it is not noticeable. Stop at the right center front on a slight angle.

The no. 13 tip in the bag of yellow icing will make the tiny lacing around the neck on the thickest part of the ruffle. With the no. 2 tip, go around the outer thin edge of the ruffle. If the ruffle has had a chance to set a few minutes, it will be easier to apply the edging.

Now for the arms and legs. Take the bag of violet icing with the no. 12 tip. Hold the bag at a 45-degree angle on the right side where you think an arm should be. Apply pressure until the frosting makes a thick continuous arm. Pull the bag very slowly. Turn slightly to form an elbow and stop the pressure at the wrist just before it reaches the front edge of the cake. Now add the left arm following the same technique. This is called figure piping.

Humpty's legs are done in the same manner as his arms using the no. 12 tip on a bag of violet icing. As the icing in the tip is apt to be a bit dry, squeeze about ⅛ inch out. Wipe the tip and proceed. Hold the tip against the right front; then apply pressure to hold his leg in place. The pressure applied with a clean moist tip makes the frosting stick. Pull away slowly still applying pressure; come over the front of the cake to form his knees; then go down to his ankle. Release pressure and the frosting will stop flowing. Pull away very slowly. Now do the left side. Be careful not to make the legs too far apart.

With the no. 104 tip on a bag of pink icing, apply the ruffle around the wrist. Start on the left side with the thickest part close to the hand. Apply pressure and make a slightly forward and backward motion to create the gathering. Go as far as you can to the right of the wrist, holding the thickest part of the tip so that it forms a circle around the purple arm. Do the other wrist.

Now do the same thing around each ankle by starting at the left side and going to the right. This is a little more difficult because of the angle and will take more time.

Tip No.	*Uses*
2:	ruffle edging, eyes, nose, mouth, and ears
3:	mortar outline for bricks or stones, gloves or mittens
7:	boots
12:	jacket, piping for arms and legs
13:	inner ruffle lacing, star buttons
68:	leaves surrounding wall
104:	ruffles
193:	drop flowers

After the ruffles are completed on the arms and legs, apply the yellow trim around the wrist and the ankles with a no. 13 tip. Change to a no. 2 tip on the yellow bag. By this time, the ruffles will have set so that you can directly apply the icing to the thin edge of the ruffle without any difficulty.

With the no. 3 tip on the bag of white icing, form the gloves by putting the tip directly in the center of the ruffled circle. Apply pressure and rotate the tip slightly to form the back of the hand. Form the thumb by placing the tip on the inside of the mound and applying a little pressure. Stop pressure and pull away. If you pull away before you stop the pressure, Humpty will end up with sharp claws! Just away from the thumb, apply 4 fingers in the same manner.

Or, to make mittens, start in the same manner by applying pressure and rotating the tip slightly to form the back of the hand. Continue this a little further till it is in the proper proportion. Apply a thumb.

Finishing Touches

With the no. 2 tip on a bag of black, do the eyes, ears, and nose, applying the tip directly onto the icing (see fig. 17-25). Ears are indicated with a C placed to each side of the head.

For the bow tie, use the no. 2 tip and black icing. Start in the center front where the ruffles meet and hold the tip straight up. Form a circle and come back to the center front; then do the same on the opposite side.

Place the no. 68 tip on the parchment bag with green frosting. At the base of the wall, position the tip and apply a little pressure to give it body so that the leaves will stand up against the wall. Do this around the cake, having some of the leaves cross and others drooped over (see fig. 17-25).

The hat is optional and is done by removing the no. 12 tip from the violet bag and placing the coupling directly on top of Humpty Dumpty's head. Apply a great deal of pressure and the frosting will mound over the head; then pull up a point. If the point is not sharp, wait a few minutes for the frosting to set slightly and shape it with your fingers when it is not sticky. To make a ruffle around the edge of this mound, take the pink bag with the no. 104 tip. Place the thickest part of the tip against the mound, and make the ruffle with an up-and-down motion. Yellow frosting is used with a no. 13 tip to add the lacing where the ruffle joins the hat and a no. 2 tip on the same bag to follow the ruffle around the edge. Do the pom-pom with the no. 2 tip in yellow.

The boots are made with the bag of black icing and the no. 7 tip. Insert the tip directly into the center of the yellow circle at the base of the pink ruffle. Apply pressure and pull down slowly; then pull your bag upward to form the heel. Apply more pressure to form the foot; then pull up, releasing pressure. This will form a point, rather like a pixie shoe.

Grow the Flowers

You have almost reached the end. All the canvas bags that you have used, except the black and gray, will now be used for the drop flowers growing around the wall. Place tip no. 193 on the violet bag. Hold the bag straight up and apply pressure. As you do, twist the bag from right to left. Stop squeezing, push the tip down slightly into the flower, and pull away. Make 12 to 15 drop flowers scattered at random around the base of the brick wall. Do exactly the same with all the other colors, transferring the tip from color to color. In this particular case, there is no need to wash the tip. When you change from 1 bag to the other, the colors will be variegated, making it all very effective. (This tip is excellent for making candleholders as well. When the bag is squeezed from left to right, build up the frosting so that a candle may be placed on a plate or a board or even on the cake.)

With a no. 2 or 3 tip on a bag of yellow icing, squeeze a little dab in the center of each flower.

Use the no. 13 tip with pink frosting to make 1, 2, or 3 small stars down the center front of Humpty's jacket. With the no. 2 tip, put a little drop of yellow in the center of each star button.

Now for the final touch. The no. 2 tip is washed once again and placed in a parchment bag with the red frosting that was mixed earlier and kept covered. Carefully form a circle for Humpty Dumpty's mouth to give him that "Oh" expression.

This cake is an excellent project for using leftover frosting. You do not have to follow my suggestions for colors but can use your imagination and create your own Humpty Dumpty.

80

SUPPLIES

Two cakes, 13- × 9-inches
125 to 150 assorted flowers
150 leaves in various lengths

All the flowers should be made and dried (see Chapters 3, 7, 8, and 9) before baking the cakes.

The 13- × 9-inch pan with rounded corners is excellent for many numbers. While your cakes are cooling, trace the bottom of the pans onto a piece of paper to form your numbers. See fig. 17-30 for measurements.

After your cakes have cooled, place the pattern over the inverted cake

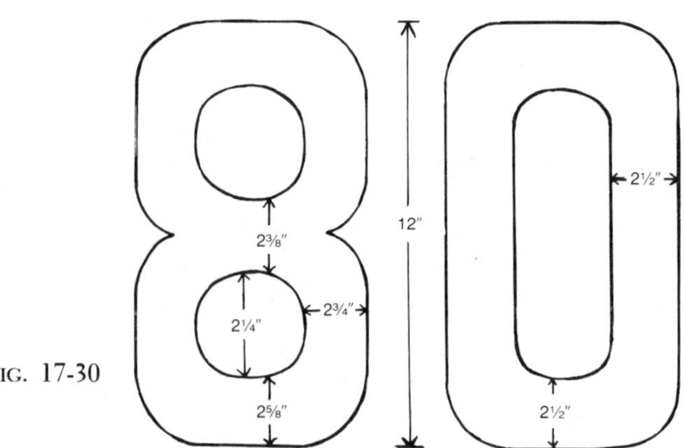

FIG. 17-30

and cut out the pieces. Carefully work with the blade of the knife straight up to get a clean cut of cake or crumbing will be very difficult.

Mark the center of the board for the cake, and place the 0 about ½ inch to the right of it. Crumb it.

In order for you to do the roping in between the 2 cakes, trace the 8 pattern on a piece of heavy foil. Place the cake on the foil on a flat cookie sheet with the side that will be next to the 0 close to the edge so that it can be easily transferred onto the board. Crumb the 8.

When the glaze on the 0 is dry, do the roping around the outside base with tip no. 22, and use tip no. 20 to do the roping around the 3 other places. Do the roping at the base of the center of the 0 first and then do the top edges.

On the 8 cake, glaze only the side that will be going next to the 0. Do the roping on the lower edge just at the indentation. Carefully slide the cake in place. Finish glazing and add the roping, using the same tips as used on the 0.

Fill the top area with flowers and leaves. Always put a little dab of frosting underneath each flower and place it at an angle.

Book Cake

SUPPLIES

13- × 9-inch cake
40 to 50 large white and yellow Shasta daisies with large yellow centers
60 to 70 leaves

For those who enjoy curling up with a good book I do not recommend the Book Cake. For a delightful any-occasion cake, it is both unique and attractive, with a surface that adapts itself to many decorating ideas.

The objective here is to learn how to cut and shape cakes. This basic lesson in the art of cake construction will enable you to execute other ideas. You may not produce the Great American Novel, but it will be a delicious book.

Once you learn how to cut a book cake, you can make it in any size from 3 inches to 3 feet. There are pans available for making a book cake, but they come only in 1 size.

For a very large book, you would have to make several cakes. Trim the side edges to remove the brown part; then place the cakes side by side. Needless to say, all cakes must be the same size. (Both sides do not have to be exactly the same height for a book may not always be opened in the center.) In this way, you can make a cake as large as a kitchen table. To have fewer joinings, use your largest roasting pans. If the cake has to be transported, be sure you can get it through all the doorways on the way. Place your cake on a board approximately 2 inches larger on all sides.

No matter what size cake you are using, it may be cut into the shape of an open book. With a long sharp knife, cut about halfway down into the cake directly in the center. Starting about 2 inches from the center, trim a very little; then curve your knife inward toward the binding (fig. 17-31). Cut the outside edges of the cake at a 45-degree angle to shape the slant of the pages (fig. 17-32). Remove as many of the loose crumbs as possible; then crumb the entire cake.

FIG. 17-31

FIG. 17-32

Wait until the top of the cake is completely dry before you glaze it to keep the crumbs from coming to the surface.

When dry, glaze the top surface (open pages) with a metal spatula dipped in hot water and wiped dry before using.

If you have a doily or a rough-textured board under your cake, put a double thickness of waxed paper on the board up against the cake. The comb must slide easily over the "pages." Be sure the frosting is creamy without air bubbles. When making your frosting it should be mixed very slowly.

Now frost one side of the cake with a generous amount of frosting. Starting at the left-hand corner with the finest side of the comb against the frosting and the edge firmly against the board or waxed paper, slide very slowly to the next corner. If you are not satisfied, add a little more frosting to your edges and try again. You may have to do it 2 or 3 times before you get satisfactory results. Complete all sides (page edges); then remove waxed paper. If you want the edges to look like an old manuscript, keep going over the page edges with the comb. It is very effective.

You have now completed the basic steps in preparing the cake to be decorated, regardless of its size or the specific occasion for which it is intended.

Make the roman numerals out of white run sugar (see Chapter 11 and photograph). The book cake shown in the photograph was designed for a bar mitzvah party, and the roman numerals represent the 10 commandments. These numerals are done in Royal Icing.

For outlining the top surface of the pages, make a C design (fig. 17-33) or make a reversing C (fig. 17-34). Try it first on a piece of waxed paper. With a no. 16 tip, holding the bag of white frosting straight up at the center crease of the book, squeeze a C. It might be a good idea to connect the Cs until you get the rhythm. Go all around the top edge. One advantage of working on glazed frosting that is dry is that you can remove the border if you are not satisfied.

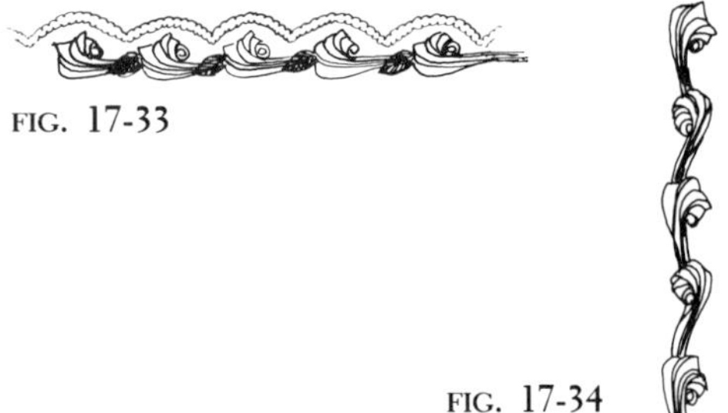

FIG. 17-33

FIG. 17-34

With a no. 3 tip and yellow frosting, outline the inside edge of the C motif with a slight zigzag design. Make a green leaf using a no. 66 tip where the tail of each letter C goes under (fig. 17-33).

The book cover is simulated using a no. 104 tip on a bag of green frosting. Start at a corner with the thickest part of the tip against the cake and touching the board. Apply pressure to make a continuous flat border without stopping until you reach the next corner. Follow this same procedure all around the base, butting the frosting at the corner. If the edges look lacy, that will now show. Apply another layer in the same fashion, but this time reverse the tip. This is a little more difficult. The thin part of the tip is against the cake.

As soon as this is completed, take the blade of the spatula, dip it in hot water, quickly wipe it dry, and give the seam a final touch to smooth it.

The book cover may be eliminated if you use a heavy border of flowers that would obscure this detail.

With a no. 30 tip and white Basic Frosting, do a slight zigzag motion all around the base of the cake. Place your flowers and leaves as shown in the photograph. With a little Royal Icing under your numbers, arrange the roman numerals on the cake.

If you wish to make a bookmark on your cake (fig. 17-35) use tip no. 104. If a wider ribbon is desired, use a larger rose tip; for a narrower ribbon, use a smaller tip. The bookmark may be placed on the left or the right. The thin part of the tip will be the center of the ribbon. With that in mind, place the tip on the top section. Your bookmark should begin at the base and come up over the top edge. Apply pressure and very carefully bring the bag up over the border and down the page of your cake. Continue squeezing until you reach the desired length. Stop pressure. When you pull away, create the angle you want for the ribbon end.

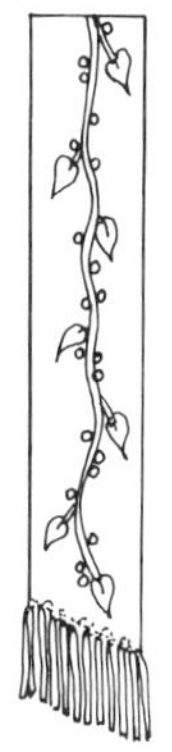

FIG. 17-35

Start the next part of the ribbon by overlapping the thin frosting about ¼ inch and follow the same instructions.

Immediately use a hot dry spatula to smooth the seam. Now that the ribbon is completed, add the fringe. Put the no. 1 tip in the bag of frosting and place the tip against the edge of the ribbon. Squeeze and pull out slightly; then release pressure but keep pulling. After a few strands you will be able to regulate the length of the fringe.

APPENDIX

Guide to Supplies and Methods

Aluminum measuring cups

These cups come in a set of 4: 1/4, 1/3, 1/2, and 1 full cup. They make excellent dry measures and can also be used to bake portions of the Jack-in-the-Box and Humpty Dumpty cakes, or small parts of any cake you might want to construct. Treat as you would any baking pan, filling with batter two-thirds to three-quarters full.

Angel cake pan

This baking pan has a cylinder in the center and comes in different sizes. The round pan is more popular, but square ones are also available. It may be used to bake any type of cake. The pieces of metal extending beyond the top edge are used to rest the pan on when the cake is removed from the oven and inverted to cool.

Angle

A straight line formed from a common point.

Ateco tips

Domestic standard decorating tips made of nickel silver. They are of excellent quality and are recommended for the projects in this book.

Baking pans

Any container that will withstand the heat of the oven may be used to bake a cake. Saucepans are good, as are aluminum measuring cups, but be sure not to put pans with plastic handles in the oven.

Basic Frosting

A frosting made with pure vegetable shortening, confectioner's sugar, salt, and water (recipe in Chapter 1). It is used to crumb and glaze cakes, as well as to decorate. It handles easily and is used for many of the projects in this book.

Bulb

To bulb is to make a series of ball-like shapes, one immediately after the other.

Butter cream frosting

This excellent frosting for any type of cake is often used for French pastries. This icing can also be used in decorating bags, but the results are not as good as with Basic Frosting. Recipe is in Chapter 17.

Cake pans

Any container used to bake a cake should be filled no more than two-thirds to three-quarters full of batter.

Cleaning brush

This is a specially designed brush used to clean decorating tips. It is made of stainless steel with a broom brush on one end and a tubular brush on the other.

Confectioner's sugar

A very fine sugar used to make no-cook frostings. Always sift before measuring and do not use the sugar with dextrose to make decorating icings because it will not be firm enough to work with.

Cooling rack

A metal rack used to cool cakes evenly after their removal from the oven.

Coupling

A device placed in tne canvas decorating bag to simplify the changing of standard decorating tips. Large tips are placed directly in the bag for they will not fit on the standard Delrin coupling.

Crumbing

This term describes a thin layer of soft frosting spread over the surface of the cake to set the crumbs.

Cupcake liners

Available in paper and foil in a variety of sizes, these liners are used in cupcake tins when making small cakes.

Decorating bag

Plastic-coated canvas decorating bags can be used many times. After each use, wash in lukewarm soapy water, rinse, and let stand at room temperature until thoroughly dry. Do not use hot water for it will make the bags porous.

Decorating comb

A triangular or ruler-shaped instrument with different-size teeth, the comb is used to make even ridges or lines in frosting.

Double thickness

Two layers of frosting, one on top of the other

Dowel skewer

A ¼-inch dowel is sharpened at one end and used to make roses (see Chapter 3). It is also called a rose dowel.

Drop flowers

A tip with a metal nail in the center is used to make attractive flowers with one press and a slight turn of the tip.

Fan

To keep one end of the tip in position while swinging the other end from left to right.

Garland

A wreath or rope of flowers and leaves.

Glassine doilies

Plastic-coated, grease-resistant, paper doilies with lace edges are used under any baked product.

Glazing

This term describes the second layer of frosting put on a cake over the crumbing icing. The hot dry blade of a spatula then smooths the frosting with long strokes (see Chapter 2).

Glycerin
A colorless, syrupy liquid used to thin dried-out or too thick paste colors.

Hat pin
A long straight pin with rounded head.

Hot dry blade
A spatula dipped in hot water and quickly wiped dry.

Layer
A single thickness.

Lazy susan
A platform with a ball-bearing mechanism that allows the platform to turn. It's a great help when decorating for turning a frosted cake can be difficult and messy.

Level
A flat even surface. A small device for leveling.

Meringue Powder
Powdered egg whites. Excellent for making Royal Icing.

Mock roping
A rotary motion with a continuous flow of frosting.

Nails (decorating)
Decorating nails come in different shapes and sizes and are used to make flowers that will dry before being placed on the cake. A no. 7 nail is the only one used for projects in this book.

Paintbrushes
Fine 00 and 000 brushes are used to paint lines on flowers made of frosting. Best results are obtained when painting is done before the frosting dries.

Parchment paper
Triangular pieces of paper are used to make disposable paper cones for decorating. These are especially helpful when you need only a tiny amount of 1 color of frosting; parchment bags can be used with or without tips.

Paste colors
Available in a variety of colors in small jars, paste colors are excellent for use in other foods, as well as in frosting. Never add water to paste colors in the jar. If the paste is too thick or dry, add glycerin to soften.

Pattern
A shape to serve as a model or guide.

Pear drop
A design in the shape of a pear.

Puff
A rounded mound of frosting.

Pipe
To apply pressure and form a design.

Roping
A roped effect is created by using a plain or round star tip (see Chapter 6).

Royal Icing
Excellent for making flowers and run-sugar designs, it also frosts dummy cakes (Styrofoam). It should be used to make decorations but not to frost cakes for it hardens and is impossible to cut.

Run sugar
Softened Royal Icing is used to fill in outlined designs (see Chapter 11).

Scoring
Using a knife or spatula to cut into the cake or icing just enough to leave a guideline for decorating. For example, the top of a cake is scored evenly for a lattice-work design to be applied.

Spatula

An 8-inch spatula (with a 4-inch blade) is used to frost cakes and fill decorating bags. It's indispensable.

Storage containers

Frostings that do not contain anything requiring refrigeration, such as eggs, may be kept in an airtight container at room temperature. A glass jar, with waxed paper covering the top before the lid is screwed on, is ideal for Basic Frosting.

String work

Fine lines done with Royal Icing.

Swag

A loop hanging in a curve between 2 points. Drops are made between swags, and the swags are covered sometimes with leaves and flowers to make garlands.

Tape measure

A narrow strip of tape for measuring.

Template

A pattern.

Tier

To place one tier above the other. Or the layer of cake itself.

Tips or tubes

Cone-shaped metal objects, inserted directly in the decorating bag or attached to the coupling, have different openings to form a variety of designs. Wash in hot soapy water using a cleaning brush especially made for cleaning tips, and rinse thoroughly with hot water.

Tweezers

An instrument for grasping and holding small objects.

White flavorings

White vanilla, almond, lemon, or mint flavorings should be used when making decorating frosting to avoid adding color to the frosting.

Suppliers

Parrish's Cake Decorating Supplies, Incorporated
314 West 58th Street
Los Angeles, California 90037

Maid of Scandinavia
3244 Raleigh Avenue
Minneapolis, Minnesota 55416

August Thomsen Corporation (Ateco)
36 Sea Cliff Avenue
Glen Cove, New York 11542

Warner Jenkinson Company of California
P.O. Box 16787
17500 Gillette Avenue
Irvine, California 92713

Cuisena Cookware
Tetbury Priory Ind. Estate
Tetbury
Gloucestershire
United Kingdom

Index